Welcome

"Come Sit With Me"

Spirit of Numerology

Joice Ashly

Blessings on your
journey through your
numbers & destiny.

In the Spirit of Numbers
Love
Ashley
8/29/94

Spirit of Numerology

Copyright © 1996 Joice Ashly

ISBN 0-9649077-1-2-0

Library of Congress Catalogue Card Number: 96-096226

First Printing, December 1996

Author: Joice Ashly
Concepts for Illustrations: Joice Ashly
Artist for Illustrations: Mary Jo Willis, Phoenix, Arizona
Cover: Artist, Delmary, Sedona, Arizona
Format and Typography: Martha McLelland, Salt Lake City, Utah
Publisher: Self-published

I am privileged to have the cover of this book gifted to me by the renowned artist, Delmary, of Sedona, Arizona. As my dear friend she offered to do a painting for a chapter in my book to represent the Age of Kaliyuga. The painting was so extraordinary, as is all her work, that I decided to use it as the cover of my book. Delmary has mastered the 15th Century Dutch Flemish technique of glaze painting. Her works have been used for numerous magazines and book covers. Her artistic creations are found in collections around the world through POGS, CD labels, international greeting cards, puzzles and twelve original works of collection plates for Franklin Mint. She is a classic artist who expands your consciousness through her unique expression of colors and composition. Her remarkable painting is a complement to my book. If you are interested in contacting Delmary or want information regarding her work please write to:

Delmary, P.O. Box 2044, Sedona, Arizona 86336.

The

West and East

Meet in Prayer

PRAYER OF THE WEST AND THE EAST

This book begins with a prayer to offer light to the readers and to the author, the bestower of the knowledge. Below are two different versions of prayer: the West and the East. The first prayer is from the West glorifying the "Divine Mother Mary". The second is a Mantra from the East requesting "Highest Illumination and Blessing".

Prayer of the West:

"MEMORARE: PRAYER TO OUR LADY"

Remember O most holy and gracious Virgin Mary, that never was it known that anyone who fled to thy protection, implored thy help or sought thy intercession was left unaided. Inspired in this confidence, I come unto thee, O Virgin of Virgins, my Mother; to thee I come, before thee I kneel, humble and sorrowful. O Mother of the World "incarnate" renounce not my petition, but in thy mercy hear and answer me. Amen

Prayer of the East:

"GAYATRI MANTRA"

OM BHUR, BHUR SVAHA, TAT SAVITUR VARENYUM,
BHARGO, DEVASYA, DHEEMAHI
DHIYO, YONAH PRACHODAYAT

God, we meditate on thy divine light. Bestow blessings on us so that our intellect may rise to the highest consciousness. Enable us to meditate, be successful in life and realize God. O, All Pervading Light, manifesting through the solar circle, illuminate our intellect.

"Ganesha"

A popular diety considered auspicous to invoke the blessings of prudence and prosperity at the commencement of any undertaking.

TABLE OF CONTENTS

Spirit of Numerology

Eastern Numerology
is
The Search For Balance
from
"Zero To Nine"
with
The West Merging With The East

Joice Ashly

Prince Hirindra Singh

DEDICATION

Prince Hirindra Singh

In this book I unveil a wealth of information about a unique system of eastern numerology that I learned from Prince Hirindra Singh. Prince Hirindra, born in Patiala, India, is an internationally known lecturer and teacher. He grew up amid splendor in an Indian palace. His father, once a powerful sovereign, ruled a providence of India before India's independence. At the age of 23, Hirindra left the palace to develop his own lifestyle and to satisfy his spiritual longings. Hirindra studied the system of eastern numerology which I use in this book from a master yogi in India, residing in the Himalayan Mountains.

I am privileged to have studied under Prince Hirindra. Under his personal tutelage I gained expertise of this unusual system of numerology. In 1985, we traveled to India together. Through Hirindra's background and knowledge of his homeland I was fortunate to experience the wonders and spirituality of India in both its fullest pageantry and its somber poverty.

Dear Hirindra: Your friendship has given me the impetus to publish what I have learned from you, as well as what I have discovered through my own experiences. I feel blessed to make this book a reality instead of a dream. You are the catalyst that gave me the foundation to build this house. This book unveils a wealth of information that I have mastered concerning the sacred mystery of numbers.

Dear Reader: Hirindra and I represent masters of this unusual system. Through his interpretation you learn of the spiritual and past-life analysis; through my interpretation you receive the more worldly and futuristic analysis. Both aspects are powerful. To have a reading with us both is like experiencing the Shiva and the Shakti.

THANK YOU PRINCE HIRINDRA SINGH OF PATIALA, IN THE SPIRIT OF LOVE THIS BOOK IS DEDICATED TO YOU AND TO ALL INTERESTED SOULS.

Ananda Shakti

Ananda Shakti is the spiritual name given to me by the esteemed Satguru Sant Keshavadas when Hirindra and I were guests at his home in Oakland, California, in 1987.

*To all who are a part of this undertaking
"Thank You."*

ACKNOWLEDGMENT

Beloved Sant Keshavdas, of Bangalore, India, is a mystic and has one of his many temples in Oakland, California. During one of my visits with Sant Keshavdas in Oakland he said to me, "Ananda Shakti there is nothing that is impossible when you have tremendous faith in God; you have that faith." I want to thank him for those encouraging words. With that faith, I have written and published this book.

"Thank you" to all my friends and family who believed in me and inspired me to write this book.

I owe many thanks to Phillip Quartullo, Scottsdale, Arizona. Without his assistance in *numerous ways* this book may not have come to fruition. He purchased a computer for me to use which was a tremendous blessing in writing this book. I am deeply grateful for his support as the vessel in helping me to accomplish my dream.

To my dear sister, Nancy Winn, Scottsdale, Arizona, thank you for your professional insight in editing and proofreading.

Thank you to the talented professional artist, Mary Jo Willis of Phoenix, Arizona, for the beautiful art designs and to the renowned artist, Delmary, of Sedona, Arizona, for her illustration of Kaliyuga.

For providing proofreading I thank Michael Sullivan, Missoula, Montana, my dear friends, Junitia Payne, Nashville, Tennessee, Susan Baker, Oil City, Pennsylvania, Sherry Blake, Phoenix, Arizona, and my Aunt Priscilla Frasher, Columbus, Ohio. Marty Wolf, Sedona, Arizona, thank you for your help in the title of this book, *Spirit of Numerology*.

Dear Margaret, thank you for your self-giving dedication and devotion in the formatting of this book. You are truly special.

I express my deep gratitude to my dear cousin, Leonard Pietrzak, of Federal Way, Washington, for his generous donation toward the publication of this book. May God bless his remaining years with longevity, health, love and peace. Thank you, Leonard.

FOREWORD of the WEST

Over the years, I've dabbled a bit with numerology. Never on a professional basis, of course. Simply for my own entertainment and exploration. There is, after all, something fascinating and mysterious about numbers in themselves. Oh, yes, we take them so very much for granted now, forgetting what a quantum leap in humankind's intellectual evolution they made when early geniuses in Sumer first learned to count -- then to add, subtract, divide. Well, after that, it was only a few thousand years before an astronaut was walking on the moon.

All in all, I must say that Joice Ashly's *Spirit of Numerology* is the most thorough book on numerology that I have ever read. If there are any applications of numerology that she does not cover, I can't imagine what they might be. It is readily apparent to me that Joice has spent years mastering her art and that she has made an exhaustive study of the many applications and implications of numerology in the lives of the individual spiritual seeker.

And while she delves into the mystical and the mysterious wonder of each numeral, Joice does it all in a very easy to read, conversational style. She invites us on the very first page to come and sit with her -- and the book soon begins to feel exactly like we are sitting across from this attractive and well-informed lady in a relaxed and informal atmosphere -- perhaps with a cup of coffee or tea before us -- as she cheerily explains all that we might wish to know about the harmonics of numbers, the link between numbers and the planets, the significance of our birthdate, and the wonder of our very own destiny number.

This is a book that you may use as a workbook, a tool, an instrument of self-realization and personal enlightenment. It is a book that you will find yourself picking up again and again, allowing it to become a valued companion on your life path.

Brad Steiger, Author of
One With the Light
Revelation
The Divine Fire

FOREWORD of the EAST

Numbers are everything. In the great Vedic Upanishads it is said at the beginning there was only One. One was without a second or Adwiteeya, and from that One came many. The whole of the Universe with its diverse forms of creation, is a continuum of vibrations within the numbers. These numbers encompass all forms of life, including the most intelligent species called man. In the proven hands of one as Ms Joice Ashly, these numbers are cracked open to present life's ups and downs in all its colours and shades.

The science of numbers achieved a high level of development in the hands of the ancient and Vedic Hindus who saw life as patterns of numbers. Numbers and frequencies are vibrations. Sound, light and energy are also vibrations. In India, the science of numbers was called "Sankya Sastra" and was based on a correct understanding of the law of periodicity. The vibrations that are attached to the various alphabets was developed by the Rishis of India through intuitive means and a science of interpretation was developed. This science plays an important role in Prasna or Horary Astrology and has been dealt with in Prasna Marga, a classical work in Sanskrit on the subject.

Ms. Joice Ashly's approach of deciphering numbers relative to life-events and situations is quite novel, and of course radically different from that enunciated in the Sankra Sastra. Through her vast background in esoteric lore and her wide experience in counseling, she has been able to evolve a system on the basis of allied disciplines cast from the Gregorian year of birth, plus date, month and time of birth. She also reveals one's vocational preference and choice of mate. Her theory that people born in the same month or year but different dates will react with different responses of behavior while sharing a similarity of outlook, merits a careful study.

Ms. Ashly divides behavior patterns into nine main categories defining specific attitudes and tendencies, inspired by the nine Navagrahas of Vedic Astrology. She also links the planets with the numbers, claiming that numbers like planets have orbital major and minor cycles. This task is made very easy to understand by Ms. Ashly's keen mind and powers of perception of life events.

I have gone through the draft and found a lot of hard work has gone into the book. This exposition of numbers is hoped will help to enrich ones life, filling it with a new awareness. I wish the author all success in her forays into the world of numbers.

Gayatri Devi Vasudev, of Bangalore, India
Professional Vedic Astrologer
Associate Editor of *Raman Publications* (Astrological Magazine)
Daughter of B. V. Raman, Chief Editor

INTRODUCTION
Purpose of This Book

Spirit of Numerology is a book based on eastern numerology. It is about the spirit of numbers beyond the year 2000 and how the quality of the numbers will change due to the emergence of the number 2 beginning with the year 2000. This system, I believe, is unlike any system ever used in the West or East.

The method used was taught to me by my mentor, Hirindra Singh, who learned it from a yogi in the Himalayan Mountains of India. Because this unique system originated in India, I feel it is appropriate to present this book as an eastern system of numerology. The science of ancient numerology had its beginnings in India. This book is presented to guide each reader to understand the method used and to bring about an awareness of numbers as a step toward guiding you into the realm of your own self-mastery. Allow this book to be the flame within you that imparts bhakti (love) and muda (pride) into your prana (life force).

Crystal balls, palmists, astrologers, tarot readers, psychics, prophets, spiritualists, channelers, regressionists, hypnotists, past-life readers, yogis, gurus, masters and teachers of mind control, have become well-known words to a large number of people in society. The word psychic means a non-physical phenomenon, unexplainable by physical interpretation, yet sensitive to esoteric and supernatural forces. Psychic means being able to foretell the future, describe the present and capitulate the past. It is a phenomenon that cannot be described or explained by orthodox scientific means. It is a pseudo-science that has become very popular and powerful in our society and is captivating even to many skeptics. Through the influence of the mystical sciences, many people seek to gain an explanation of the resolutions of their personal destinies and worldly conditions. As we journey through the global festival of this vast universe, there are many individuals who are searching to be guided through personal transformation. The curiosity of many seeks to draw understanding and guidance from the mystical sciences into their personal value system. There is a thirst and hunger to gain access into the future through the supernatural forces. It always has been and always will be a universal marvel when individuals can gain mastery over the arcane forces of nature. Life today seems to be based on the distinction of one's importance and status rather than one's good deeds or moral character.

We live in an auspicious time. Life in the 1990s is becoming very transformational on many levels. Somehow, people are attempting to find happiness and fulfillment through external and physical stimulation. We are in a propitious period in history where the earth is moving through fundamental changes, stirring the belly of the earth. This transformation involves a marked change not only in our lifestyle but also our attitudes. Unsettling conditions usually create fear and arouse emotions for many individuals as a result of uncertainty. This great transfiguration taking place on earth is affecting many lives through a depreciable lifestyle. These conditions stir people to seek answers and guidance through metaphysical or spiritual advice. Many seek to lift the veil of the future through esoteric wisdom when rationalization disputes or rejects theoretical knowledge. In times of stress, pain, depression, mental anguish or unfulfilled desires, people probe for explanations that will guide them to alleviate their anxieties and uncertainties. In the quest for enlightenment, certain individuals seek metaphysical or esoteric philosophy to expand their consciousness and to find truth in the purpose of their future. Behind the physical form is an eternal form. The mystery of life cannot always be understood as we try in vain to endure our struggles and trials in life. Make each life experience an opportunity for productive learning.

People frequently ask what led me into the metaphysical and spiritual realm and how did I get involved as a practitioner of these sciences. My own interest in these subjects came about through the death of my infant daughter. I was raised as a strict Catholic in my younger years. Although I no longer practice Catholicism, I continue to have a deep devotion to God and the Blessed Virgin Mary. As a young girl, I would spend many hours in church sitting in front of her statue, feeling very contented and peaceful. On many occasions I would lay flowers at the feet of the statue, or light candles to obtain a special wish through her intercession.

I never endured the negative aspects of Catholicism that many of my friends or acquaintances have. In fact, I revered the Catholic religion, the mass, the clergy, the beliefs and all the sacred ceremonies that were part of Catholic traditions. I attended mass every Sunday and on school days. I never complained about attending daily mass because I accepted that requirement as a Catholic student; in fact, I felt it was a rewarding experience. Accepting the intense religious training and traditions to which I was so dedicated was easy for me at that time of my life.

To me, Baptism, First Holy Communion and Confirmation are traditional rituals which have their own special value and symbolize a spiritual ceremony. With deep respect for the religion that I inherited through my parents, I never sought to believe there could be other religions or spiritual philosophies that had value or merit. I led a sheltered life, with limited exposure to the outside world or other religions and kept close friendship with other Catholics.

In January of 1968, when my family and I tragically experienced the crib death of my one-month old daughter, my religious beliefs were significantly shaken. I already had given birth to two sons, and she was the long-awaited, cherished daughter. Her birth was a fulfillment of joy that I am unable to explain. She was going to be blessed with everything I had yearned for as a young girl. Without a doubt, she would be pampered, spoiled and loved unconditionally.

I will never forget January 11th. In the early hours of the morning, my beloved daughter's soul, without warning, left her body. I was completely shattered by this experience and tried to find some answers to ease my painful loss. I was devastated spiritually, mentally and physically. Her death took the sap from my spirit and left me emotionally drained. I analyzed myself and my life to find some reasonable explanation for her death. I was a committed Catholic who lived honorably and tried to do everything right in life. How could this happen to me? How dare I be punished so severely when I tried my best to live a decent and respectful life. I was a good soul, and I could think of no reason why I was being punished with the loss of my child.

I went to a therapist who urged me to count my blessings and to be grateful for my two healthy sons. Nonsense, I did not want to hear that, I was in pain; so, after a few sessions, the therapist was history.

I also went to visit with a priest who was a friend of the family. He tried to tell me through his authority that God wanted her spirit back to make her an angel. He tried to explain that God has the right to give life and to take life, and we have to accept his authority with trust and faith. Well, to me, God had no right to take my child's life. I did not want an angel in heaven; I wanted an angel on earth. I wanted her alive and in my life, and I could not accept the therapist's nor the priest's explanation of her death.

In December of 1970, two years after my daughter's death, I attended a lecture on psychic phenomena and reincarnation. When I saw the advertisement in the daily paper, I knew I had to attend. After hearing the lecture I felt I had gained an understanding that helped me to feel I could finally accept my daughter's death and release her spirit that I clutched so tightly in my chest. It was the word "reincarnation" that opened a door within me like a buried, hidden tomb, waiting to be discovered. The lecture awakened my suppressed spiritual instinct which I had never before known. I felt at home with this new philosophy of reincarnation and meditation. This awareness was the beginning of my journey into spiritual evolution. As my knowledge of reincarnation increased, so did my acceptance of my child's death and my renewed love for God.

Today, I no longer feel anger and resentment about my daughter's death; in fact, I feel gratitude that I was privileged to have had my baby girl, even if was just for one short month.

I am a Christian who believes in the higher power of God. I believe it can be helpful to have a religious foundation in life for those who desire it or for young children. A religious foundation teaches devotion to God through prayers and ceremonies and can be important to children in the early stages of development, but as an adult, I can no longer accept the limited beliefs of most religious institutions. For me, to be religious or spiritual does not mean I have to belong to a religious organization to acknowledge God as the Higher Power. As an adult, I feel free to make my own choices about my personal religious beliefs.

I now possess a higher level of perspective and devotion to God which assists me in attaining that spiritual supreme bliss. I am now more fervent about my spiritual faith than when I was a practicing Catholic. I do not feel God is about religion, but about righteous living, spirituality and the belief in eternal life. At this time in life my devotion is to the Heavenly Father to attain my spiritual growth, not to a religious organization. I did not get to live my dream with my daughter through the physical realm, but I do live my life through her spiritual intercession, which is some compensation for other unfulfilled desires.

This book is being written to share what I have learned about numerology. I believe knowledge is meant to be shared with others and not kept in a storehouse of secrecy. Today, more people are becoming curious about their numbers and how these numbers affect their lives. This book is an indispensable source of information about eastern numerology, and the method used is easy to understand, even for a novice.

This book is informative in helping you to understand numbers. It will serve as a tool that will be useful to better understand yourself as well as others. Read this book slowly. Do not just skip to certain parts or chapters that appear the most interesting to you and think you understand the whole range of information about the numbers and how they interrelate. Acquaint yourself with the entire subject matter. Digest the material in this book until you extract the basis of understanding useful to your awareness, not only of yourself, but also of others. The interpretation of the numbers will generate a prompt curiosity and will motivate you to become more engrossed in the subject. I feel this book can awaken and stimulate your curiosity while providing in-depth information to better understand others and your own inner being.

The material in this book is basic numerology, simple enough for a novice to understand. The teachers of western and eastern numerology will find this method an educational and beneficial addition to their respected system. The interpretations in this book can add deeper meaning to all the basic numbers of numerology to help achieve a more expansive background into the peripheral vision of numerics. This book on eastern numerology will help you to understand the ancient art of divination through a system that is unique and orderly. In the description of the numbers, every element forms a clear and distinctive individual characterization. The science of mathematics is a sacred science and is universally accepted. Numbers are used in practically every event of our daily lives and the world cannot exist without numbers.

Numbers in a birthdate are a repetition of constant application through major and minor cycles acting like a network of electricity, sending currents to each other. To achieve your destiny number, a methodical arrangement of numbers is calculated by adding up all the numbers of your birthdate, using the day, month and year. Time of birth is also a factor. I modify these combinations of numbers to form an analysis of all the influences. Also used to interpret the individuality of a person are three wheels of fate that distinguish the intellect, emotions and materialism. All three wheels together and separately act as a conductor of energy representing three numbers within each of the three wheels.

There are two orbital cycles of major importance that are also used to govern an individual's attitudes and outlook in the progression of life. One is a major 9-year cycle, the other is a 9-month sub-cycle. The numbers used in these cycles are taken from the sequence of numbers in the entire birthdate of the individual. The destiny number is the final sum of the total numbers in the birthdate. Each of these numbers is used separately as cycles of orbit to challenge your life. The 9-year cycle is the major period and the 9-month cycle is the sub-major period. Minor and sub-minor periods of 9-weeks and 9-days can also be used. I do not assign importance to the minor periods. It is not that the minor periods are not important, they just do not have the significance of the major periods. One has to learn to live life on a daily basis without concerning oneself with every minor incident.

Another cycle I work with is the personal year ,which is from one birthday to the next. This personal year number changes systematically every year in sequences from 1 to 9. I use the personal year number because the energy is instrumental as another transmitter of current which presents diversity to the year in question. The annual cycle of the personal year definitely affects the 9-year challenge. If you are in a conflicting 9-year cycle and the personal year is positive, you can add tranquillity to an otherwise difficult period. The degree of success or hardship during certain periods of life will be altered by the 9-year challenge number, the 9-month challenge number and the personal year number. We create and govern our individual life experiences by the way we interpret events. Our thoughts are like rolls of film passing through a projection. If we do not like the picture we must change the film.

The sciences of numerology and astrology are not meant to predict the future, but to provide assistance and insight into one's identity. These sciences are used to analyze a person's character and to assess one's weaknesses while encouraging individuals to build on strengths. They can also determine a favorable cycle or the best time to make decisions or major changes. The interpretation of all the primary numbers unveils many characteristics of the personality. This identity is meant to foster self-reliance through personal understanding. A person is born through karma (action or reaction of results from a previous lifetime that affects the present actions) and in this lifetime must live through dharma (righteous way of living or proper conduct through truth and purity). *It is my understanding that karma is the cause of destiny, not the result of destiny.*

The concept of mathematics originated in India and has achieved great scientific progress with the numbers. Numerology is known to be one of the oldest arts of the mystical sciences. The intrigue of this science has become increasingly popular. The concept of numerology is similar to the science of astrology, but without the spectrum of the planets, signs and houses. There are many different systems of numerology. All variations are used to identify individual personality traits through the power of the numbers. Use this book and other books of mystical sciences to help in varied life situations. I use numerology and other sciences as a tool to reinforce positive qualities and to help me identify my limitless potential. The sciences help me to dispel maya and to help me connect with mind, body and soul.

It is difficult to explain in a book how to interpret the combination of numbers because there are so many dimensions. As a student you will have to work with many charts and combinations of numbers before you can predict with any accuracy. To interpret a chart for any individual, it is important to have a full understanding of the influences of all the numbers. A strong destiny number with a weak directional number can have conflicts of interest, and the destiny number will fight to have its own way. The destiny and psychic numbers are never at odds with each other, even when they are opposite to each other. But when the directional and destiny numbers are not in harmony, they will be antagonistic to each other. It's like wearing clothes that are too tight for you; you feel the discomfort. It does not mean that you cannot have a contented life; it just means stressful situations or the crises that you encounter will always seem more difficult than normal. You feel like you are constantly going through life always falling short of your goals, or that any efforts you put forth to reach your accomplished desires are always through undue pressure. The only way to overcome the external catastrophes is through spiritual tools and the disciplines of your individual development.

I hope this book will be a guiding light to those who use it. Individuals are all like ripples in the ocean. We are not bodies with souls, we are souls with bodies, expressing ourselves in this vast cosmic universe. We are not human beings here for a spiritual experience, rather we are spiritual beings here for a human experience. Although we are all separate ripples in the ocean, we exemplify the principle of oneness within the ocean. It is impossible to see the ocean as part of the universe if we cannot see ourselves as just one bubble in the ocean, separate and unique in shape and form. We are all the oneness of bubbles in the ocean, and the ocean would be less without all our little droplets. What we are all searching for in our society is a sense of communion with each other and with the cosmic parent in this mighty ocean of life. Allow this book to be a lifeboat to carry you across the waves of ignorance.

FATE OR FREE WILL:

We all have free will, yet we are all fated. Free will is going beyond nature to use our prerogative in this life. Every one of our actions, thoughts and wishes are a link to the wheel of birth, death, and rebirth.

I gave birth to a baby who died a crib death. This tragedy was not my free will; however, it was my fate. My choice was to give my daughter life through birth, but it was destiny's choice to cease her life. Together, it was our joint karma for her to be born, but I have no conscious realization of that agreement.

Karma determines our condition, both in this world and in our next life on earth. Karma is choice and effort. Destiny is the consequence of that mysterious choice and effort which provides the explanation of our existence. You cannot work through destiny; however, you can alter your destiny through the natural law of action and reaction which is the law of reincarnation. Deeds and thoughts are seeds of good and bad, consisting of your actions as they relate to karma. I believe on some level we all chose to live in this world and, because of that decision, we have to act out the actions of our karma.

Many people have been going through some difficult times adjusting to many unexpected changes, especially in the past few years--some all of their lives. Life with its twists and turns is very uncertain. People are being compelled to transform to a constantly changing world and to prepare for a new age which calls for more flexibility. The American dream seems lost in a struggling future. Sometimes it can be quite uncomfortable to see your life change dramatically when outside forces come crashing down. Do not allow yourself to live in guilt, fear or worry about the future. Joy and happiness are states of mind. Work to improve your thought patterns, your soul, your spiritual growth and seek attunement with divine spirit within your divine presence.

Submit to yourself spiritually. Accept your destiny or karma, even if it is with a sorrowful heart. Place your devotion in God's hands. Pray for enlightenment, guidance and strength to grant you blessings. When life seems most impossible or unbearable--that is when you must not quit. Always continue to make the effort to succeed, even when you lose faith. You can never tell when the grace of God will respond to the sincerity of your efforts and prayers to change the course of your destiny.

In your darkest hours you must trust your spirit to lead you from the dread of darkness into the universal light. Light allows you to see, and it is that life-creating radiance on which you must mold your destiny. In the light you are in your spiritual vision, while in darkness there is cold, fear and doubt, blinding you into spiritual inactivity. When confusion is removed from thinking, obstacles to happiness are destroyed. Allow yourself to be liberated from the bondage of life and death. Your thoughts are the cause of your bondage and suffering, and yet at the same time, your thoughts can be the rewards of salvation when you focus on the spiritual path.

It is the liberated mind that learns to experience eternal joy, and it is this joy that is everlasting. What you hear in the darkness of your soul, you must speak in the light of your spirit. Dear Soul, be absorbed in union with your true being and shine in your radiant light.

OM SHANTI (peace and love). My love goes out to you beloved souls. May we all become manifestations of spiritual energy in action. Let us unite and take flight and always know that God is truly the "Wind Beneath Your Wings".

"Godess Gayatri: "Blessed Virgin"

The feminine principles of love and peace that will guide us into the new millenium of the 2 energy.

Numerology is the only science through which we can analyze in-depth millennium psychology. As mankind enters the new millennium of the 21st Century through the 29th Century, we will have a grand awakening to a new vibration of the feminine energy. The female principles of love, peace and unity will be expanding to a new vibration.

The number 2 symbolizes female energy as it represents the "we" consciousness. Two is a number of compromises and will bring people together through peace in every situation. However, first, there may be a downpour of fear and pain to prove our faith and to demonstrate our love to the Supreme God.

Fear works; it brings people back to God when they have drifted away. When people are absorbed in religion they live with fears and man-made doctrines; when absorbed in God there is no fear, there is only love. To help overcome fear become God-realized, accepting fate with faith moving your will into action. As mankind moves forward to a new age, people will be expected to bring about an evolutionary leap from one cycle of life to a brand new millennium. The wisdom and power gained through this forward evolution will be the emblem of light that will shine to carry you into your journey as you move forward into the new millennium beyond the year 2000.

The last millennium has been dominated by the power of the number 1, which rules the male ego and the "I" consciousness. The next 1000 years will be influenced by the number 2, which is the female influence and the "we" consciousness. The male and female numbers are definitely different in emotions and expressions. Male energy needs to do good to feel good; female energy needs to feel good to do good. In society the male is seen as the symbolism of protection while the female is viewed as the symbol of service. The universal millennium beginning in the year 2000 will bring together 1000 years of peace after the year 2027.

In the world of numbers 1 is considered active, egocentric and autonomous, while 2 is cooperative, receptive and sensitive. It is not wrong that people desire an ego, because as humans we can never completely eliminate the ego, but must direct it to allow the "I" and the "we" to flow together in teamwork. The search to experience ONE-NESS requires that individuals deal with the TWO-NESS. The last 1000 years of history was governed by the patriarchal system which activated generations of highly ambitious people who were powerful, self-governing and sought personal status. Many people in government and religious organizations in the past millennium were motivated to face risks in life for the purpose of personal attainment, material wealth and world superiority because of global economic competition. As society moved forward, it became evident that because of extreme diverse beliefs, individuals have become suspicious of government, religious institutions and each other. People are becoming concerned about the doubtful future.

Both 1 and 9 are odd numbers that manifest masculine assertiveness. Number 1 is the physical flame of energy and never loses its glow. Number 9 is the spiritual flame of wisdom and knowledge and never loses its invisible power. As a male-dominated society in the past millennium the world has made more advancements in science and technology than during any other millennium, but has not made satisfying significant gains to advance women in the professional realm. Scientifically, politically and with religion, the world continues to experience a transformational cleansing. Mankind must place more emphasis on the importance of human conditions in life, not false values of patriarchy.

What does all this transformation mean to global existence? In the past generation, have not many of you felt that you have lost the glow of your flame and at times even lacked trust in your own spiritual faith? The universal competition of the past millennium has created a challenging and provocative period between people and countries. Many powerful individuals were led by their egos to gain material wealth and to claim all their desires. In our present lifestyle individuals feel continuous pressure to strive to do better and to have more in life? Was anything more coveted in human goals than self-importance and material wealth? Many people desire to be leaders, demand status, recognition, power and wealth at any cost. For many, today's dream is to be permanently happy and wealthy, but this dream is becoming more difficult to attain.

During the 1900s many powerful and wealthy individuals influenced our lifestyle and changed our economic world in many ways-- leading mankind to social upheaval that will transform many lives in the next decade.

The past millennium produced an abundant lineage of dynamic male personalities, as well as a few females--both favorable and unfavorable in forming our society. America thinks it is a republic; but for women, there is still a lack of equality in religious and government institutions, although the gap for equality between both genders is beginning to narrow as we enter the new millennium. The world has steadily lost assurance of the future as a result of egocentric leaders who lack integrity for political and economical justice. The division in social order is due to the unstable changes and pressures of a runaway government. The message to the world should not be "What can I do for my country?", but "Together, what can we do for our country, and what can our country do for us?" Many people talk about the "we" consciousness, but practice the "I" consciousness. We need to put the "I" behind us as a society and help to transform life into the "we" awareness to maintain unity with mankind under all circumstances.

As you attempt to sort out life's values and meaning in the coming millennium, do the right things in your behavior and actions; not because it is expected of you, but because it constitutes harmony in your highest spiritual achievements. Society can no longer tolerate a corrupt government, dishonesty or egotistical political leaders who make decisions compromising their integrity for power and self-importance. There are numerous officials who are more concerned with their political appearance and status than they are with ethics or human conditions. When people expose and protest against the unorthodox villains of the political battlefield, society should take the necessary steps to eliminate their influence.

The number 2 as a figure is interesting when you picture my hypothetical explanation . I see the curved upper half of the number

2 as the female on a pedestal and the bottom line of the number 2 as the male, the structure of the pedestal that balances the Shakti (female energy). The bottom line of the number 2 becomes a 1, laying down its strength to become the backbone for the upper crescent, shaped like the female. The bottom line of the 2 is the support base holding the vision of the female on his pedestal to honor her as she rises to lead mankind into the new millennium through the nurturing qualities of her 2 energy. Two is ruled by the moon and both are feminine qualities which will lead and uplift humanity through a true spirit of nourishing life in the next millennium. The bottom single line of the number 2 represents the male "I" and the upper crescent of the number 2 represents the female being elevated to a position of high regard and adoration.

The male figure can no longer be the dominant force in the next millennium. The male, by laying down his 1 to elevate the feminine principle of the 2, will become the significant strength to sustain the female energy so she can open her spirit to embrace the "we" doctrine in the next dynamic millennium. Through love, unity and diplomacy, she will work with the masses to pioneer a new spirit of justice and world peace. It is important for people to become less self-absorbed and more unified so mankind can enjoy and appreciate a world of harmony and togetherness.

The upper half of the numeral 2 is the flow of the crescent moon being held upward by the support of the number 1 male force, creating the foundation for body, mind and spirit. Remember that 1 comes before 2 and 2 is dependent on 1 to provide the important foundation for the female energy of the next millennium. As you transform your consciousness from the "I" principle to the "we" principle, you will form a relationship of opposites that will change your life into the golden age. Each of the 9 numbers will expand and alter their influence through the feminine 2 vibration and the awaiting wisdom of the Shakti.

The female energy of the number 2 is beginning to rise, and people must embrace it with openness to gain idealistic harmony for all humanity. Change is the law of life. The future appears uncertain, as everything in life seems to be deteriorating around the world--the weather, family, government and belief systems. Absoluteness of established traditions are diminishing as life preservation becomes more unpredictable, and people struggle to maintain jobs, a comfortable lifestyle and faith in a better future.

Whenever there is a radical or major change in the world as there will be in the next decade, there will be fears that create anxiety in individuals. Many people find it difficult to accept changes, whether in business, their environment or personal life. It is easier for people to accept old habits and patterns of past events, even when they cause unhappiness, than to adapt to new changes. Many people already sense a void in their lives, feeling alone and vulnerable--creating ponds of emptiness and depression. The future in this world is uncertain with too many egos and minds attached to the world of materialism adding to a sense of greed. People need to let go of material desires, more now than ever, and break the mold of the materialistic belief system which government and society created in the past decades. People must create a new platform of unconditional love and unity as we all go forward into our journey and into the new millennium of the year 2000.

The scriptures advise people to keep faith, hold high values and remain positive in times of adversity and change. Many people are anxious about the prophesied coming of the Messiah. My impression is that it will be a spiritual revelation of affinity between the mind and the heart heading toward a new social order--the heart representing the female principle, and the mind representing the male principle. Many have different ideas about what the next millennium will be like. I feel it will be an increase in faith and different forms of spiritual values--through personal spiritual experience, rather than religious doctrine. The patriarchal system of worship is still common in most religions today but the matriarchal system is gaining importance. Souls of both genders walking this planet together will share the roles of individualism in the coming millennium.

As people move into the future of worldly turmoil, there will be an increase in personal soul searching as people will question the atrocities that will take place around the world. Mankind needs to rise above the material influences and reject the negative traits of lust, anger, pride and greed. This process requires spiritual processing and philosophical understanding to remain positive and to keep faith.

The activation of the 0s in the year 2000 will begin to be felt in 1998. The 0s will add power and intensity to the next 29 years as we embark upon the next decade. Personal growth and re-evaluation of social and structural systems will be required so society can begin to heal and unite people who feel limited by lack of finances or education, or feel incapable of taking charge of their own lives. Many people could end up feeling like they are hopelessly wandering, lost in a darkness of worldly despair without hope or without faith, proceeding forward in their ambivalent journey.

Faith in a higher spiritual power will be necessary to heal people throughout the world--where you are today and where the next millennium will take you. In the coming decade (2001 to 2009) there will be two pairs of 0s. During the era of ancient mythology or Judeo-European history there was a lot of interest regarding the mystery of spiritualism; this interest is returning, especially as we come closer to the 21st Century.

There are many questions about life that cannot be answered by mankind and must be left to faith and trust. I believe the two 0s connected with the evolving feminine energy of the number 2 from 2000 to 2010 will have a very profound mystical effect on the world. It will be a new era in spiritualism and social justice where people may experience an awakening of a global civilization. Eventually, I anticipate there will be a one world government with a unification of all cultures and contact with civilizations beyond our galaxy.

After the year 2000, the world will focus on becoming more of a service-oriented and nurturing society through the influence of number 2s ruler, the moon. Eventually everyone can hope to be part of a society of peaceful coexistence. It will be like going from "sunset to sunrise," the dusk of the night always being darkest leading us into the dawn of light.

In 1969, the renowned Yogi Bhajan told his followers, "You may start life with the individual consciousness, but you will have to go through group consciousness to reach universal consciousness." Humanity will begin to see the value of group consciousness as the way to survive on this planet in the next 1000 years. The "2" energy is the catalyst which will bring on a more balanced lifestyle. It represents sensitivity, feelings, gentleness, cooperation, patience and negotiation, striving to bring peace into the next millennium.

Two will represent the Age of Aquarius, bringing people together to create a world where all will work toward greater individual responsibility in a supportive and unified way to live more peacefully on this planet. Starting in the year 2000, the 0s along with the number 2 will be the force of energy that will lead humanity through the darkness of uncertainty. This chaos could add to the uneasiness of mankind's emotions, forcing events which will encourage people in coming together in peace and unity.

Life in this world's present condition is similar to that of an ocean. Whenever there is a turbulent storm raging in the ocean, there is not much anyone can do about the blustery conditions except wait until the storm calms down, because nature's fury controls the ocean. We can no longer ignore the calamity surrounding many nations and individuals on this great planet. There is a crying out in our universe to find answers for many weary individuals as they fight for survival in the midst of transformation, especially in certain countries. Many people who live in the doom and gloom of darkness, fear the uncertain economy, losing their homes and jobs. Life is lacking in quality and security. There are burdensome tax structures, a runaway crime rate, a dishonest government, various viral attacks, lack of individual morals and many countries at war with each other. These are not easy times for many people. It takes a lot of courage to maintain faith and optimism.

We are living in difficult times known as "Kaliyuga". The eastern philosophers call this the age of ignorance, conflict and ego-oriented motivations. Many people seem to be lost in the pursuit of material greed and sensuous pleasures. Because of this pursuit impermanent physical phenomena becomes more important than the permanent spiritual phenomena. Approach life with a new awareness, for divine order can only come from divine chaos. Everyone will have to become more flexible in meeting changing times. Just as waters of small rivers and lakes merge into the vast ocean, the ocean receives all the waters whether polluted or clean. Eventually the undercurrent sinks the pollution to the bottom of the ocean or washes it to shore.

The personal crisis of any individual is just as traumatic as a mass crisis. As individuals and as collective groups, we need to uplift the entire lifewave of society to help each other and to fight for a more balanced existence. If the Eastern Philosophers are correct and we are in the age of kaliyuga (which represents evil forces), then humanity in all its struggles must unite to move upstream into the light of attunement and peace. As masses of people begin to come together, we must reach out to help each other and join hands in unity to seek the light through transcendence rather than destruction. As hands reach out to join hands, color, race and culture will become unimportant and will have little significance in the human goal to achieve peace and harmony. Remember, whatever the color of the cow, the milk is always white and the blood is always red. The world, as a whole, needs idealism and altruism to find the answers to questions as mankind enters a new dynamic millennium.

There cannot be global consciousness without the "we" energy. Humanity must strive for syntheses of planetary consciousness, working towards unity on all levels of cooperation and understanding. As you approach the new age do not allow the temptations from energies of the dark forces to block your spirit and faith. Learn to let go of the past and your fears so you can embrace a new and rewarding tomorrow.

The future of tomorrow is today. You may not understand the future, but you must not worry about it. The present is the only time you have for certain. Be aware of today and the revolution of events that will force the world to expand into a more appealing tomorrow. Accept the future with great faith and trust for the past is the reminder of the future and the future is a continuation of the present. Let us work together as a society toward positive solutions for the benefit of the world to become more unified. Society needs to become the "we" and not the "I" consciousness. Allow the power of your soul to connect to one soul and then another, continuously connecting to others until all souls have moved toward self-actualization in group consciousness reaching universal consciousness.

The world must not be viewed through maya. Realize that our security is ever changing and will not be sustained through future transformation within our society. As the world gets closer to the new millennium of the year 2000, new survival skills must be learned as many people will lose the luxury of material security. Look at the meaning of life experiences from two sides until you are able to bring it to uniform expression.

A thirsty person who sees a mirage of water while walking in the desert heat will run toward the illusion to satisfy the thirst. You must not run to a mirage when you are disillusioned, instead you must use discrimination when aroused by vague illusions. When you are no longer lured by the appearances of the world or your illusions, you will then reap the benefit of eternal bliss, which is beyond your present reality.

> *We create a living by what we earn financially.*
> *We establish a life by what we earn emotionally.*
> *We harvest a lifetime by what we earn spiritually.*

MANTRA FOR THE AGE OF KALIYUGA

To be chanted daily to destroy all evil effects of this dark age of kaliyuga.

HARE RAMA   HARE RAMA
RAMA RAMA   HARE HARE
Rama, remove all pain from the world.

HARE KRISHNA   HARE KRISHNA
KRISHNA KRISHNA   HARE HARE
Krishna, destroy the sins of the world.

The Age Of Kaliyuga
by
Delmary

THE DESTINY NUMBER PREFACE

YOUR YEAR	YOUR MONTH	YOUR DAY		YOUR DESTINY
1 9 3 7	4	1 8	=	6

1 9 3 7 $(1 + 9 + 3 + 7) = 2 0 = 2$
Month $\qquad = 4$
Day $\qquad = 1 8$
$2 + 4 + 1 + 8 = 15 = (1 + 5) = 6$ the destiny number

To learn your destiny number always put the year first, the month, and then the day. Add together each individual number to get the single remainder of all the numbers. The destiny number should never be a double digit number, unless it is with a 0. Use the above sample to help find your destiny number from your birthdate.

DESTINY--_Something to which a person or thing is destined. A predetermined course of events held to be a restless power or agency._

The numbers in numerology are viewed as an abstraction. They have no physical existence, but rather a spiritual realization. The numbers in your birthdate are a collective force of actions and accumulations of your past lives. Every individual creates his or her own destiny and is born to meet that destiny. Numbers are the inevitable inheritances of life. The most important number of all your numbers is the _destiny number_. It is how you begin to understand yourself. It is equivalent to that of your sun sign in astrology in relating to your destiny signature. However, no single factor of just your destiny, psychic or directional number should be taken as the decisive potential. Carefully examine all the numbers in your profile to have a completed picture. Interpreting your life with just one number is like looking at the face of a person without seeing the nose, eyes and mouth. All factors are necessary to be effectual.

The destiny number is the main character in the part you act out in the performance of your life. It reminds you that as an individual you are a mystery ultimately to be savored, but not to be solved. You are free to make choices; however, the options you choose will reflect the values you have for yourself in life. The thoughts you entertain determine the type of world you choose to live in.

As mortals everyone wants to experience the greatest joys in life; to have a powerful presence, be knowledgeable, and to gain the respect of peers. Everyone would like to be spared from sorrow, poverty, pain and fears. Reincarnation is meant to develop the maximum of your potential so you can plunge into this great ocean of life with a life preserver without sinking to the bottom to be able to experience material, physical and spiritual blessings.

All individuals have an obligation to their souls. Life must be lived through strengths and potential. The greatest difficulty for many people is lack of self-understanding or not knowing the direction to focus toward. Discover the unconscious obstacles that keep you in the prison of your consciousness and deny you your true destiny. Use the numbers in your birthdate to understand the relationship between your personality and your soul. Claim the unique individual you are. Know how your mind and actions are influenced by the combinations of your numbers.

It is true you reap what you sow. The body is like a field that needs to be harvested. If you sow bad seeds you harvest negativity. When you work with the best seeds you harvest great deeds. Some gardens take longer to mature than others, depending upon the soil you have to work with. Remember, weeds grow in both bad and good gardens and must constantly be removed so they do not take over the healthy growth. You are the farmer of your field, which is the soul, and you are responsible for taking proper care of it.

Failure to understand your mission can push you back a whole incarnation if you refuse to follow the guidance of your higher self. It is important to recognize the soul-stirring events in your life which force you to face yourself and to bring your hidden secrets out into your awareness. The first place to begin understanding is with your birthdate. Add all the numbers in the year, month and day and reduce the total to a single digit number. Use that single digit, called the *destiny* number as the beginning stages of your development. The numbers in your birthdate reveal the mold of your characteristics in which the process of fate cast your destiny, revealing your destiny for your soul's growth.

The destiny number is the beginning of a sequence of numbers that will be used to formulate a profile of your individuality. The destiny number never changes as your birthday never changes. You cannot change the day nor the time you were born in order to change your destiny. Your soul knows the purpose of your being. I know people who change their birthday to change the destiny of their fate. Rubbish, I do not accept that theory. Your true birthdate will guide you to the experience of your soul's purpose. You cannot prevent or avoid the developmental principles of your fundamental premise. When you do not know your true birthdate, an alias birthdate should not be assumed. To change or accept any birthdate is bogus and under those circumstances the mystery of that ignorance is never unlocked. It is best to live life in your present incarnation, knowing that your destiny is not to be established. Avoid taking on a birthright that has no value to your real development. Your birthpath is your journey, and if there is no valid proof of your birth, then use this lifetime as a journey of adventure, allowing faith and fate to deliver you to the peace and purpose of your soul. You must surrender to the order of the universe to maintain the true purpose of your birthright. It is a mathematical principle that you are the embodiment of your birthdate from birth till death. Changing your birthdate will never change your original blueprint. An apple tree will not bear oranges and an orange tree will not bear apples.

The destiny number is similar to the sun sign in astrology. It is the soul's purpose and significant of your individual development. It is how you want to shine. The numbers are symbols of expression. The power of that expression has an element of distinct factors that affect the nature of the number. The planetary element of your astrological month, sign and the destiny number determine how the destiny number will express itself through that planetary energy.

There are four planetary elements that define the energy of your number: fire, earth, air and water. When you know your astrological birth sign and your destiny number, you can decipher the function of the element with which your number is associated. The numbers 1 through 9 will be integrated with one of the four elements. This integration is essential to the function of the destiny number. A destiny number of 1 will have a different reaction to the life flow if it is in a fire element than if number 1 would be in a water element.

Number 1 in a fire sign will be motivated by an excitable competitiveness, and number 1 in a water sign will be motivated by a more emotional competitiveness. Each element has its own vibration which constitutes a unique expression in the destiny number. Below is a list of the astrological signs and their corresponding element.

SIGN	DATES			ELEMENT
ARIES	Mar	21 -- Apr	19	FIRE
TAURUS	Apr	20 -- May	20	EARTH
GEMINI	May	21 -- Jun	20	AIR
CANCER	Jun	21 -- Jul	22	WATER
LEO	July	23 -- Aug	22	FIRE
VIRGO	Aug	23 -- Sep	22	EARTH
LIBRA	Sep	23 -- Oct	22	AIR
SCORPIO	Oct	22 -- Nov	23	WATER
SAGITTARIUS	Nov	23 -- Dec	22	FIRE
CAPRICORN	Dec	22 -- Jan	20	EARTH
AQUARIUS	Jan	20 -- Feb	19	AIR
PISCES	Feb	19 -- Mar	20	WATER

(In the above list, some of the dates overlap, because in certain calendar years the birthdays can begin or extend to those days)

When you determine your destiny number and your planetary element from the above list, you will be able to focus on the relevance of your number and how the expression will be communicated. Every number has a different energy. Each number in one of the four elements will use that element to help perfect the individual quality in the expression of that number. You incarnated into this lifetime with your destiny number with a specific planetary element to reveal the forces of how you must use your destiny number. Your destiny number and the mode of the element it represents is important in how you use your potential through the use of your will. As you acquaint yourself with the interpretation of your destiny number, observe the primary purpose of the developmental nature of its planetary element. When you understand the essence of your nature and how it functions, then you can understand your mission and the wave of reincarnation that drew you into the ocean of life.

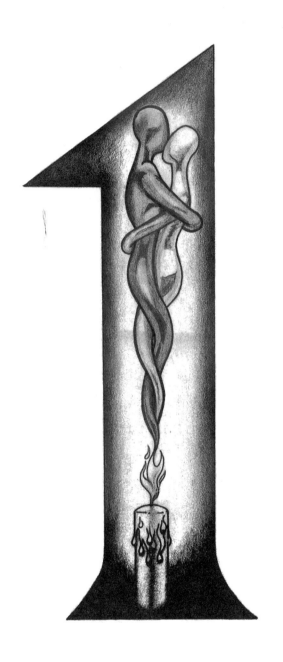

The Flame of Life

Androgynous Lifeforce

DESTINY NUMBER 1

The Alpha of all life-force is the beginning of your first breath of prana. Your heart starts to beat and the development of your journey on earth begins. One is the outburst of energy like the first glimmer of dawn that brings light to the day. All number 1 individuals are regarded as a single phenomenon having a powerful force which can nurture the spiritual growth of fellow human beings. Similar to an arrow, your thrust is forward and forceful. The number 1 wants to run before walking. It is masculine in nature. One is independent, likes to stand alone, desirous of personal power and determined to accomplish worldly achievements. Destiny 1 people also have strong leadership qualities, need a lot of freedom and will rarely ask for help from others. The ego is strong and actions are impulsive and overwhelming, just so number 1 can be first.

Never concerned with the past, number 1 always looks enthusiastically to the future. However, there is such an ironclad determination to lead and to win that the energy may manifest in reckless behavior or aggression, causing you to lose your centeredness. Your opinions are strong, and your outspoken nature will make you say things you may sometimes regret. You have little patience for people with opposite viewpoints because you are very sure of yourself, and do not trust the advice of others. One is associated with independence and leadership, needing to perform actions with initiative and force. This expression can make the individual appear selfish and self-centered, always seeking self-importance. One is strong, direct and conveys courage, to do, to dare, to know. It is the straight and narrow path upright in body and character just like the number 1 signifies. One stands for the beginning of man's being, and the "I" entity is your primary thrust into life.

A well-developed number 1 with both feet on the ground can represent a true channel of pioneering spirit which makes the person unique in vigor and enterprise. With the courage and audacity to succeed in life, you will pursue your goals relentlessly, even if it is a tug of war. Most people who are a 1 destiny have a very silent and serene nature, yet they are dynamic individuals who endure a lot and can be quite controlling, but you would never know it upon first meeting them. One can often be a loner number.

Similar to the number 7 you enjoy many friendships in life, yet you need a lot of time to yourself and do not feel obligated to anyone. The faith and belief you have in yourself is so strong you react like a soldier never thinking of the danger only the performance. Satisfaction in achieving your personal goals presents itself when you use strategy and avoid impulsive reactions. Always complete projects you begin. Learn to develop your character beyond the ego desires to achieve quality not quantity.

In competitions, number 1 is not concerned with the prize; winning is everything. Your greatest satisfaction comes in achieving the desired goal so you can move on to your next challenge for new excitement and adventure. The contributions you make are not always acknowledged, nor will others always appreciate your exuberant vitality. You will benefit the most when you work independently, not in a subservient role. Vocations where you will excel will be in using your skills to promote yourself or to promote others who will empower you. Your constant aim is to conquer and to accomplish; however, in your driving force remember that you can be unreasonable if you are not controlled. Number 1s can be most successful when using talents with tenacity and patience, not force. Many accomplishments can be within your reach when you allow your endless energy and enthusiasm to soar. Be productive in your conquest for material success. Learn to understand the reality of the real world. Sometimes number 1s can ignore aspects of reality, thrusting themselves into the fire, only to get burned. One is autonomy, not uniformity; so if you are a number 1 destiny, apply the tools that keep your life in balance and make this lifetime a special experience.

Most number 1s are very particular about public image and will go to extremes to receive recognition or to be popular in many social circles. Even though you are capable of being a lone-wolf, you want to be friends with everyone and you will go out of your way for friendships. Unfortunately, you do not always make a reliable companion because of your restless nature. If you already have plans with someone else and something more exciting comes along, in your venturesome spirit you will go with the second choice. Your social invitations will be viewed as opportunities that will benefit you the most, or the invitation that sounds the most exciting. As a result of your dynamic magnetism, smooth charm and self-confident individuality your company will be sought by others. To others you reveal a cheerful, exciting, entertaining and animating personality. Because of these viable assets, you will acquire public favor, gain power, be respected and have good fortune. You will benefit through many friends and business associates because of your goodwill towards others. You are always willing to help a friend regardless of the situation.

The last half of life will be your greatest adventure with less restrictions and more freedom in your life. Problems in the first half of life are due to uncontrolled desires and lack of discipline in controlling actions, especially during early years. Gather knowledge from what you learn in your life experiences to mold life to be fertile and useful. In the working world number 1 will never retire, for retirement to a 1 is the end of existence.

Although you easily rush into romantic situations because of a warm and passionate nature, once you make a commitment, it will be forever. Both males and females, especially the males, will have many opportunities for romantic involvements and many friendships. The opposite sex can be your weakness as a result of your strong sexual urges and your passion for forbidden fruit. You require a partner who is physically and sexually compatible, or it will be easy to stray. As a lover or mate, you can be very demanding, especially a female--always wanting to have the power and control. Even though you may be possessive and jealous of the one you love, you can also be a big flirt, expecting your mate to be understanding. It is not uncommon for you to possess animal passion and yet be unemotional in romantic liaisons. To be in love with one individual is not necessarily important to be happy or to be sexually involved. To be loved by many is more to your spirit, since it is easy for you to fall in and out of love. Although once you decide to mate with someone exclusively, you are capable of being loyal while your interest is in them. The person you choose as a lifelong mate should be strong, independent and self-confident. Your companion should be willing to allow you to take the lead, or to at least let you think that you have it!

OCCUPATIONS BEST SUITED FOR 1s:

business owner, entrepreneur, corporate director, management, promoter, chauffeur, aviator, supervisor, engineer, attorney, military, police officer, politician, disc jockey, transportation driver, race car driver, athlete, religious leaders, yogi, FBI worker, sales, waiter, cashier, mechanic, fireman, musician, telemarketing, construction, hunter

As you swim upstream in the ocean of life, you will be the eternal flame that burns bright to light the way for others, never losing your brilliance. Use the passion in your enthusiasm to ignite inspiration in others as well as in your personal desires as you go forth into this adventurous world. You do best when you are your own person and allow your uniqueness to shine. Live life freely with integrity and allow your desires to achieve the impossible dream. You are the beginning, not the end. You are the seed of new growth and the profound liberator of mankind. In you is the flame which illuminates the world, bringing light and energy into your life and the lives of others. You must take lead in the dance of life.

The Yin and Yang of Life

The Male Supporting the Female Premise

DESTINY NUMBER 2

The Shiva and Shakti of eastern philosophy. Two is a beautiful reminder of the support and understanding it takes to have a loving relationship. Two is the partnership number which seeks to serve the world through a marriage of perfection. The union is not necessarily of two intimate individuals, but the union of the masculine and feminine natures within the soul. Tied closely to the pulse of humanity, a 2 is most effective when interacting with groups of people or in public communications. Attracting people from all walks of life comes easy because of the cordial and sincere disposition, which is 2s greatest asset. Most 2s are talented in areas of music, cultural art, counseling, or in fields connected with beauty because of their artistic sensitivity. Two is the ebb and flow of all emotions and it will show in the dual personality of the individual. A destiny number 2 is under the rulership of the planetary configuration of the moon which is the embodiment of pleasure, love, and emotion.

Like a pendulum that moves back and forth, 2 is the continual movement of balance and imbalance,expansion and contraction, spirit and nature. Individuals with a 2 never weigh situations; they either reject them or accept them. Your patience with people, combined with your strong communication skills help to keep you objective and centered enabling you to keep your environment serene. Blessed with a strong persuasive personality you can be powerful as a leader of large groups. Your power lies in the ability to be the bridge that can unite people to get projects accomplished and deadlines met. Two understand the difference between a compromise and a truce to keep peace. This awareness is a primary attribute to the life force of all groups to become involved. You are able to see both sides of a situation in solving problems, whether on a one to one basis or with a group.

Number 2 is a pair of opposites, always breaking away from the number 1-- but remember $1 + 1 = 2$. Although 2 is generally good natured and unassuming, it is always aware of its rival and will always be protective of its own personality. In many ways 2 is like the weather. When it is a beautiful day, 2 will be on top of the world--full of sunshine and enthusiasm. When it is a dreary day, 2 will fall to the moods of depression--full of fears and phobias, vacillating between highs and lows.

Being an impressionable and intuitive being, be careful of living in a world of fantasy--not wanting to accept the responsibility of pressure or negative conditions. As a destiny number 2 you always seek to have someone dependable in your life and with whom you can confide your hidden insecurities.

There is a natural ability to mediate between groups to promote compromise making you a strong and effectual force as Earth Mother or Earth Father. When charm is used with a diplomatic approach you will radiate love and inspiration. Do not be enslaved by vanity, pride or insecurities that tempt you to satisfy people's needs just to keep their favor. Avoid becoming easily offended or upset when people's remarks and criticisms affect you personally, or when those remarks oppose your point of view.

Two is essentially a well-balanced individual, but when you do become angry and lose control, you will drag everything out of the closet that has ever angered or troubled you especially if you have not dealt with past problems as they occurred. As a number 2 you require a lot of attention and compassion in your life. Deep in you lies a dual personality that can be a mischief maker as well as a peace-maker. At your worst you can be malicious, cruel, even deceptive, if it helps attain your purpose. Remember, the 2 can stand for "two-faced"--saying one thing and meaning another. Two is the number of polarity both positive and negative. When life is financially and emotionally fulfilling you will move with harmony and grace, and when it is not, you become emotional and depressed, brutalizing yourself and others.

Your feminine soul understands color and rhythm and this is why you display a natural talent in your creative ideas. Whether it is in your home or profession, your refined taste will bring many compliments. You will also be able use your talents such as dancing, writing, music or painting as a tool for relaxation and enjoyment. Social gatherings, an evening of good conversation or just friendly dinner parties will contribute to your well-being, because you love being around people.

In your lifetime you will experience several loves, but with those involvements there will also be some heartaches. With a tendency to get too emotionally involved you express your sentiments in a devouring love, demanding the same in return. Even though you are involved with someone in an abounding way and that person becomes your total anchor, you still need a lot of outside stimulation and social interaction with friends and family. A strong fear of being alone or being lonely sometimes prompts a 2 to stay in an unhappy or unfulfilling relationship. But when you are through, it is over, and it is useless to argue about what went wrong. Marriage and love are very important to you because they add to your sense of security.

Partnerships are important, and you will always profit from them, whether it is in business or in a marriage. Two has the ability to attract a strong mate with the potential to acquire material resources through them, allowing you to live a comfortable lifestyle. The power of personal attraction and charm make it is easy for you to influence others. Therefore, you will always prosper in a career focused on service to others, working with groups of people or using your creative talents.

There is great emotional attachment to sexual sensations and pleasures that can lead you to licentious behavior. In a desperate longing for closeness, you can become too vulnerable just to have emotional and sexual gratification. Do not allow sexual desires let you fall prey to others by being available to a variety of partners or predisposed to sudden infatuations. Your obsessive quest to satisfy your sexual appetite could paralyze your true talents. The wheels of life should always be in balance to avoid putting pressure on yourself or on others. Use your head and your heart as the rhythm of energy to perform actions that keep you functioning at your very best.

OCCUPATIONS BEST SUITED FOR 2s:

artistic designer, musician, actor, dancer, entertainer, host, mediator, translator, politician, cosmetologist, therapist, seminar lecturer, teacher, secretary, jeweler, social worker, creative service representative, chef, fashion designer, telephone operator, flight attendant, nursery school teacher, importer and exporter, nanny, landscaper, gardener, housekeeper, art dealer, interior decorator, sculpturer, graphic artist, sales person, printer, counselor, customer service representative

As you swim upstream in the ocean of life hold hands with the universe, Know that you are a sensitive and cooperative soul who carries the power of personal charm to attract your blessings. Your ability as a diplomat and the consideration you show others will help you become effective and respected in society. As the Yin and the Yang, you are able to bring balance and love into this great ocean of life. Although you may not always receive the public attention you deserve, the result of your teamwork and cooperative efforts will bring you admiration and appreciation. Allow your grandeur and spirit to permeate everywhere you go and in everyone you meet. You are the essence of Earth Mother or Earth Father and your loving energy will be an experience from which all may benefit. When you love as one, two will always benefit.

The Trinity of Life

Father, Mother, Child

DESTINY NUMBER 3

The sound "OM" is symbolic of the Trinity and balance manifesting creation, preservation and disintegration. Threefold is the essence of your oneness--Father, Mother, and child. Three is the triad of perfect balance containing the physical, mental and spiritual generative force. Threefold has many forms such as past, present, and future. There is an old saying: "Everything happens in threes," or "I'll give you three guesses." Your essence is the spirit of immortal youth. At heart, 3s are like playful children, full of buoyancy and optimism. Always outgoing and generally happy-go-lucky, this youthfulness makes the number 3 popular with adults as well as children.

The extension of yourself is your charm and social magnetism. Your natural gifts lie in your ability to be warmhearted, friendly and extremely sociable. The characteristics of the number 3 are to be expansive, communicative and entertaining. Blessed with literary talents and verbal skills, positions of public speaking, creative writing, publishing and journalism will be of interest to you. Any subject you present will be skillfully done, stimulating and humorous due to your melodramatic actions. Your conversation is like an interesting story full of drama, spice and imagination. Many writers and directors have 3 as a destiny number because 3s like to play out their fantasies in the real world. You love the attention focused on you while you speak, so you can be chatty and long-winded, never running out of things to talk about.

Due to a friendly nature, people often overlook your imperfections. You never seem to worry about anything and feel that whatever will be, will be--and you accept that. Of course, everything always seems to turn out favorably for you regardless of the situation, almost as if you have divine protection. Your subconscious fantasy is a motivating factor to your creative thought form. Often inspired by your creative ideas, you never stop to think that these ideas originated from your fantasies. You carry within you a joy that is always present. You heal others through your gifts of words, wit and wisdom and you have the luck to succeed without even trying. It is very important to broaden your philosophy to attract opportunities. Remember, prosperity does not always mean financial wealth but the innate wealth of your natural abilities.

Another ambition you have is a desire to travel extensively. The world is like a playground--just waiting to be explored. You love to be boundless in your journeys, with freedom to roam wherever your curiosity leads you. You will cultivate friendships with people from all walks of life because you view everyone as your friend. Foreign travel is something you will definitely do if time and money allow. It will not be unusual for you to take many short weekend trips in order to satisfy your penchant for roaming.

Because of a propensity to communicate with many different individuals on all levels, a destiny number 3 should be versed in foreign languages. If you cannot stimulate your curiosity, you get easily frustrated and will go to extraordinary means to be mentally superior. Absent mindedness can be a deterrent to your focus because your mind is so expansive and curious that before an idea or thought is finished, you are on to another. In spite of your self-assurance and intelligence there are a lot of hidden fears which can block your confidence. Objectivity is necessary when dealing with others to avoid becoming shallow. Avoid allowing sarcasm and bluntness to be your non-redeeming quality.

You are not only child-like, but can be childish, especially when it comes to getting your own way, even behaving in a spoiled manner. The planet Jupiter rules the number 3. Both Jupiter and 3 have qualities of childlike behavior along with their benevolent wisdom. Both symbolize spirit and matter united by the mind, being threefold in manifestation. Three's basic needs revolve around diversity, excitement and challenge. These basic skills will promote intellectual reinforcements to any goal consisting of intellectual reasoning or communication.

Your warm bubbly personality is the spark of life that ignites positive enthusiasm in others. Encourage people to reach greater achievements and help others to feel good about themselves. Your aim in life is to rise to any occasion. You will never be satisfied with a subordinate role or any unfulfilling job. It is important to expand yourself in the philosophical realm, but also to meet your desires in the creative world.

Broaden your life through your love of travel and in the mastery of your communication skills. You are definitely a forerunner who can do something important in life. Positions of authority are best suited for you, especially where trust and expansion of authority are required. You do not like to be challenged by authority and when you are you become quarrelsome, making as many enemies as friends. Avoid expecting too much from life or people since it will only lead to disappointments and undue pressures for you and for others.

When you overcome negative thinking and see your experiences as learning situations you will benefit from them. Keep your attention focused on what you love to do so you can expand your vision to become a reality. Through the passion of your vision and magical powers of communication you will eventually achieve ultimate success in whatever you pursue.

It is your nature to constantly persevere to gain wealth rather than to live in moderate surroundings. Although much of your life will be surrounded by luck and good fortune you must make a conscious effort to work hard to achieve your acquired success. A 3 knows how to turn negative situations into incredible opportunities.

Home and family will always play an important role in your life, regardless of your status. You make a wonderful parent because of your childlike imagination and enjoy spending a lot of quality time with your children and family. Relatives could impose themselves on you because of your good nature and willingness to be of help to them. But you do not mind, because you view helping others as being supportive to them to maintain peacefulness in their life.

You may have several serious relationships and possibly several marriages striving to find the mate best suited for you. You need a partner who is intellectual, interesting and fun to be with or you will become disenchanted and dissatisfied with the relationship. Once mated 3s are capable of being monogamous and sincere to the individual they share their affection with, having a long and happy life together.

Definitely a person who likes to flirt 3s could have many sexual companions. Attracting the opposite sex is very easy for you. Do not allow your sexual passion to interfere with your friendships by mingling both. Your sexual weakness can cause difficulties in your relationships and could be responsible for confusing love with friendship.

Regardless of your station in life, you will be fortunate in your relationships and friendships and thrive in social situations. Most 3s are blessed with a comfortable home and will be able to attract opportunities to attain extraordinary success.

OCCUPATIONS BEST SUITED FOR 3s:

entertainer, broadcaster, TV position, publisher, printer, pilot, flight attendant, nursery school teacher, traveling salesperson, marketer, clown, cosmetologist, physician, banker, jockey, broker, attorney, advertiser, car salesperson, construction involvement, lecturer, foreign language interpreter, writer, personnel counselor, administration, horse trainer, gambler, journalist, clergy or religion vacation

As you swim upstream in the ocean of life, the magic of the 3 will be your good fortune allowing you to look at life optimistically and to become the sunshine for others in their darkness. You are an inspirational soul who will touch many hearts through the value of your unique and cheerful personality. Speak loudly with spirited enthusiasm as you profoundly express yourself in the world through your skills of communication. You know how to create cheerfulness and weave the web of happiness for others to renew their spirit as you travel on your journey. Your smile is like a brilliant light that glows. Others will realize the value of your joyful and benevolent spirit as the key for them to become light and cheerful in finding their happiness in the universe. You are the trinity of the past, present and future.

Home
Sweet
Home

The Foundation of Life

What We Build Our Life Upon

DESTINY NUMBER 4

Somewhere in the highest mountains sits a pot of gold and although it may take a lifetime to reach it through the sweat of your brow, you will attain your dream. You are the foundation of all the numbers; the 4 cardinal points of the cross, the 4 seasons, and the 4 elements of air, earth, fire and water. The forces of the 4 will bring about changes during your lifetime from all directions for you to establish a lasting foundation built on sacrifices and struggles.

When you carry your cross know that you have spiritual help to fulfill your destiny. Your power and success will be measured by the strength of your spiritual rod and not the anguish of your sacrifices. Without a 4s laborious efforts there would be little accomplished in this world. You are not unlucky, boring or simple as you are labeled. You are invaluable to society and the world at large in harvesting perfection. Born to express yourself through a stable and orderly life, it is paramount for a number 4 to keep life within specific bounds to avoid adversity. As probably the most responsible and dependable of all the numbers, your one weakness is that you take yourself and life too seriously. Governed by a strict self-discipline and a sense of duty you will exercise caution and prudence in your path to success.

Four is a material number representing a grim struggle for existence. The tendency to be selfish, gloomy and negative develops from the slow progress that transpires through your misfortunes and limitations. Not afraid of work, you are afraid of failing to meet your own expectations. In fact, you always tackle all your projects with great steadfastness and purpose. It is important to you to do a job efficiently and you will not be rushed until you near perfection. This sense of self-discipline can keep you isolated and alone.

To achieve success, 4 must labor with the burdens of hard work and a rigid schedule while awaiting golden opportunities. Any project that calls for dedication, endurance or problem solving is your forte. It is important in your daily schedule that your work is physical and yet you must have projects for mental stimulation. You are not an idealist, your mind works through logic and practical beliefs.

You possess a rare loyalty of character, regardless of your strict and overbearing discipline. People, in time, will come to respect your principles. Being too rigid or forceful with family or friends can be exasperating and burdensome to them, alienating you from the people to whom you want to be close to. There are times that a 4 needs to be more flexible and resilient in expressing opinions. Do not allow rigid qualities to sabotage your progress, but enable you to see that there is more than one solution to any problem. Encourage others by giving positive reinforcement and taking a sincere interest in others.

Honor other people's opinions by overcoming an unyielding nature. There are situations when a change of plans or accepting another point of view can actually add new life to a dead-end plan, bringing unexpected happiness and success. Flexibility requires unselfishness on your part. Your cooperation can only help you to lay a solid foundation to achieve success for your future.

Ease up in life and release some of your defenses to become more trusting. You will actually feel like you have more freedom with less worry. Learn to overcome the rigid limitations you put on yourself and others. Not everyone can keep up with your expectations, nor do they care to! Being too frugal and overly cautious without being visionary will cause you to overlook unique opportunities for success.

An intellectual approach to life, proficient work habits, and discipline will be the strength that eventually helps you to achieve your life accomplishments, but not as quickly as you would like. Nothing will come easily to a 4 the first half of life. The second half of life will bring many bounties of blessings if you are patient. See experiences as your teacher the first half of your life. The wisdom you gain from your life experiences will make you a better teacher to others when you become the master.

Give form to whatever you do and although the timing will always seem off, never give in to the obstacles that are put in your way; instead, see them as a spiritual task. Limitations are part of the learning process 4 must endure. On many occasions you may want to give up under the constant pressure. With dedicated perseverance continue onward, never allowing weakness or procrastination to control your character.

A destiny 4 does not deny you your due reward in life, it just teaches you to acquire patience in the unfoldment of time. Maturity will bring you your treasured goals, even if it takes 40 to 50 years. Remember that something wonderful is worth waiting for. The years of wisdom and maturity can be your "pot of gold" as your reward when you eventually reach the top of the mountain. Just as it takes time to grow a tree, the true beauty of your inner personality also takes time.

Family and friends can benefit greatly from your strength of character. Remember, people are human beings, not robots. Guard against getting too set in your habits, not allowing yourself to be happy or to have fun. Let go of responsibilities and problems by spending quality time with family and friends, for this earth is meant to enjoy as well as to serve. Because you take life so seriously it is very important to occasionally take time to unwind, hang loose and appreciate all that life has to offer. Your only limitation is yourself.

Career or personal problems should never be carried into your social activities. Do not bore friends or family members with pressures or worries that they are not able to resolve. Learn balance in your life by knowing the difference between work and play. Dance to the tune of fun and relaxation, accepting all social invitations regardless of how bogged down you are. When working long hours and problems begin to make you feel depressed, remember, take time to relax.

Do not be afraid to show affection or to be spontaneous with your feelings, especially with loved ones. Learn the art of giving love giving and being compassionate. When you become less serious in your attitude toward security and more light-hearted in your spirit to have fun, your dreams will seem to materialize much quicker.

As a 4 you are usually cautious and practical about love, but in your need for love you sometimes can be ruled by your heart and not your head. Make sure your emotional responses are appropriate to help you, not hinder you. Listen to your inner spirit as your safety valve to keep your emotions balanced. Never neglect family or home by placing them second as a result of your worldly ambitions. Remember, you have a responsibility to both your family and career.

Though you are a loyal partner in marriage or a love relationship you are not an overly romantic individual. You live life with total sincerity and dedication to the one you love because you frown on divorce even when the marriage is without gratification. As a 4 you can be a great lover when you want to be, however, you do not always put a lot of importance on romance or in displaying your affections. Four is seldom sexually overactive, unless other numbers in the profile prove differently. Always bear in mind that you fear opening to your emotions, but remember to be human and to touch base with your heart and feelings on a daily basis.

As a parent you are very loving and proud, but also very strict. You respect rules and regulations and live life with discipline, wanting your children to abide by the same discipline. Be careful in parenting--it is important that you do not take away your children's freedom or limit their personal expression, influencing emotional dependency or rebellious behavior by retaliating against your strict rules. Although your actions and behavior come from a place of love, your discipline can be too severe and painful, needing balance. Maintain a loving image and express your love openly for your family's emotional health as well as your own.

OCCUPATIONS BEST SUITED FOR 4s:

business owner, builder/construction, land developer, realtor, mechanic, electrician, carpenter, accountant/CPA, brick layer, stock broker, housekeeper, tailor/seamstress, lab/medical technician, policeman, laborer, factory worker, industrial agent, supervisor, meat cutter, rancher, restaurant/motel, antique dealer, grocery clerk, repairman, doctor, manufacturer, manager, chemist, organizer

As you swim upstream in the ocean of life, know that you are in the hands of Father Time. You will set exemplary standards of achievement through establishing order in any organization you direct. You were born to bear responsibilities and to see the practical side of life in laying a secure foundation for others as well as yourself. In your life's journey your virtues will be sincerity, dedication, dependability and industriousness. You posses a rare spirit of traditional values that will provide you with the success and respect you merit. Know that God is your refuge and the remover of all pain. Your life performance will serve actions of righteousness as you are deemed the sustainer of the Universe.

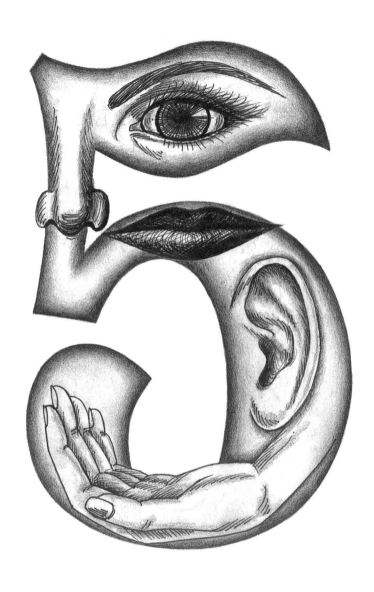

The Experimenter of Life
The Five Senses: Sight, Smell, Taste, Hearing and Touch

DESTINY NUMBER 5

Five is the dividing point of the numeric spectrum of 1 to 9. You are the middle of the road and life needs to be a series of experiences and freedom for your soul. You are the number of the 5 senses and the 5 pointed star reminding you that you are both human and divine. The 5 virtues of love are understanding, compassion, devotion, patience and honesty. The five deadly sins of fear are anger, greed, lust, pride and attachment. You are responsible for the use of these five senses to enable you to rise to the heights of the fountain of altruism or to sink to the bottom of the ocean of austerity. Learn to balance life and to realize that personal power commensurates with abilities and effectiveness. Five has the ability to bridge and communicate thought forms with feelings between spirit and body. You are often the catalyst for change but must be less unconventional and more responsible when given free reign.

There is no limit to the possibilities of your talents. Involve yourself in a vocation that requires a variety of physical and mental activities. Having a high-strung, volatile and restless disposition requires that you use positive direction in your goals or you could lose sight of your objectivity and become non-productive.

Be an individual of strong character, independence and intelligence. Rely on these strengths to accomplish your mission. Five's love to gain in knowledge and your interests will need to expand to various subjects. You are quick to learn and always eager to add new ideas to your thinking, trying to have inside information on many subjects. Your perceptive nature has the propensity to detect opportunities to be used to your best advantage. However, your intellectual attitude can make you appear cold and intimidating, which could keep you at arm's length with friends or business associates. Avoid being too unconventional in your thinking and decision making. Do not make demands in your work environment or in relationships for it will create undue stress for both.

Be discerning in all activities and avoid being obsessive to achieve freedom of your being or your personal development. When moderation, discipline and focus are used in your objectives, good fortune and accomplishments will be reflected in your successes. Others may perceive you as intelligent but also as insensitive and impatient. Regardless of how you appear, remember, you are a warm and kind-hearted human being.

With a nature as curious as a cat's, this curiosity will motivate you to expand your personal development and to participate in stimulating activities. It is important to always improve yourself so you respond confidently to challenges in your career, friendships and adventures. You are a gifted and articulate conversationalist, but must avoid being too one sided in your thinking and decision making. Bring balance to some of your narrow-minded attitudes so you can experience the nine lives of the curious cat, but with the discernment of an intelligent being.

The number 5 at its worst can be belligerent and unreasonable, especially when feeling trapped, confined, or out of control. Being the midpoint of the numbers 1 to 9, your personality is a dichotomy of desires and extremes wanting to be part of the pleasurable excitement and to be well-informed intellectually.

Like a seesaw in life, you either experience the pinnacle of grandeur or the declination of despair. Allow your positive points to prosper. Acknowledge your unique abilities to acquire wealth, success and happiness. Project your magnetism with your intellectual talents to master your individuality.

Do not eclipse your human qualities by getting stuck in procrastination over nagging reasoning. In your assessment of any circumstance, use both head and heart to become truly balanced. Be very clear about your goals and what you expect to achieve from life.

Friends, acquaintances, buddies, companions and business associates will always be plentiful in life if you openly desire them. Life will be adventuresome, yet it can seem monotonous, depending upon your mood. As quickly as you become friends with people, you can as easily become bored with them. Five wants to be constantly stimulated and will seek out companions who will satisfy that intellectual hunger. In your conversations with others avoid using tactless comments that can be offensive, especially when you are tense, restless or depressed. Your comments to others could appear insensitive in your quest to be open and truthful.

Your over-bearing personality will be a challenge to others in your personal relationships, especially if you attract a strong partner who also likes to be in control. Sexually, you are very alluring and attractive to the opposite sex. As a result of this sensuality you will have many opportunities for suitors or lovers, if you so desire. Your sexual appetite can vary from one extreme to the other, indulging yourself in sexual fantasies, or on the other hand becoming totally celibate.

Choose a partner who is compatible with your unpredictable and restless nature. Your charm and your sensuality are the magnets that will draw people to you. Your sexuality is not always external; it is your internal passion which makes you desirable and a mystery to others. Family will always be very important to you in life, especially as you become older and more mellow. Relationships with your family depend on your ability to be objective, compassionate and non-judgmental.

Learn to be more content in life by not responding to all your compulsions or physical weaknesses. Love for your family and mate must be unconditional, without expectations and without trying to force others to change their ways to suit your needs. Commitment to your spouse emotionally and spiritually is fundamental to a happy marriage and your well being. Choose a partner who is compatible and is understanding of your nature, so you can reach ultimate happiness in both marital bliss and career. When you are not happily in love you will experience a lack of interest in life which could lead to health and mental problems. When you become despondent and lonely it is difficult for you to make productive contributions to life or to find successful resolutions to problems. Your partner needs to be your best friend, your lover, your mentor and emotionally strong enough to handle your powerful and changeable personality.

OCCUPATIONS BEST SUITED FOR 5s:

administrator, physician, medical tech, personnel director, salesperson, travel agent, photographer, teacher, phone operator/technician, linguist, interpreter, athlete, journalist, reporter, editorialist, computer engineer, merchandiser, dancer, ambassador, foreign trader, professor, graphics researcher, analyst, producer, stenographer, painter, artist, scientist, court reporter, pilot

As you swim upstream in the ocean of life, diversity and flexibility will be your greatest challenge. Your spirit has the intensity and intelligence to cultivate all the adventures that life has to offer. Allow your uniqueness to be expansive to explore all the ponds in the universe. Push the buttons of others as you become the expander of thoughts to invigorate all boundaries. You are the bridge between the conscious and the unconscious. You are the center of life because of your placement among the numbers. You are the transmitter of knowledge and with your radiance you will able to transform mankind from the shadow of darkness into the sunlight through the magical light of the five-pointed star reflecting the ocean of life.

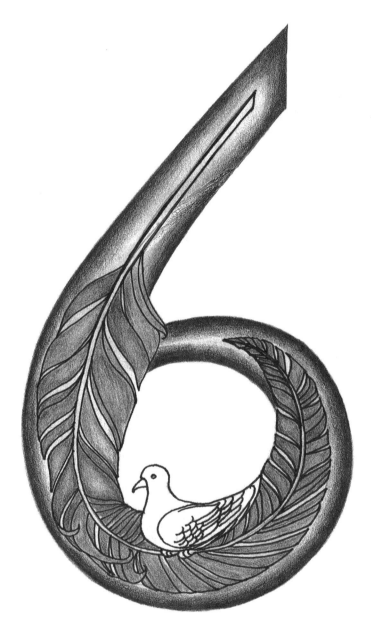

The Nurturers of Life

The Dove of Love and Peace

DESTINY NUMBER 6

You are the principal of the Yoni Shakti (power of the womb) and the maha Shivling (phallus) united in the number 6 energy to activate the feminine energy of creation in the garden of love. Your grace and charm are the personification of the feminine energy representing balance and harmony of the soul and body. Six is the two trinities (3 + 3) which seek wholeness, perfection and tranquillity. Your life needs to be free of daily clutter and the crude realities of life to be able to experience complete serenity and to blossom fully.

Being under the influence of the planet Venus, you have an inborn artistic soul with a heart of compassion. The romantic side of your nature always wants to live a life of illusion, not wanting to be exposed to the adversities of life. Being sensitive, you are aware of the feelings of others and enjoy being helpful to everyone in the universe. In doing so you also want to be appreciated and recognized for your good deeds.

The number 6 is a feminine and sensitive number. It is the number of love--symbolizing a gentle and passive nature that produces idleness, especially when there is lack of purpose. Your mission in life is to serve others and to be their support system through difficult times. In the physical world you must evolve through your labor of service, bringing love and happiness to every living thing.

In life always emphasize truth, sincerity and kindness. Through your helpfulness to others you will benefit and enjoy the contentment of feeling needed. For this reason, to gain favor you will have a tendency to want to fix everyone's problems. Your magic touch has a healing influence and your sincerity will help you attain public approval.

People will always seek you for your support and guidance because of your compassionate nature so it is important that you exemplify a stable personality to be respected for your viewpoints. Although you are very independent, your emotions are quite co-dependent with strong needs to be nurtured and taken care of. Your emotional dependency makes it difficult for you to experience wholeness unless you are being loved by another--feeling that love is a necessity to your emotional stability and not a choice. Learn to overcome this fear or it will manifest hindrances in your relationships as incompatibility and an inability to relate to others in a healthy way.

Known to be contradictory in your attitude; you are either too interfering or too impersonal. Avoid being overly sensitive to the slightest provocation or rejection or it will limit your ability to be rational. Whenever someone offends you, you become invisible by avoiding contact with them. Behind your awakened spiritual nature there is a mysterious character that is sometimes difficult to understand and you often feel misunderstood by others--and you are.

When you become the captain of your own vessel in life you will experience a tremendous source of inner strength. In your personal life do what you think is justified whether or not others agree with you. Underneath your sweet, docile temperament lies a stubborn and unyielding spirit. You do not allow anyone to interfere with your personal concerns and demand to have your own way when you feel you are right.

When you go deep within your soul you know how to concentrate to acquire the things you want, but not always the things you need from life. To be effective you must draw spiritual power from within; retreat to a quiet environment free from external confusion when you can or you will find it difficult to concentrate. Your soul is like a fragile flower that needs serenity, light and sunshine to be happy and to blossom.

At some point in your life you will be drawn into the spiritual realm as a result of your strong psychic powers or through a life crisis that will awaken your spiritual instincts. You are an idealist who needs to work hard at finding tranquility in your life, since life seldom runs smoothly for you. When you manifest the positive qualities of your nature and have complete trust and faith, you will find that you will be taken care of by your guardian angel regardless of your crisis.

Your strong psychic sense provides you with the necessary insight into humans which will be helpful in reading the thoughts of others. This intuition will help you to align the intuitive with the intellectual aspects of your mind to fulfill your spiritual insight. For your spiritual growth in this lifetime, you may have to give to others more than you receive, demanding nothing in return.

Physically and spiritually you will be blessed with inner and outer beauty. Most 6s are blessed with beautiful eyes which have the glow of mystical wisdom. Elegant in your stature and dress, you will package yourself in an attractive way. Home decorating will also be a creative outlet which comes naturally to you with your balanced sense of color and design. A 6 is always the perfect host or hostess or the perfect guest in another's home.

Due to your strong magnetism, charm and friendliness, you will be blessed with many wonderful friendships. People may come and go in your lifetime; however, you will always leave your special touch in the hearts of others because of your caring and giving nature. You care about your friendships, giving of yourself unselfishly.

You are happiest when you are in love. Love is the basis of your world and centeredness. It is characteristic of your nature to want to be dependent on another individual. You live life through your fantasies and seek to be showered with the nectar of love, because it feeds your gentle and loving soul.

Marriage is a very important contract to you. You take it very seriously as the ultimate goal to a successful journey in life. Your devotion to your spouse is unparalleled. You will make many sacrifices for your partner and your children especially when there is a strong emotional bond, but when there is not there you will find it easy to stray. Marriage can become the basic purpose of life for you and the love you receive makes it worth the sacrifices you choose to endure.

Genuine is the love you give to others. Yet, with all these attributes of loyalty, dedication and nurturing your relationships are never easy and you can be taken advantage of. As a result of attracting the wrong kind of person you may never experience the true fulfillment of love or may never find the perfect mate. Dissension between you and your partner can build into guilt because of the obligations you sometimes feel toward your mate, especially if the partner is unappreciative and unloving.

Realize in life that you cannot fix everyone's problems. Learn to accept people and situations for what they are. Many people in life will impose upon you for your help or advice leaving you feeling guilty if you do not respond to their needs. Teach others to heal themselves to bestow true love and spiritual healing to others. Share your personal experiences of miracles. Be the divine intervention for others when their boats capsize in the ocean of life, or when they feel they have lost sight of their direction, but do not try to become the captain of their ships.

OCCUPATIONS THAT BEST SUIT 6s:

counselor, healer, nurse, medical tech, social worker, welfare worker, psychologist, travel agent, airline worker, housekeeper, religious servant, teacher, beautician, interior decorator, florist, librarian, nursery school, veterinarian, office personnel, ballet dancer, skater, waitress/waiter, baker, cake decorator, chef/cook, grocer, nutritionist, lecturer, nanny

As you swim upstream in the ocean of life, use your heart and the embodiment of your kindness to bring love and joy to the world. Help to blend and balance the natures of the human and divine to a more perfect expression. You will be a fascination to many who cross your path and whose life you affect with your sparkling charm and grace. Because of your service to others, faith in God, sixth sense and your sense of duty, you will reap the rewards of success in the spiritual and financial domain. With your mystifying inner beauty and a heart for healing, people will be attracted to your presence, enabling you to restore harmony into humanity. In life, you will be a teacher of love, truth, kindness and spirituality, expecting nothing in return. You are the invisible power that bestows compassion to mankind through your soft heart and loving nature.

The Mystery of Life

The Fountain of Sacredness and Intellect

DESTINY NUMBER 7

From all beliefs in the world 7 is the most sacred and mystical of all the numbers, because 7 is the number of perfection. Seven is considered the number of perfection because it is associated with the creative forces of many expressions. Every 7 months the body tissue is replaced by new soft tissues, and every 7 years we have an entirely new constitution to our body. Seven is the number of days in a week and it is also the day of the Sabbath. It is stated in the *New Testament* that 7 sentences were spoken by Jesus before He died. There are 7 colors of the solar spectrum that make up the rainbow. The body has 7 psychic centers within it. There are 7 musical notes of the musical scale and 7 tones to the human voice. It also represents the 7 knowledges of mysticism, the psychic, occult, secrets and the mystery of time. Seven governs many other spectrums too numerous to mention.

Seven is the mystery number. Every man is an island, and your peripheral vision is an extension of that philosophy. Your mission is to raise your own consciousness and the consciousness of mankind beyond the physical realm. Mastering skills throughout your life is necessary to your survival. Continuous knowledge must be acquired by you to educate society to help to uncover the covert conditions of life. There will be times you feel and understand the mystery of life and many times when you do not. It is easy for you to be dissolved in your spiritual consciousness by the illusions of the material plane.

In your search for wisdom look for the right path that will help you in your personal growth and yet be the power that lights the way for others. You will be constantly drawn into discontented experiences until you learn to acquire unshakable faith and trust. Learn to discern between illusion and reality so you can combine understanding with righteousness of action. Your actions cannot be merely the force of your mental thoughts but of complete fusion of your mind, body and spirit.

Your emotions lie deep within you and for that reason your ultra-sensitive and impressionable nature can be destructive to your spiritual idealism. Unless the people who surround you know that, they may find you difficult to understand. By nature you are truly sentimental, idealistic and refined; however, 7 gets discontented easily by lack of physical gratification and imperfections in people's character. When you fall in love do not be led by illusions which could eventually be destroyed by reality.

Because of a lone wolf nature you are not always popular and you seldom go out of your way to be a friend to others, although others will seek your friendship. It is not that you dislike friendships or socializing, you just enjoy and value your time alone. You do best when alone enjoying the silence of your own world.

Life for you can be a playground of sensual pleasures if you do not learn to resist the temptations of the opposite sex and your overactive sexual drive. You have a low energy level, yet high aspirations. Hard physical work or pressure will cause you fatigue and oppression forcing you to isolate yourself from the social scene. Vocations that require mental strategy, not physical labor, are best suited for you.

Pull together all your knowledge and experiences in this lifetime to complete the development of your spiritual growth. Learn to accept situations and people at face value to help relieve stress in your life. Your temper can be fierce when out-of-control and you can become confrontational when intense about something. Your quest to understand people and life will help you develop the understanding that is necessary to benefit the people who seek your knowledge. As a seven, you will become an authority on any subject that fascinates them.

Absorb knowledge from all sources in your intellectual passion, but do not let your conscious, rational mind become a hindrance to your higher mind or your spiritual desires. Maturity in the second half of your life helps you to succeed in life more easily. You have the capacity to set goals with high standards for your place within the world. Let opportunities unfold for you by letting go of your fears. Guard against self-pity. Live according to the rules and disciplines of life and opportunities will present themselves in mysterious ways.

One of the dangers a 7 must be aware of is a weakness to alcohol or drugs for the thrill of the elation, only to become addicted. As a destiny 7 you are not always absorbed in material luxuries of life; instead, you put more emphasis on the everyday comforts and pleasures. Many times it will be hard for you to make decisions and you may try to overcome your desires by escaping into alcohol or drugs to avoid opposition or controversy. Drugs and alcohol are addictive vices and though they are tools used to soothe your pressures, they will affect your mind and hinder your accomplishments. Life is not easy for anyone. Although situations will not always be what you hoped for, in your own mysterious way you try to survive because you do believe in miracles.

A difficult issue for you is to open up and share your inner feelings. It is not often that you open up to others because you bury everything inside of yourself. Releasing tension through your addictions usually becomes an unhealthy habit. Allow your creative energy and your vivid imagination to help you gain your self-confidence and to reach the pinnacle of achievement you desire and deserve. Mingle with people who are intellectual and stimulating so that they can broaden your insights. Be a deep thinker and become an avid reader to discover the mysteries of life. Become more purposeful and frugal with your resources by not squandering your money. Give great attention to details for if you do, you can perfect anything you set out to accomplish. Discover what you enjoy doing most, master it and then let your higher self guide you to your destiny.

You will enjoy many social and meaningful friendships, but will commit slowly to a close personal relationship. Like most people, you enjoy love, understanding and security. You do not always accept friendships at face value, for you are too skeptical. In your need for constant approval others will find your personality difficult to understand and may take your silence as a challenge. This could work against you and expose you to criticism or unjust attacks. Sevens have deep fears of rejection and will deliberately hold back on emotions until they feel safe. Once you feel contented and secure in a relationship, being generous and passionate with the one you love will come more naturally.

As a young adult do not let romance distract you from your professional pursuits. It is better if you allow yourself to mature and become responsible before you become permanently involved in a relationship. You believe in a lasting commitment even when it is shallow and that is why you should be slow to commit. When you decide on the mate you want for life you are quite capable of staying in that union for a lifetime. It is rare for you to leave a marriage or relationship even when the love dies, unless the decision is beyond your control. Even though you feel obligated to stay with the individual in an unhappy situation, you will seek love and happiness outside of the marriage. Your inner peace will come when you are happily involved in a relationship that is loving, nurturing, positive and secure. This inner peace within you will reflect into your professional success and spiritual unfoldment.

OCCUPATIONS THAT BEST SUIT 7s:

scholar, inventor, fields of medicine, nursing, stockbroker, computer tech, chemist, dietitian, engineer, criminologist, cinematographer, insurance agent, detective, secret agent, bartender, plumber, repairman, scuba diver, fisherman, mystic, astronomer, geologist, accountant, cruise personnel, importer/exporter, merchant, sales, religious zealot, scientist, teacher

As you swim upstream in the ocean of life, your search for wisdom and perfection with your unique magnetism will have a great influence on issues related to spiritual awareness. At heart, you are a traveler and should try to fulfill this desire by visiting other states and foreign countries. Seven is the number of the great divine mystery and as a result of this, scientific research and unsolved mysteries will be pursued by your thirst and hunger for undiscovered knowledge. You will be a constant student using your intellectual insight to solve problems, constantly developing the intelligence hidden within yourself. The fountain of knowledge that comes from your higher consciousness will be the divine message to inspire mankind and womankind to dispel the fear of darkness.

The Evolution of Life

The Lower Material Lessons of Earth
Transformed to The Higher Spiritual Dimension

DESTINY NUMBER 8

You are the hourglass of heaven and earth, the spiritual, the material and the symbol of balance. Eight is the number of evolution transforming the pains and pleasures of earth to the greater realities of the higher spiritual dimension. As an 8, once you have conquered the realm of the earth circle and accomplished your karmic lessons of the material world, you then rise to the eternal circle of the 8, evolving into a new form of life.

Remember, the "pot of gold" is not always found in the federal bank; it may be found in the temple of your spiritual book. Spiritual and material balance is needed to capture the mastery of this number. Eight is twofold in the nature of the two circles: one representing failure, the other success. Tilt the hourglass sideways and it represents infinity, but without movement. Personal power, self-confidence and mastery of your abilities are just some of the characteristics you will strive to acquire in the physical and material world.

As a number 8, you may experience personal difficulties until you surrender and detach yourself from the material world, freeing you from the bondage of materialism. You can become a victim to your own greed until you understand that the purpose of life is not the achievement of power or material assets, but liberation from them.

Governing comes naturally to you with your excellent logic and broad-minded viewpoints. These qualities will be influential to help you to achieve opulence and success. The native of this number is usually built with strong fiber and indefatigable energy, not only to endure life, but to balance all social and economic problems. Your orientation is toward logical reasoning and evolutionary progress to attain mastership.

Your sole desires in life are to have status, respect and to be victorious in the material world. This could eventually become your battlefield if not kept in proper perspective. Learn to keep balance in your life and to realize that the power is not within you alone, but it is given by divine providence. You have to rise above self-righteous willfulness to bring forth a greater virtue in order to conquer all earthly conditions. In this incarnation it is important you unite your soul with its purpose, but first you must break the bonds of materialism that bind you the tightest.

As number 8 you are difficult to deal with because you are constantly driving yourself to do better, not only putting great pressure on yourself but also putting pressure on the people around you. You intend to reconstruct everything you can because the thought of responsibility or transformation does not intimidate you. Your aim in society is to rectify the imperfections of life while building a notable reputation for yourself. You have an obsession to demonstrate your power until you have equalized the positive and negative forces within your nature. But this obsession makes you misunderstood by others and steers you away from your mission.

A woman with a destiny number 8 can have difficulties in personal relationships because the nature of this number is to control and be in command. This need for you to have authority has a propensity to flow into your personal life. Being a workaholic whether male or female is a course you generally take in stride, accepting that as the normal flow of life. As you mature and use more balanced judgment you will be able to mellow your strong character. But, first your character must be molded by the hot irons of experience.

Your success and lifeforce will come from helping others to acquire their good fortune. Numeric profiles that have a strong 8 can always expect to have financial wealth or financial security in their lives especially when it is kept in proper perspective. If you misuse or abuse that perspective, you could end up with financial problems and even financial loss.

You are definitely an extraordinary individual who will enjoy many opportunities in your vocation, but will also find opposition from your peers in your competitive drive to excel. Eight does not like to lose and can be a formidable foe, using whatever force necessary to get what is wanted. One of your strong qualities is your ability to be a good judge of character. This asset will play an important role in your execution of authority. If an individual deserves recognition or praise, you will be the first to grant it. Your manipulating nature will enable you to exercise a great deal of power and control over others to get them to do what you want.

Willpower, determination and your recuperative energy are assets which will help to see you through your obstacles and difficult times. Ultimately, you always seem to triumph and learn from your mistakes turning failures into successes to bring forth your supremacy.

You have the spirit and intensity to project yourself in the public realm to produce abundantly. Eight does not like to accept anything but the best from life, and that feeling is also tied to your personal relationships. A lot of your friendships will be with mature individuals who have achieved success or associations who have influential backgrounds and can benefit you professionally.

In your home environment you have a tendency to dominate your mate and to be in control. If you marry an individual as commanding as you, you may find yourself in competition with them or in power struggles. Choose a mate who will accept your supreme authority to avoid constant conflict in your marriage. You are a proud person who can be consumed with having a beautiful home, elegant furniture, expensive clothing and a classy car as signs of your material success. Even though you can be a loving spouse and a wonderful parent, you will not allow the demands of your home life to interfere with your professional ambitions. It is important for you to show your family a lot of love and understanding. Try to focus more on their emotional needs than on the material comforts you can offer. Your overbearing attitudes and the demands you make on your mate and children can jeopardize the happiness of your marriage or personal relationship. In your aspiration to acquire wealth and prominence, avoid getting too wrapped up in yourself--overlooking the needs of your family or those close to you. Do not be afraid to shrink your pride so other people will not feel insecure around you.

Sex is a powerful tool that can be misused or abused in your life, affecting personal relationships. Although your sexual desires are strong, you do not always make a very romantic love partner.

Adding tenderness and feeling to the way you express your affections and being more understanding of your partner's needs will benefit you both significantly. Learn to humble yourself to enhance the survival of a relationship, or you may live unhappily ever after. It is necessary for you to relax and be human, so you can grow old, healthy and happy.

OCCUPATIONS BEST SUITED FOR 8s:

director, manager, supervisor, executive, administrator, realtor, stock broker, judge, lawyer, land developer, government employee, postal worker, pro golfer, IRS agent, police official, space engineer, financier, investor, CPA, court reporter, physician, entrepreneur, court official, efficiency expert, psychic, politician, investigator, athlete

As you swim upstream in the ocean of life, yours will be a journey of harvesting and success. In achieving your peak of performance, reach out and lend a helping hand to those less fortunate than you. Attain the genuine state of humanness in your mortal form, so you can transform that perfection into your immortal spirit. Your blessings will become another's gain as you help others to achieve confidence and become accomplished on their journeys. When you demonstrate great wisdom and use your special talents with knowledge and compassion on all levels, you will bring about greater harmony and peace to yourself and to humanity transforming their lives and yours. Learn to heal the fever of the material desires within you in order to have the balanced vision necessary to evolve and to live in the heart of the true master.

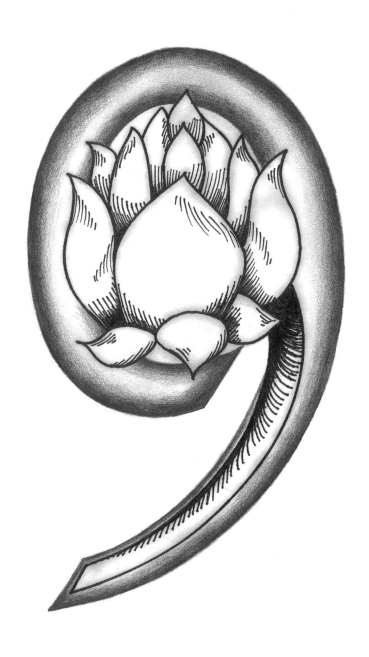

The Teachers of Life

Moving Single Mindedness to Group Consciousness

DESTINY NUMBER 9

You are the Omega, the end of the journey. The human form in your many incarnations has been wonderful and full of experiences and now it is time to move up to the lotus of eternal bliss. Nine is the number of initiation which must be experienced before you can graduate to your final journey of eternal bliss. If you withdraw and do not accept or conquer all your tests in this lifetime, your initiation can be set back a whole incarnation.

Life as a 9 is not always easy. Each individual must choose which psychological or spiritual tools to apply to transform oneself. Seek a spiritual environment to gain personal growth and try to be around people who are spiritually awakened in seeking the guidance of your Higher Self.

Your human desires will constantly test your weakest characteristics. How you accept and deal with the challenges brought forth will be the deciding factor of whether you will successfully pass the initiation. The single line in the number 9 is the human form, and the round circle of the 9 is the circular lotus of bliss. The single line stands for oneness in consciousness and moves upward turning into a circle of universal consciousness.

The circle of the 9 is the lamplight of the universe lighting the way for the physical form. You carry the light with you wherever you go. As you become perfected it will shine for you, leading you from the darkness into the light. This life is the passage in which you prepare for the eternal journey. What your soul has not completed in previous incarnations, the destiny 9 will confront in this lifetime, to deal with all past karmic issues. Nine is the number of completion, not endings. According to Christian doctrine--at the 9th hour, Jesus died upon the cross, but actually rose to another dimension.

The lifetime of the number 9 engulfs the energies of all the numbers, 1 to 9. It is the flow of the "Alpha and the Omega," a powerful force that originates outside of the human consciousness transforming your spiritual growth.

In this journey of life you need to relate to the ideals of universal brotherhood. Walk your path according to your beliefs, not accepting others lifestyles. You will always experience a feeling of being different from others, as if you were from another time or place. Your heart's desire is to touch the heart of the world, and yet to feel no attachment to it. Your love for people cannot be a personal distinction, but must be universal so you can reach out to many.

Nine is born to be a humanitarian and must be dispassionate and impartial to personal sentiment. Yet, it is important for you to be a very sensitive and loving individual, sympathetic to the needs of mankind. Your revolutionary urges can get you into struggles with people because you do not always accept advice or listen to sound judgement.

You will have a large circle of friends so be careful whom you trust. Partnerships are something you enjoy, yet you are at your best when working independently because you do not like to be tied down to anyone else's rules. Your "know-it-all" attitude can make you very bullheaded at times and difficult to reason with.

Try to deal effectively with your extremes in behavior and your unreasonable demands. Your nature vacillates between being introverted or extroverted. As a 9 you like to lead an irregular lifestyle, never knowing from day to day what your reaction to life will be due to your constant distractions and impulses. Adapting to changes in life is easy for you since you create most of the flip-flop in your life. Also, punctuality is not your strongest virtue as a result of your preoccupation with what you are doing at the moment.

The vibration of this number demands universal love. This lifetime must be lived out by making others happy first and yourself second, having to give more than you receive. You must be willing to give without expecting anything in return and to truly do it from an open heart or you will hold angry feelings. It is almost as if you are being asked to take a broader view of humanity through your own self-sacrifice to reach a higher awareness through unselfishness. Define your specific goals in this lifetime and integrate them into the divine perfection. Attribute this reasoning to the understanding that in this lifetime you are in a completion cycle, getting prepared to advance to a new dimension.

This lifetime is a gift and as a destiny 9 you must value and cherish each experience you encounter. Practice compassion and the understanding to contribute to your universal outlook. Focus on a positive outlook. In your deep concern to raise the consciousness of the masses, you can be the catalyst in helping people in their lives to make a positive difference. Your role to mankind is that of a parent and teacher. Inspire people to focus on the joys of their lives, rather than their sorrows. Life will bring you many tests when you are most vulnerable. Your spiritual growth depends on how you personally meet these tests.

Part of your universal purpose is to encourage others to learn true love and forgiveness. Ease their pain and grief through your unconditional love. Be willing to educate mankind to be independent of you and anyone else. People need to be self-sufficient, accepting responsibility for their own actions in life. You should not do for others what they can do for themselves. It is easy for a 9 to take control of the lives of others because 9 craves personal power and admiration. You must be the change you wish to see in others.

It is important for you to reach out to many in life, including people of different cultures, rather than to serve just a few. Be of assistance to other's needs before your own, then let go to advance your soul. Your service to others must be for mankind's highest good. Being of service to others does not mean you cannot expect to achieve recognition or financial gain in your spiritual development. It also does not imply that you should not be paid well for your services or be recognized for your merits. It only denotes that your mission in life is not solely for your personal recognition or to pursue financial wealth. The more you give, the more you receive. Remember, your good deeds and achievements will never be overlooked or forgotten, and your rewards will be great.

You will always be surrounded by people having many acquaintances from all circles of life. Making friends comes easily to you because of your friendly and unique personality. Even your clients or business associates will be attracted to you, playing an important role in your achievements.

Marriage for you is not always a happy experience and can even be painful. Loss in relationships from your overbearing demands or expecting too much from those you love can lead to separation and divorce. Your desire is to have a happy home and marriage, yet your independence can be the very obstacle that prevents you from achieving that desire. Remember in personal relationships there are two people involved with two diverse personalities. Although your true feelings are not always visible to those you love, deep within you is a very loving and warm individual. Make sure you wear glasses of reality when you choose a mate, for you have a tendency to be impractical where love is concerned. To attain personal happiness, cooperating will make the difference between success and failure. This is your lifetime to make it right.

OCCUPATIONS THAT BEST SUIT 9s:

teacher, massage therapist, psychologist, professor, engineer, politician/statesman, funeral director, artist, journalist, printer, painter, wallpaper hanger, celebrity, bartender, chemist, psychic, designer, nutritionist, travel agent, aeronautic engineer, astrologer, TV personality, writer, counselor, physician, religious practitioner, salesperson, computer technician, scientist

As you swim upstream in the ocean of life, your journey will be to provide wisdom to the seekers who cross your path and to help raise them to higher states of consciousness, finding your spiritual blessings in their achievements. Using your highest ideals, your strong principles, your unique individuality, and your humanitarian ways will serve you best when you serve mankind. Recognize the advantage of your presence and your vital being. You are last, not least, of the numbers, and it is up to you to raise the vision of the world with your humanitarian vision and your unconditional love. You are the embodiment of inspiration to help bring victory and righteousness to all living beings and to serve in raising mass consciousness to spiritual perfection.

The Seed of Perfection

ZERO or the ZIPHER

Rulership with the Sun

Zero is omnipresent. It is without beginning, and it is without end. Timeless; genderless; supreme in principle; neither first nor last; zero embraces all the numbers 1 through 9, weaving its perfection to have universal harmony. Zero is the acting energy which extends into all things and connects to all the bodies of numbers.

Zero is eternity, symbolizing the universe. It is the beginning and the end, working through the spiritual approach. It is the mighty "O"cean of life that contains the realm of numerical potency through the spiritual egg. The 0 is the yoni (womb) that takes in the power of the seed through the lignum (phallus), which is the number to its left that fertilizes the egg. The egg becomes symbolic of life form that radiates both stillness and motion.

Zero is symbolic as the birth of the soul seeking to manifest an expanded consciousness. In this lifetime the individual has to find true meaning of the material and spiritual world without extreme obsessions. A feeling of failure or elusiveness may have been carried over from a past incarnation. The soul feels a division within the spirit and must unite with a number to become a more dynamic force.

There is an urgency in this lifetime to push yourself to your physical limitations. The struggle is within your spirit and body which your mind alone cannot understand. But through your own efforts and actions, you will be able to resolve the limiting struggle. Through positive transformation and accepting new thought waves of understanding, the soul will have the ability to expand beyond the level of mind and matter.

Within everyone is the seed of perfection, whether you have a 0 or not. When the shell of the egg is broken, you are freed from physical limitation, having the opportunity to gain mastery over the spiritual and physical plane within your potential and your destiny.

The number to the left of the 0 in your birthdate, is the indicator of the point of evolution that you must reach in this entity. If you have more than one 0 in your birthdate use the one that is associated with your day or destiny number first, then your month, and last your year. The year is only used if that is the only 0 in the birthdate and is considered generational, but it still has its importance. Anyone born in the same year has the same number and will have a special connection to you and to all those born during that year.

The connecting number to the left of the 0 is the seed that fertilizes the egg and points to the direction of your evolution. For example, if you are born in 1990, 9 is your indicator because 9 is to the left of the 0. If born in the 10th month, then 1 is the indicator. If born on the 20th day, then 2 is the indicator and if you are born on the 30th, then 3 is the indicator. The connecting number to the left not only points to the direction of your evolution, but to the knowledge you must possess. The talents with which you were born and right actions are needed to survive in the mighty ocean of worldliness.

If born with a 0 in your birthdate, whether it is in the year, month, day or in the final depositor of your destiny number, you are considered an old soul. When you have 0 in your day of birth or in your final destiny number, it is significant because it is most powerful. The 0 in your birth month is the second strongest placement. When the 0 falls in the year of birth it is the weakest, but still felt. When there are two or more 0s in your entire birthdate, you really have some karmic cleansing from past actions which cannot be shirked or left unnoticed.

Every effect in this lifetime will be preceded by a cause. The effects of your past actions continue to live on in your body through the bondage of limitations. Nothing is exempt and everything you experience in life counts. With a 0 in your birthdate you are able to fashion your fate through the partner of the 0. When you achieve perfection in your experiences, you no longer work through the 0, you become the 0, complete in form. Zero represents a life where you have to give your all or nothing.

Spiritual people, particularly with 0 in their birthdate, feel they were born to fulfill a purpose, or feel destined to achieve some significant accomplishment in this lifetime. Frustration and anxiety about life or fate can leave you mystified or rudderless the first half of your life. If you are a soul without focus you can waste a great portion of your lifetime in suspension until you realize the burning desire of your purpose. Life for a person with a 0 can be like a buffet table at a brunch with too many choices distracting the appeal of the main course Be willing to go beyond the pleasure of the bountiful selections and focus on the main course, or the principal preference of what you love most. Allow yourself to be drawn to what you require to fulfill your desires.

When you have one or more 0s in your profile, your life depends on the accomplishments of your previous existence as a result of previous actions (or karma). When a 0 is part of your final destiny number do not drop it to a final digit because it is an integral part of the number it is associated with. For example, if you add all the numbers in your birthdate and your final destiny number is a 10, 20 or 30, you do not drop the zero for it is power to the destiny number, but you still interpret the 10, 20 or 30 as a destiny 1, 2 or 3. They are separate energies but their power is connected to each other.

Destiny numbers are more powerful in their effect when they have a 0 with it rather than a singular destiny digit of 1 to 9. Zero is an element, not a number. The numbers 1 to 9 are like flashlights with their own batteries, The 0 is like a lamp that needs to be plugged into current (similar to an electrical plug into a socket) before the light can shine to add greater light and energy. Whatever number the 0 is energized into that number becomes the battery of energy and the functioning activator for the 0. Zero and its companion number always associate together, for the 0 is not accidental but a deliberate conscious presence of the subjective subconscious to experience spiritual significance through their shared attachment. When you have a 0 you are dealing with two forces because 0 does not act alone. It is important you take the partner of the 0 into consideration. The 0 is a circuit of energy and the source of power is the partner (the number to its left), being the protector of that source.

The soul is influenced by the cause of past perception. Perception only determines the object of perception, not the act of perceiving. The soul is spiritually free and is not the same size as the body. It works as a powerful energy and is instrumental in the intelligence of the struggles and the sacrifices you perform. Whether or not you can recall your past lives is not important; your past experiences from other lifetimes are inscribed in your soul. Do not brood over the past nor worry about the future, only the present is in your hands. Self-realization is the only gift with which you can leave this earth.

Zeros in a birthdate will experience restless and disagreeable conditions for an individual in the first half of life. Success is usually attainable after the age of 45. Children who will be born in the year 2000 will have an absence of significant numbers in their birthdate and could lack in energy, but will be auspicious in element. It is written in the *Upanishads*, a holy book of eastern philosophy, that souls born in that year will be reincarnating to achieve mastery in the spiritual traditions and teachings. The individuals will not only be old souls, but also high masters and teachers who will return to become prominent and highly developed beings to bring wisdom and guidance to mankind and womankind.

Individuals with a 0 always strive to be in control of their destiny and will rebel against authority or any limitation that will hamper this freedom. If you have a 0, you fear not being in control, and can become obstinate and irrational when you are not. You have an unusual personality that cannot be molded by society or your environment. With a 0 in your birthdate you are capable of achieving recognition and prominence in your lifetime. Gain mastery of your spirituality by your willingness to open your life to a higher infinite source of power.

With a 0 in your birthdate you are basically very insecure the first half of life, yet you will always display a healthy ego to the world. When you can recognize the imbalance within you, you can then understand your feelings and will be able to open yourself to greater dimensions.

At certain periods in life you will find that you will experience certain limitations and dissatisfaction in your personal accomplishments, dissolution of attachments, and even withdrawal until you become the personification of divine perfection. Zero is not an occurrence of one experience, but rather an evolving recurrence of many experiences both human and divine.

You have the original ideal of spiritual perfection within your being. Awaken it through the highest quality of integrity and by application of moral correctness. Through proper motivation and understanding the rhythm of your numbers you can become aware of that purpose.

Cycles and events in life will unfold when you personally apply yourself to be of service to mankind. Through unconditional acceptance of your birth status, never hinder or limit your potential, regardless of the environment into which you were born. Be willing to accept what you cannot change and to change what you cannot accept.

People with a 0 in their birthdate cannot live in the shadow of the ego or fade into the shadow of disguise to the number to which 0 is connected. The 0 must become the light that illuminates the number in its darkness. However, the only way that can happen is when the 0 humbly surrenders the ego and becomes the lighthouse for mankind and womankind.

The inner self must strive to discover what it needs to accomplish spiritually to fulfill manifestation of the soul's destiny. Become centered within yourself. Lay down your offense and defense to bring your source of power into manifestation. In numerology, nothing happens by chance, but it can happen by choice. When you discover the soul's purpose there is no more resistance. Release yourself from the constant state of fear, whether it is in the subconscious or the conscious mind.

Zero gives you options, and the option you choose can be a test within itself. Survival is the theme of your existence when you have a 0 in your destiny. Find the understanding and power necessary to transcend the forces of limitations that 0 represents in your destiny. Zero knows no beginning; it knows no end. It just continually evolves, giving constant movement to the life force of the individual-- good or bad.

The purpose of 0 is not to determine whether it is positive or negative, or to feel doomed if you have it in your birthday or because we are entering the year 2000. The true purpose of 0 is to provide options to explore and to discover the special lessons designed for your spiritual growth. It is evident that 0 is concerned more with the inner spiritual principle. It is formless, yet takes on form as soon as it represents a number symbolically.

Be open to the purpose of your existence so peace and tranquillity can be obtained in your lifetime. Without total surrender of the ego you cannot begin your journey. Zero is regarded as sacred because it does not represent a quantity but a quality. It is the beginningness and the endlessness, the Alpha and Omega.

The 0 is eternal, resembling the "O"cean of the universe. Similar to the ocean, it commands respect. Zero can be the cemetery of life or the fountain of life--full of penance, but also full of bliss.

THE FOUR ELEMENTS OF
AIR - FIRE - WATER - EARTH

The element of the number with which the 0 is associated is an important consideration. There are four elements to acknowledge: air, fire, water and earth. Each element has a mode of expression that will integrate with the numbers and will determine how the numbers and the 0 will project itself.

Each number has its own beneficial powers, displaying the benefic or malefic actions of past lifetimes. The elements of air, water, earth and fire have fundamental qualities that determine how that element will serve your destiny number. When you know your strengths and weaknesses, you can handle most situations, regardless of the influence. Bring balance and well-being into your entire life, destroying all your negative limitations. Until you strengthen your relationship with yourself, you will never really feel complete or attain true, satisfying happiness. Your purpose in life is served best when you understand what is available to you to create the type of life you value.

The air element is communicative and social.
The fire element is energetic and enthusiastic.
The water element is impressionable and demonstrative.
The earth element is practical and conventional.

The air signs are Gemini, Libra, Aquarius.
The fire signs are Aries, Leo, Sagittarius.
The water signs are Cancer, Scorpio, Pisces.
The earth signs are Taurus, Virgo, Capricorn.

Following is a brief summary of 0s interpretation with the four elements and its importance. When you interpret the 0 with an element it is similar to the energy of one's nationality. It is like having two of the same number, instead of one. Think of it as being "twins with individual personalities".

The elements of air, fire, earth and water are derived from the month of your astrological sign. If your destiny is a number 1 and your sun sign is in Aries, then the element is fire and you are a 1 number with a fire element. If you are a number 1 and your sun sign is Taurus, you are a 1 number with a earth element. A number 1 in a fire element and in an earth element will forge through life with similar aggressiveness of the 1, but with different energy. One with a fire element is like a race car going forward in motion. Number 1 in an earth element is like a army tank moving forward but at a much slower pace, yet both will knock you over if you get in their way. The numbers and the 0 work through the element with which it is associated. This is discussed more extensively in the Destiny chapter.

The elements of air, fire, earth and water are important to consider as the 0 will react with considerable difference to each element--each element has its own mode of expression using energy differently. The element of air, fire, water and earth gives a clue to the manifestation of the 0's personality and nationality.

ZERO IN THE EARTH ELEMENT:

There is a great need to succeed. You must learn to enjoy life and laugh a lot more or you will become too solemn, revealing a nature that is pensive, insecure, or unhappy. A person with a 0 is a sensible individual, loyal to everything in life. You are usually connected with business or earthly professions. Your nature can be obsessed with security, family, and material prosperity; yet, you are the salt of the earth. Although you can be overburdened in mind and body, you hide your stress so others only see you in a positive way. Be careful in your eagerness to help others that you do not do more than your share, neglecting your own mission in life. Even though success does not come easy you must make every effort to succeed -- *study those who succeed.*

ZERO IN THE WATER ELEMENT:

There is a great need to find fulfillment through love, home and marriage. You have a strong need for privacy and can be too emotional and possessive in your need for affection. You are extremely sentimental and enjoy showing your strong feelings openly and lovingly. Avoid becoming too self-absorbed and feeling sorry for yourself when life does not always fill your emotional desires. Your strong psychic powers and your sensitive feelings can bring on distressful conditions, because you are vulnerable and sensitive to your environment. Balance your visions with goals that you can achieve and that will provide you with security to avoid becoming despondent. You want to see good and beauty in everything around you and cannot bear adverse conditions that generate unhappiness or insecurity. Project yourself with a successful self-image to enhance your success. Your creative potential is unlimited.

ZERO IN THE AIR ELEMENT:

There is a great need to have mental expansion and versatility in your lifestyle. You are influenced by the power of intelligence, education and philosophical ideals . If you are not centered or balanced there will be opposition from your self-awareness and your perspective. You are the eternal communicator who is friendly, popular and interesting to be with. You can be an indispensable friend, but a merciless enemy. Definite in your ideals and ambitions about your life, you will make every attempt to fulfill them. Be careful in your enthusiasm as you are easily led from your own ideas by outside influences for the sake of diversity. Learn how to help yourself and others to be healthy in mind and spirit. You are the master planners, being noble-minded and socially inspiring. You are sensitive about your importance, prestige and honor to fulfill your aspirations.

ZERO IN THE FIRE ELEMENT:

There is a great need to convey leadership abilities and authority when 0 is in the fire sign, especially when the associated numbers are 1, 5, or 8. Competitive and bold in your outlook, you set out to achieve your ambitions never looking back as you hastily push yourself forward. Avoid being impatient in your thoughts and actions.   Being too hasty in wanting to get things done may only end up with you making mistakes. This impatience can be difficult for others who have to deal with you, especially if they are laid back. You are a power person who is constantly engaged in exciting activities to promote your public image. There is a lot of unpredictability in your emotions and desires in your quest to experience life--yet your inspiration and zest for life help you to be the popular person you are. Most of the time you are a jovial individual who loves good times and all that life has to enjoy.

THE ELEMENT ZERO
WITH THE ASSOCIATED NUMBER

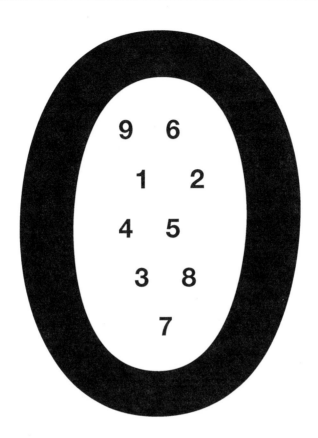

0 with a 1 ---------- You are able to plow through any obstacle because of your super achieving personality and your vigorous energy. Highly competitive, you are obsessed with the need to be important to fill a deep insecurity. You can be like a bottle filled with propane gas under the heat of the sun, waiting to explode. In your demand to have it all in life you will even neglect your home and family to achieve what you desire. Your mission in life is to be independent and to be a pioneer. You want to do it your way and will challenge any personal or personal limitations in your path. Learn to lead like Gandhi in an enlightened way to become the trailblazer who guides others across the ocean of struggles, after you have first tested the waters.

0 with a 2 ———You can be emotionally dominating and possessive and yet be very dependent upon others. People view you as very friendly, affectionate, and appreciative and to you that is important because of your strong need to have approval from others. Your values of love, compassion and nonviolence are the requirements for expanding pure consciousness. Your supersensitivity makes you appear shy or inhibited, and you will become dispassionate when you are not compensated for your loving ways or your good will. The key is to accept and love yourself for who you are. You are not always reliable with your changeable personality, and it is easy for you to get off track, especially because of your fears. Your mission in life is to work with groups of people without criticizing others and to inspire the altruistic side of life reflecting wisdom, truth, and warmth.

0 with a 3 ------------ You are like the jolly elf who is extremely extravagant in your spending sprees, not understanding the necessary value of saving for a rainy day. Although your nature is usually happy and friendly, in your stubbornness you can be quite uncompromising. You like to be in control and strive to constantly improve your life's conditions; however, you are not always serious enough about life or persevering in your discipline. Too much of your spare time is devoted to social contacts and friendships. You are a likable person who is fun to be with, attracting both male and female friendships. Fields of communication, teaching, sports, courier, or a travel related vocation will suit your personality and lifestyle best and can be most rewarding for you. Your mission in life is to be light-hearted. Use your humor and good nature to cheer others without overshadowing your objectives or your goals.

0 with a 4------------There is a great need to prove your self-worth and to overcome deep insecurities trapped in your subconscious mind. You will be faced with many anxieties and obstacles in your home life and with family members. Much of your strength of character will come with maturity, due to your life's lessons and the respect you will earn for yourself through your perseverance. You tend to be very self-righteous in your need to be right, and yet you can be humble and understanding to those you love and respect. Do not limit your potential because of obstacles created by menacing difficulties, but instead allow the winds of time to blow you steadily and safely to your destiny. Your mission in life is to accept your crosses without hostility and to rise above self-pity to become the bearer of wisdom.

0 with 5----------You are the problem solver. Full of bright ideas, you will always have many irons in the fire as you feel the need to have back-up plans in case the original plans do not succeed. You do not object to working with others as long as you are in control. When you are not in control you can be quite stubborn and narrow-minded, lacking in patience and sensitivity. People do not always trust you because of your hidden motives--always trying to use people to your advantage. Your position is the center of the numbers 1 through 9. You are seen as the center of the head and of the heart so it is important to bring balance into life-form. Your mission in life is to use both your heart and analytical mind to project your unique ideas into perfection through all the five senses. You are the polarizing beam between the numbers to balance opposites, and must be the universal intermediary to pacify opposing forces.

0 with a 6----------There is an overwhelming need to be loved and have emotional security. You have an exciting, sensual, demonstrative and faithful nature, but it can be too sensitive and needy for fear of being lonely. You are always more in love with your partners than they are with you. When you feel rejected you can become quite cruel or will sink into depression. In your need to be loved, avoid being self-sacrificing and clinging. You have a lot of creative abilities, but if you are not practical in goal-making you could end up dreaming your way through life-- preventing you from living out your dream. Stop trying to reap love through personal suffering, instead reach out to the suffering of others through your love and understanding. To affect others your mission is to give love freely without an expectation and to communicate a loving manifestation. You are the precious link in peace and harmony that binds through the spiritual love force.

0 with a 7————There is a great need for you to be experimental in life; however, your instincts are not always reliable and can be easily led astray by friends, drugs and alcohol. Divided by reason and emotion, you are a humanitarian who can see the purpose of the past and still have vision for the future; however, you are not always practical in the present. With your nebulous nature and biased view of reality you must be careful not to be disillusioned as you partake of what the mind believes to be the truth. Although you are basically a loner and peace loving, you will join groups and causes because of your patriotic commitment to an ideal. Your mission is to use your intuition, intellect and heart to promote spirituality into the mental and physical aspirations of the world.

0 with a 8 ———— Love of power and freedom make you quite daring in your revolutionary need to reform worldly conditions. It is important to your growth for you to try everything life has to offer never wanting to have personal limitations. There are many sides to your intense personality, and you need full expression and freedom to dramatically display all of them. All your worries are based on the fear that you will lack power and material security. Be careful of your urge to transform others--first resolve the complexities of your own identity. Even though you are an intellectual individual, you are also impetuous and unconventional. Use your heart and mind to guide you, for together they will always know what is right. Your mission in life is to be responsible and adaptable as you use your talents and power to make the world a better place in which to live.

0 with a 9 ------------ Practical builders of economic and social reforms you are emotionally restless individuals who seek freedom in speech, relationships and careers. Although you appear open minded about most subjects, you are very opinionated in your thinking. You always try to change your environment when it does not suit you or your needs. Even though you are totally independent, you love to be around people because you fear being alone. You behave in a very unpredictable and unconventional manner and appear to others as eccentric and unusual. You can think your way into or out of any circumstance. Learn to see life from two perspectives to find a common ground in your head and in your heart so you can live happily in this world. Your mission is to use your unique and magnetic personality to help rectify injustices in the world and to unite people as a group in helping mankind to solve problems.

PSYCHIC NUMBER OR DAY OF BIRTH

This is your own special day, the day you took life to meet the self. The day your body and soul merged into one and you presented yourself as a guest to the human race. Through your birth you take on physical form to go forth in an eternal quest to begin to know yourself through your birth numbers and to strive toward self-mastery. Apply the spiritual principles of your psychic number to awaken your talents and to utilize your individual powers You are the pathway to your own life. No one can walk the days of your life for you and no one else can find that inner you, except you.

The seed of divinity is within you and you must go forth to rekindle the flame of human possibilities. This is accomplished through spiritual awareness, self-study, self-understanding, self-growth and self-evolution. As your path progresses you must leave the smaller self behind and focus awareness on your greater self. Self-mastery and self-realization can be the pathway to the God within you. It does not matter what religion, denomination, or race you are. What matters is whether or not you walk in the divine light. You are answerable only for the measure of your own actions. Therefore, focus your attention on positive actions, thoughts and desires to increase your divinity and to attain serenity of mind.

When you seek the devotion of truth the doorway of wisdom will be open to you. Life is a school to help teach you to fulfill your reality by the experiences of inner growth and where the wisdom is found. We are all separate individuals, yet we are connected to each other like an aspen tree. An aspen tree has one main root, and from that root many trees develop. Remember, the way to grow outwardly is to first grow within. Use the information in this book as a message of light to awaken your unfulfilled self to enter into your birthright.

The psychic number which is the day you were born is an important dignitary in your numeric composite. It is the window to your personality, the external side of the self. The psychic number is what people observe when they first meet you, before they even get to know your soul identity--which is your destiny number. The destiny and the psychic numbers are never in conflict with each other even when the numbers are not in harmony, because they enhance each other--similar to the Moon being a reflection of the Sun, both have their own personalities.

I like to think of the day that you were born as the stone in the setting of a ring. The hand that holds it has its own personality; the setting of the ring has a personality, and the stone in the ring personifies the energy of all. Stones are like people each having their own personality--different in size, weight, color, brilliance, and shape. Imagine the setting of a ring as the destiny number, which includes the day, month and year. The hand that wears the ring is the directional number (time of birth) and focuses on how the ring finds its fulfillment. The stone is the day of birth, reflecting the first impression of your personality, and gets the most attention. All are separate in their unique personalities adding to their versatility, yet they become linked with each other creating a bond of oneness.

The best and simplest way I can explain the psychic number is to think of it as the impression people have upon first meeting you. Imagine you going to someone's home for the very first time. As you walk up to the doorway you form an opinion of that individual based upon your first impression of that house. When you enter the home you get another opinion. Both opinions can be similar or very different depending on the personality that is projected.

The psychic number works through the feelings of intuition and wisdom. Your psychic number is your awakened nature, and your destiny number is your soul's purpose here on earth. You need to spiritually awaken your mind through your intellect to gain mastery over your destiny and to have a connecting awareness of mind, body and spirit. Each number has its own vibration learning to work together with the other numbers in harmony to find a common vision for your welfare.

The psychic number never challenges the destiny number; they mirror the balance of each other in their personalities. The destiny number is the stronger force because it is the inner personal power. The psychic number is the outward radiance of your personality and together they have a profound relationship. The energy of all the numbers is needed to provide versatility into your journey and to the pathway of all your experiences. Therefore, use the guidance of the sacred numbers as a map to seek your destination.

(WHEN THE SOUL FINDS THE NECTAR OF WISDOM IN ONE'S LIFE, THEN THE PATH ON THE JOURNEY IS NEVER ONE OF HUNGER AND THIRST, BUT OF DIVINITY).

1-1-1-1-1-1
DAY 1
1-1-1-1-1-1

You are like a young stallion not wanting to be controlled or tamed. You appear regal and self-assured, yet like the young stallion you are untamed. As a child and as an adult you will seek independence and self-reliance. Often people are left with the impression you have a strong ego and the determination to match it--and you do. You are definitely an extroverted person who is eager to be visible in your public image. You are number one and that is your personal advantage to achieve authority by the strength of your will. Even though you project a pompous persona, you are a big-hearted soul and will be the first to help a friend or family member when in need.

In the professional realm or in your personal life, unless mellowed by your other numbers, you are outspoken, self-centered in your outlook and not always considerate of other's feelings. Enforce self-restraint in your impulsive and reckless ways or you could face perilous hazards. Being quite self-sufficient, you do not like to be told what to do and, in your belligerence, can even become bad-tempered when others do. Yet, in your own feisty and loveable way you are a very social being, always attracting friends due to your adventurous and friendly personality.

When it comes to having patience, a day 1 is not always victorious because of your quick temper. It causes you to become argumentative when frustrated. As quickly as your temper flares though, you regain composure acting as if nothing ever happened. You never live in the past, so confrontations are easily forgotten by you--but not always by your foes. Allow your enthusiasm, adventurous spirit and motivational skills to be the spark that sets you on fire, not your temper.

You will be rewarded for many achievements in your lifetime because your determination to succeed helps you to reach your accomplishments.

You are the person who keeps the ball rolling and gets life out of stagnant situations. For you life is a revolving door. No one knows better than you the limitless horizons open to all and for day 1, life will always be from the song "I Did It My Way".

2-2-2-2-2-2
DAY 2
2-2-2-2-2-2

By nature, you are a sensitive, cooperative, refined and sociable individual. You always show other people consideration, and you are definitely a team player. Your preference is to work with partnerships or close association with others rather than working alone. Your vulnerable nature can be extremely emotional and moody. You always want life to be balanced, yet you always find your life disrupted or in chaos. When people first meet you they see a calm and easy-going exterior. However, inwardly you have the tenacity of a bull dog especially when you cannot have your own way. Like it or not, you often feel unappreciated for your good deeds; taking a negative attitude towards life or wallowing in self-pity. Your sole purpose in life is to develop human understanding.

Make your own decisions and stick to them to avoid having undue stress and disappointments. You can be your own worst enemy when you procrastinate or when you try to capture balance by sacrificing your ideals. Two is dual in nature. Because of this duality it is sometimes difficult for you to hold firm to your own principles.

In your desire to please or make others happy, you may not always express your true feelings openly. Remember, your first responsibility is to yourself. When you are happy and confident others will accept your ideas and respect you more for your decisiveness.

You love to be caressed and kissed as long as the affection you receive is not superficial, but helps you to feel secure and cherished. Definitely a people person, you love to be surrounded by friends, family and loved ones. Your diplomatic skills and friendly approach in helping others will put you in touch with influential people who will assist you in the pursuit of your goals.

Two is a feminine number with a tendency to be passive and lethargic. When the spirit is disheartened it is important that you face your difficulties with logic and with an affirmative outlook. Be willing to accept small opportunities to achieve significant successes. A cooperative attitude along with your gracious manner will eventually propel you to favorable circumstances. Once you have set your feet firmly on the path to your dream, your efforts will not go unnoticed. It is through other people that you will receive your greatest rewards. " People Who Need People" are the luckiest people in the world, is a song that was written for a 2.

3-3-3-3-3-3
DAY 3
3-3-3-3-3-3

Happy go lucky, your optimistic personality and good humor make everything you do a spirit of joy. As a result of this pleasant spirit you will be sought after by many companions. You are the social networker of life opening up opportunities not only for yourself but also for others. Being quite comfortable with public attention enables you to create opportunities for yourself in fields of entertainment, artistic endeavors or vocations where there is an admiring audience. In fact, you have a knack for helping people to see the lighter side of life through your sense of humor, optimism and philosophy of life. You will benefit in popularity when you use these skills to enhance your vocation.

Within you is a child-like being who is always eager to explore the fantasies of a childish imagination. Because of this youthful imagination children and adults alike will be fascinated and drawn to you. While using your talents to bring happiness and inspiration to others always stay in the moment, for it is easy for you to scatter your thoughts. Most of the time you are happy-go-lucky and can be seen with a smile on your face, but when you do lose your composure, you become boastful, dictatorial and difficult to be around.

Avoid negative associations and influences which can leave you feeling depressed or expose you to negative influences. Normally you are not a person who is easily influenced by others, but when the good times roll you can be easily distracted or talked into risky situations. Although you are playful, when duty calls you are most responsible and ambitious always dedicating yourself to your goal. In fact, in your relentless efforts to meet with success you can sometimes cast the negative side of yourself and appear snobbish or impersonal.

To gain from this lucky number, channel your positive actions toward the enhancement of public interests and keep a high profile. Constantly keep yourself in a high profile to gain personal recognition. Somehow, even when you sense situations are not going well, hold on to your blind optimism and it will never let you down for long. You always display a natural youthfulness in your persona--and although you will inevitably age, you certainly will age gracefully. Years may wrinkle your skin, but they will never wrinkle your good-naturedness.

As a result of your popularity there will be many opportunities to have meaningful relationships, making it easy to attract romantic situations into your life. Your weakness to have a good time makes you want your piece of the cake and usually more. Be sure you do something significant with your life. Most of life's teachings must be accompanied by rules and discipline, not just having good times. With a little luck, a little effort, and a lot of faith, you can be that "One In A Million".

4-4-4-4-4
DAY 4
4-4-4-4-4

Just like the song "Through The Years", your credentials will be valued for the qualities of dependability and devotion as you are recognized as the backbone of society. Avoid becoming serious or too rigid in your orientation or your sober nature will reflect lackluster in your personality. Being too serious can bring out a lonely and unappreciated spirit, adversely affecting your friendships individuality and ambitions.

You are not naturally a social being and your pessimistic nature can affect your associations within your social and professional circles. Accept life at face value and try not to hang on to things. Stop striving to be extraordinary or achieving all your success at an early age. For you patience and time are the keys to your success. Although you are not the liveliest of creatures, you are certainly a true survivor. You have extraordinary willpower to diligently achieve your goals and to acquire material wealth.

The fear of poverty and your obsession with money invoke you to become a workaholic. Do not become possessed by earthly treasures, instead seek the value of spiritual treasures. Your lifeline to success will be brought forth through stability and hard work. Born to take on responsibility, you are seen as the foundation of society. In your disciplined lifestyle and traditional values, you will eventually gain due respect by the authority of your will and dedication.

Your protective and sentimental nature will always be loved and respected by your family. You will be very devoted to your mate and, as a parent, will be most loving and caring. Watch the tendency to become too strict with discipline when reprimanding your children. Allow them to have the freedom of trusting their judgment to express their individuality and avoid making all their decisions for them. Your love for your family needs to be expressed through understanding and affection, not through control and harsh discipline.

Love is a two-way street. Learn to give love unconditionally before you can receive. Traditionally, most people born on this day have a deep respect for their parents and elderly people, usually enjoying a contented and close relationship with them. Doing chores around the house, working in the garden, physical workouts and dining out are necessary and effective undertakings to help you to relax from the pressure of your labors.

A loving and sensitive mate will be your greatest gift and blessing in helping you to mellow. Learn to live in the moment and to always find time to enjoy the simple things in life . In the more difficult times of your life, you will always feel that "All I Need Is A Miracle" and you usually get one; even if it is at the 12th hour.

5-5-5-5-5-5
DAY 5
5-5-5-5-5-5

To have a life of excitement and personal freedom is your driving objective. You are intellectually inclined, blessed with a good memory and have a penchant for academic achievement. The need for constant adventures easily sidetracks you. As a result of your impatience and hyperactive energy, you can waste precious time always going off in different directions. You are an individual who is fearless. You enjoy being a daredevil, always wanting to tempt fate because you get bored easily. It is very important to your success that you control this need for adventure and satisfy your desires through scholarly stimulation rather than just venturesome thrills.

Because you are so headstrong, it is easy for you to lose your temper at the slightest provocation. Learn to have regulation in life or your unpredictable actions will result in irresponsible behavior, neglecting your obligations. Turn unsettled mental energy into intellectual pursuits, for inherent in you is a natural ability to be able to communicate, philosophize and debate. Your life will never be dull; however, due to your restless nature you may lack stability and fortitude. It is important to focus on goals and become proficient in your skills.

You will be able to accomplish a great deal in life when you realize that your keen mind and your enthusiasm are your strong and impressive attributes. Avoid being over-critical, misjudging people, losing your sense of humor, or forcing your ideas on others, leading to unnecessary confrontations. Learn to develop patience and understanding, especially with loved ones. These are necessary factors when dealing with family and friends. Respect and listen to others' opinions, regardless of your beliefs.

As you navigate the curves and corners of your journey try to give up personality traits that keep you locked within yourself. Establish patterns of behavior and ideologies that keep you traveling toward your journey with ease and use flexibility in both your thinking and your attitude to get the most out of opportunities and life.

You are blessed with a natural attractiveness and a sensuality which makes you inviting to romantic encounters. When you use good judgment in choosing your associations they will help to propel you to success and good fortune. Regardless of your station in life a strong faith and belief in yourself will always help you come out on top. So remember, only you and you alone can "Make It Happen".

6-6-6-6-6-6
DAY 6
6-6-6-6-6-6

Tender-hearted and caring, your human interests to help people is genuine and that is the true purpose of your mission. However, your concern to help others is also motivated by the desire to attract attention in hopes of making you more popular. It is the support and gratitude you receive from others that comforts you. Helping others can make you a notable soul, but it can also make you appear like a martyr whom no one ever appreciates. Make sure when you obligate yourself to others that you are not taking on responsibilities that are not requested of you. Trying to fix something that is not broken or encroaching on others' privacy should be avoided. Use your good judgement to attract the people who will appreciate who you are and what you do. You will often find that the friends who seek you out for your words of wisdom and support may also take advantage of your benevolent nature.

You are passive in your ambitions and prone to inertia. Working hard is not something you care to do unless you love what you are doing or you do not have a choice. Homemaking, taking care of others or doing creative pursuits will bring you the most satisfaction and fulfillment in life. Always lend a helping hand to others and your rewards will be great.

With your nurturing qualities and sound instincts, you will make an excellent mate, lover, and parent because you give so much of yourself. You always enjoy the surroundings of your home and family, providing them quality and quantity in attention. It is important that you feel appreciated for your good deeds and receive love in return for that which you give so willingly to others. Just like a flower without water, you will wilt without love and never bloom. When you receive genuine love, your beauty will shine inwardly, as well as outwardly--for females and males alike.

The opposite sex finds you extremely attractive and because of this there will be many opportunities to enjoy their companionship. You like to dress to be attractive and colorful, not necessarily to draw attention to yourself, but because you take pride in packaging yourself skillfully. For you love is life, and life is love, and you feel like love is the "Best Thing That Ever Happened To Me".

7-7-7-7-7-7
DAY 7
7-7-7-7-7-7

You appear to be a mystery to people as a result of your elusive personality and unpredictable temperament: yet people will find you lovable and charming. Emotions run deep in your personal relationships and you will be a challenge to anyone who gets involved with you intimately.

Extreme in your perfectionism, avoid becoming too critical not only of yourself but also of others. This quality is not really the personification of who you are but the illusion that you unconsciously project. You are a provocative and entertaining companion when you choose to be so. Within you are unresolved emotions that need to be released so you can experience love, joy and happiness in your life.

Not always trusting of other people, you take caution in choosing your friends, which will be helpful in keeping you from being taken advantage of or deceived. In fact, because of your distrustful instincts and emotional intensity you often appear impersonal and cold-hearted to those who do not know you well.

Spending a lot of time alone, especially in your youth, helps to get you involved in many projects or hobbies that can turn your talents into money making opportunities. Physical and mental fatigue affects your body because of your overactive mind. You are too super-sensitive to the harsh realities of life and should seek relief through enjoyable hobbies, meditation, spiritual disciplines or social activities.

Be careful that you do not waste a lot of time daydreaming, or fail to become responsible to provide yourself with the necessities of life. Accept your struggles to develop strength of character at each level of your development. Every time you experience a hardship remember, you are developing maturity physically and spiritually. Keep faith, accept your struggles as the stairs to your upward journey.   Faith in life and confidence in yourself will eventually lead you to your fulfillment.

You are happiest and most comfortable when you are in a rewarding relationship of one-on-one--not playing the field.   Avoid relationships that lack stability or substance--you do not handle rejection well. Involve yourself with someone who can match you intellectually as well as spiritually to keep you from boredom and an unfulfilling relationship.

Be open-minded in your decision making to promote harmony and good will.   Your very existence and the wisdom you receive through your intellectual pursuits is enough for you to carry on happily and spiritually until the end of your mortal life so "Que Sera Sera--What Ever Will Be, Will Be".

8-8-8-8-8-8
DAY 8
8-8-8-8-8-8

You are strongly individualistic with a natural self-confidence that will be advantageous in helping you to gain prestige and recognition.   The greater the bounties of your success, the more fulfilled in life you will be. You know how to command respect from others and can express yourself eloquently to help you triumph over any endeavor.   Through sheer stubbornness, regardless of the hurdles you must leap, you will inevitably always come out on top.   You possess the nature of a powerful being and will use this power forcefully in the business world.

With your high-energy and strong leadership skills you always seem to be in control and above remorse, but underneath that hard shell you can be as vulnerable as your prey--but will never show it. Born with a natural maturity your authority will always appear capable of handling any responsibility you encounter. Due to your ambitious and professional desires you will successfully launch endeavors regardless of the magnitude, helping you to achieve prominence and the respect of your peers and family.

The one area in life that will be your greatest challenge will be to achieve balance between your personal life, as well as your professional life. You are definitely status conscious and in your eagerness to have it all make sure you do not subject the people you love or your friendships to tyranny or neglect. When bolstering your self-image, do not do it by slighting or intimidating others.

In your quest for success, avoid the pitfalls of arrogance, dominance, stubbornness and insensitivity. These negative qualities could be your Achilles' heel. Allow the evolution of progress to expand through the mastery of your powerful being with a clear purpose of integrity, responsibility and cooperation.

In your lifetime you will find it easy to achieve many of the material comforts of life through the financial success of your career and your wise investments. The world can be your ocean of pleasures but learn to avoid making unnecessary waves because it is a lot easier to swim in the ocean when it is calm than when it is turbulent. In your journey to achieve material blessings try to remember that "The Best Things In Life Are Free".

9-9-9-9-9-9-9
NINE 9
9-9-9-9-9-9-9

"Catch a Falling Star" and put it in your pocket; never let it fade away. There will be several opportunities for you to have success and happiness in your lifetime, but you must direct your talents to helping others to find their self-fulfillment.

In your unpredictable nature there is a tendency to scatter your energies or become a rolling stone, wasting your precious time in idle preoccupation. Try to stay focused, be practical and listen to the chord of reality through your analytical insight.

To others you appear impersonal, even calculating in your approach, but that is just a cover-up of your inner insecurity. Nine is a mental number and because of this you have a tendency to worry a lot about everything. Building up pressure from stress or emotional issues will undo your temperament and cause you to act out unreasonably, and yet some of your best work is accomplished under pressure. Find the perfect balance in your mental reasoning so you are motivated by human desires rather than unconventional inconsistencies.

Because of hidden inner insecurities you can easily become moody when the attention you want is not focused on you as you thrive on approval and praise. A 9 personality is like an emotional roller coaster until you learn to transcend the difficulties in life that are necessary to experience. Relaxation will only happen when you chill out and be at ease with who you are. Learn to find your happiness within and align your values with your daily actions. Allow friends and loved ones to enjoy being with you. You have a likable personality and a funny sense of humor that will be appreciated by most people who know you.

Without a doubt, you are an independent spirit; yet emotionally you appear quite dependent because you fear being alone. Steer clear of negative and obsessive relationships. Your devotion to the individual you love can be obsessive once you give your heart. Feuding with family members or friends during your lifetime can be a source of challenge. Your quick temper and stubborn ways could affect your closeness and happiness with others.

You will need to overcome many obstacles in your lifetime before you are able to reach your pinnacle in life. Assert yourself by using all your talents especially your sharp mind and gifts of spiritual understanding. Your gift of charm will make it easy for you to relate to people in all walks of life. There will be many opportunities for travel in your life. You will be lucky in unusual ways, bringing opportunities and benefits to you because of your unique and dynamic personality.

10-10-10-10-10
DAY 10
10-10-10-10-10

"It's Hard To Be Humble" when you are dedicated to yourself. You are an individual who has intense willpower and likes to be in constant motion. Keeping busy and active is very important to your well being and restless nature. There is a strong need to help other people with their problems despite the many obstacles you endure in your own life. When you feel challenged in your personal relationships you become intense acting out in a rash and impulsive manner. Slowly count to 10 (your lucky number) before you explode or jump to conclusions.

Always speak directly, but also know how to listen. Do not allow your single-mindedness to become challenged by argumentative or opposing viewpoints. The constant challenge of your nature is a fundamental need, but you must learn to deal with it in a compromising spirit. Exercise your robust energy through athletics or outdoor activities to release frustration. Your strong self-confidence, competitive nature and adventurous spirit will welcome the challenge to move bravely forward especially to gain merit and to prove yourself.

Victory is your greatest accomplishment because you dislike losing. In competitive situations you could encounter intense defiance from your peers in your self-centeredness. Losing adds inferior feelings to your deep insecurities and this can bring out uncontrolled and aggressive behavior. Utilize your gifted talents in a way where you become a winner or a loser with a good self-image. Bolster your ego through positive actions not arrogance to get less resistance from your rivals.

Full of vitality, eagerness and dynamo, you will be an asset to any task. Become an inspiration to others who are less enthusiastic in their goals. Your life will be full of overwhelming challenges, so use your talents and enthusiasm to accomplish any feat you desire. Work toward your goals without resistance or force to bring you greater satisfaction both personally and professionally. In your lifetime you will be fortunate to have many friends who love you, both male and female. There is a whole lifetime to meet your accomplishments, so be patient. Rome was not built in a day. When your ambitions are moderated by patience there "Ain't No Mountain Big Enough".

11-11-11-11-11
DAY 11
11-11-11-11-11

"You Can Do Magic" with your charismatic personality, vivid imagination and energetic enthusiasm. Motivated by your spirit to be dynamic, creative and inspirational, you have a zeal that will be noticed and respected by others. Your magnetism and intensity will match your willpower. Either you will attract people to you or repel them due to the overbearing ways of the two 1s.

As a master number you try to be all things to everyone. With a thirst for power over your domain, you expect other people to concede to your ideas and policies. Positions rendering service to others or dealing with the public such as counseling, sales, promotions or mediating works best as vocations for you. Your nervous energy, fickle nature and independent mind makes it difficult for you to work for others.

You have the ability to inspire and awaken the talents in others by motivating them to achieve their goals. This ability produces the power you intensely pursue and personally seek. Avoid being overly concerned with what others think of you or it will get in the way of your personal principles and goals.

Whatever goal you choose for yourself, go after it with great fervor and focus. Be careful that your dreams do not become impractical or unprofitable due to your excitable and impulsive nature. Remember, you have a master number. The number 11 is two 1s in double strength adding to the intensity of the number 1 principle. As a result of the two strong 1s you may find concentration difficult or an inability to relax for long periods of time. Develop good concentration habits and use meditation as a relaxation tool to keep you from becoming unproductive in your actions.

You enjoy being the center of attention and will try to make your presence known in every situation you are in. The power of your vision can be extraordinary when it is not used to manipulate but to encourage positive reinforcement. Avoid twisting the truth to strengthen the effectiveness of your portrayal in an argument. Allow others to freely express their opinions as well.

Blessed with charm, warmth, and a friendly persona, people will find you likable and you will be a sought-after companion. You respond openly to your strong intuitive powers and can benefit from using them in your daily life. When your ego stands out of the way of your dreams your evolution will benefit greatly.

12-12-12-12-12-12-12-12
DAY TWELVE
12-12-12-12-12-12-12-12

You are definitely the "life of the party" at any social gathering. You enjoy making people laugh and make it easy for them to feel at ease while gaining the attention you enjoy. When you use your well-balanced attitude and your excellent communication skills to influence people you will be admired and sought after. People are enamored by your goodwill, bewitching charm, humor, and childlike personality.

Do not allow yourself to get sidetracked or give in to your moods of depression because it will only make you ineffective in reaching your goals. The secret to success is to remain positive, disciplined, and steadfast. Always use your talents productively for public recognition to gain personal status. Be an example of respectability to others who look up to you. You have the ability to impress, guide and be a teacher to others. Take pride in your personal achievements, but do not allow that pride to turn into pompous vanity.

Twelve becomes a 3 when you add 1 and 2 together, so you are working with the energies of numbers 1, 2, and 3. Number 1 gives the energy of

This trio combines qualities that are positive in life, 2 brings about sensitivity and values, 3 favors luck and expansion. nature and reflect a life of plenitude. It can also encourage a life of self-indulgence and extravagance with lack of self-control, keeping you from reaching your success. Each of these numbers influences your psychic personality and will favor you with many advantages, as long as you do not become consumed in your indulgences.

You love being in the public eye or in the limelight. It is gratifying to your spirit since your personality survives on recognition, adulation and drama. Regardless of what you do with your life you will always be fortunate. In your playful and dramatic personality you will be able to sing your song, "What A Wonderful World" this can be.

13-13-13-13-13-13-13-13-13
DAY THIRTEEN
13-13-13-13-13-13-13-13-13

"Who Can I Turn To" when the web of destiny makes you feel trapped in your own complexity. The aggression, ambition and dictatorial behavior of your personality could be your Achilles heel.   Intensely determined to be a success you can become an unreasonable driving force, not only to yourself but to others. Your nature seems to require constant praise and reassurance. Your first response to situations seems conservative and yet you become impatient and irritable with people who do not share your ethics or viewpoints.

With your hyper-energy and active personality you will take on responsibility beyond the call of duty, never complaining. You are definitely a doer and a planner. Having matured at an early age you understand self-sufficiency and accept the responsibility of all your personal goals with discipline and fervor. For you, being industrious and enterprising is the accepted norm, especially in your profession. You are determined and committed to work long and hard to attain the ultimate achievement of success. The process of having to make revisions can be painful for you but necessary to achieve progress in any professional field. When you see the reality of situations more realistically and not hold so tightly to your own viewpoints, you will more accurately assess your personal and professional situations.

Your vibrant spirit knows how to draw people to you, yet you are never silent if you disagree or disapprove of other people's work ethics. This outspokenness can alienate you from forming successful friendships of stability or long-lasting duration.

Be more idealistic and less narrow-minded in your outlook. In your strict discipline to attain your ambitions do not neglect the lighter side of your personality which can add joy and laughter to your life. When you feel depressed try releasing inner tension by visiting a comedy club, going to a movie that is funny and entertaining, or just watching a beautiful sunset. Allow yourself the opportunity to enjoy life to be fully capable of having a good time. Your pinnacle of success may not be achieved until the last half of your life, but the dedication and effort you apply the first half will eventually bring you the ultimate rewards of success and comforts.

14-14-14-14-14-14-14-14-14
DAY FOURTEEN
14-14-14-14-14-14-14-14-14

In your fearless and venturesome spirit you will drive your ambitious nature to attain success and material comforts. It is almost as if there is a driving force that compels you to push forward without ever questioning the motive. You will work long and hard to acquire the status and wealth for which you are destined.

You like your environment orderly, your time scheduled and your privacy to be respected. The preoccupation you have for control and independence can be carried to extremes, making you appear demanding, selfish and without feeling. There is a strong superiority complex within your aura which can be provoking at times, separating you from loved ones and close associates. Be more understanding and less obsessive in your leadership qualities, especially with your family. At times you will feel unappreciated for your dedication and good will, but it will be your suspicious and untrusting nature that gets you into trouble.

You have a sensual mystique and can be a seductive individual even though you openly make no claims to your sexual prowess. When you allow yourself to enjoy life by letting your hair down you can be a regular party animal--as fun loving and romantic as the best of them.

Be careful of what you wish for in life. You want to have whatever you desire and could be irresponsible in the way you attain it. Even though you have frugal ways, you will think nothing of going into debt for personal pleasures. In your demands to satisfy those desires avoid acting out in childish behavior always demanding what you want.

Learn to have faith in yourself and others. It is this faith that will carry you through difficult times. You work best under pressure even when you bite off more than you can chew. Your industrious nature is the key to success in any vocation when you are in a supervisory or management position. Your responsible qualities, along with your analytical mind are assets that help you to attain your ultimate success.

Avoid spontaneous changes in your life because of boredom especially with work or it could become your downfall. Careful thinking and planning should be considered prior to any major changes you decide to make.

Easily self-absorbed in your work and personal needs, it will be important to show understanding to others in life, especially those you love. In time you will come to realize that what you unselfishly give to others will come back to you two-fold in ways you never expected. One of the most basic human experiences for a day number 14 is to give freely without expecting anything in return, to feel like you are "Walking Away A Winner".

15-15-15-15-15-15-15-15
DAY FIFTEEN
15-15-15-15-15-15-15-15

With your sensual and passionate nature, you enjoy being pampered with a life of luxury and affection. Not necessarily an overly ambitious person, you are definitely a creative one. People will appreciate your diplomacy, good advice and sensitive words of wisdom as you become a pillar of strength for others.

Your life will seem fated in many ways because many of your life's experiences will seem like you are constantly having to make sacrifices for others. Personal wishes at times may have to be forsaken for the happiness of the people you love. Taking care of your family and home as well as a desire to help others is your priority. Domestic interests, such as child rearing, homemaking, gardening and family gatherings provide the stability and gratification you desire.

Although you are loving and sympathetic towards the needs of others, you are definitely not a wilting vine without a backbone. In fact you are quite an independent thinker because of a strong need for self identity. To be competitive in the world is not your main focus, but you are also not just a team player. There will be many strong interests in all aspects of your life--to be artistically creative is one of them.

In the business world you will discover that you have many talents and will be seen as an asset to any organization, especially with your management and organizational skills. Being a multi-talented person, you will be able to wear many hats quite comfortably as a "Jack of all Trades" and masterful of all.

In your attractive and elegant image you personify class, warmth, sincerity, generosity and understanding. Many opportunities for friendships will be open to you from the both sexes who will sense and appreciate your genuine qualities. You will find that animals also trust and take easily to you because of their strong instincts and perception of humans. It is your benevolent aura that will bring you good luck and blessings so "Let the Good Times Roll".

16-16-16-16-16-16-16-16-16
DAY SIXTEEN
16-16-16-16-16-16-16

Through the years your life will be extremely eventful, having one experience after another. In your need to be analytical, and exacting your mind will speculate theories for everything that happens to you. You like your feelings to be your own affair, yet you are a sentimentalist who enjoys being friendly. Be careful of appearing evasive or impersonal in your actions in your need for privacy. Your mysterious aura makes you appear suspicious and distrustful and this may not always be visible to you. Avoid shutting yourself off from the world because of your preoccupation in your personal interests. The simpler things in life generally appeal to you.

Perfectionism is a strong quality of yours which can be wonderful when the situation calls for it; however, you must realize when it needs to be controlled or it will drain you mentally. You are fortunate to be blessed with a fine mind, an excellent memory, and an instinctive intuition aiding you to do well in technical or artistic fields where you can be independently creative. Specialize in a vocation, or become a master in some skill so that your focus is directed in a practical and profitable direction. If you do not learn to focus on your objectives you could become a drifter or escapist through addictive behavior. Avoid becoming financially irresponsible or self-indulgent with your life or you will lose your stability. Too much day dreaming can lead to depression or cause you to lose your mental clarity.

Always try to live in a environment that is free from conflict, and if possible, keep away from the city life to allow you the tranquillity that your nature seeks. Work hard at putting a lot of effort into relationships or you will experience constant disappointment through them.

Fortunate in having a charismatic and stimulating personality, people find it difficult to stay angry with you. Your friendly nature will always attract friends even though you have a tendency of being self-centered.

You are a gentle soul who needs a non-threatening mate who can help you both emotionally and financially. It is easy for you to drift into unrealistic goals or obsessive behavior patterns because of insecure feelings about yourself. You are very sensitive to any criticism directed toward you, yet your attitude reacts as though it does not bother you.

Life after the age of forty will be more content and gratifying as you become more social and outgoing in your nature because for you "It's Just a Matter of Time".

17-17-17-17-17-17-17-17-17-17
DAY SEVENTEEN
17-17-17-17-17-17-17-17-17-17

Just like a hawk seeking out its prey, you observe your given situation with keen insight before you strike. You know how to express your personality with fervor and will command respect in your profession and in the business world. There is a strong ego inherent within your personality that puts you under pressure to succeed to your highest potential. Because of this strong spirit it is important to you to gain material assets and to be in powerful positions. Enterprises where you can use your effectiveness and be independent are more appropriate for you than scientific or technical fields.

Your love of money, status and material comforts will put you in the competitive arena until you find satisfaction and success in reaching your goals. Whether you are in the business world or in the social arena of life, you will have high expectations. You appear to others as an opportunist who uses charm and persuasion to get what you want. Be careful of getting too wrapped up with yourself, becoming neglectful of the needs of those you love or those who help you in life.

You tend to gravitate to individuals who are influential to help you attain your goals. Be sure you choose these individuals carefully or others could lead you to your demise. Your blind desire for success is so powerful that you could involve yourself in immoral dealings or with deceptive individuals in the pursuit of your attainments. In your quest for power, remember to use integrity and morality in all of your dealings. Avoid manipulation and misrepresenting facts for self-promotion or to maintain your views. Your attitudes govern your actions. Make sure your actions are harmonious and guided by your higher nature, never losing sight of the higher ideals.

Have strong faith and principles. Use good judgment and be careful of whom you trust to achieve your mark in the world. Remember, nothing will come easy to you in life, but with determination and sheer stubbornness you will be able to enjoy the fruits of your talents and be guided safely to all your dreams.

After the age of forty-five your life will begin to get easier and more balanced. As maturity sets in you will be blessed with considerable comforts, enjoying the later years of your life in a happy and prosperous way, so "Don't You Worry About A Thing".

18-18-18-18-18-18-18-18-18
DAY EIGHTEEN
18-18-18-18-18-18-18-18-18

Like "The Eye Of The Tiger" you are born with intellectual ingenuity, a superior sixth sense and tremendous strength of character. Your approach to life will be authoritative because you will be able to express yourself in a very powerful way. You definitely know how to influence people and will use that asset to your advantage. Magnetism, knowledge and power are just some of the characteristics you flaunt dramatically to get the attention you desire.

There is a detached sentiment in your personal and intimate relationships, wanting a loving friendship but without the confines of a commitment. It is not uncommon for males particularly to be involved in several affairs at the same time. You are unwilling to give the expectations that a commitment requires and could sadly end up with many unfulfilled short-term romances.

You strive to have status and material comforts and those desires will exceed all your other priorities. With fervor you actively persevere to attain your desires and can even direct the tides of your destiny. Through your talents, friendships or just sheer luck you are be able to exert your influence to achieve success in life. Be careful in your indulgent desires not to sacrifice the true meaning of your life for momentary enjoyment making you lax in your goals.

Do not let romance or the opposite sex lead you astray. Avoid taking unnecessary risks in life and avoid reckless behavior with the opposite sex, for ultimately it could backfire. Your grand passion could create a tumultuous effect, disappointing you with failures in career, loss of money and lack of meaningful achievements.

Strive to be broad-minded and educated in various fields to gain mastery over your skills to become an effective leader. Your deepest fulfillment will come from sharing your gifts with the world. Use your keen judgment and insight in understanding people to help to strengthen your communications skills.

Your maturing years will be kinder to you as you stabilize your lifeforce; focus on your talents and become more enlightened. In order to gain recognition and to be successful you must serve a purpose, not your ego. Your strength will come from your philosophy, spiritual beliefs and the faith of your awakened intuition.

Let go of your attachment to your ego so you can be guided by the inspiration of your true purpose in your journey. Allow your philosophical mind, spiritual wisdom and your magnificent essence guide you to your destiny.

19-19-19-19-19-19-19-19-19
DAY NINETEEN
19-19-19-19-19-19-19-19-19

You are a victor never to be conquered by your foe having tremendous inner strength both physically and mentally. With your positive spirit and optimistic attitude your life will be extraordinary for you in many ways, but never dull. Nineteen encompasses everything from the Alpha to the Omega. One and 9 added together becomes a number 1, the final digit of activation. You are the beginning to the end, and the 19th is considered an auspicious day associated with prosperity and success.

With all the virtues of a natural born leader you have the ability to make things happen. Your challenge in life is not with others, it is with yourself, and making a deep commitment to your ideals. You are like a dolphin in the ocean that spends little time in rest, always actively surging up and down, enjoying roaming around. You have a fascinating personality and will be able to use your natural charisma to achieve your ultimate objective, even using others to your own advantage when you need to.

Everything you do in life is with confidence, competence and courage. Nineteen encompasses all the numbers and therefore you will have many different kinds of experiences. With a multitude of highs and lows in your lifeforce many frustrations and delays must be endured. If you do not control your impulsive actions these limitations can make you irritable causing you to react irrationally to your disappointments. Patience is not your best virtue. When life does not go your way, or plans do not work out as successfully as you had hoped, you can easily loose your composure and pleasant manners.

Always give one hundred percent in life, whether it is with love or in business. Do not become discontented when you feel life served you lemons instead of lemonade. Continually push your spirit of independence forward, for eventually your multi-faceted talents will help you rise to a position of high esteem. Your pinnacle of success may come slowly, but you will eventually attract the rewards and recognition you deserve and which you work very hard to attain. Remember, peace begins within each person and extends to home, neighbor, and the work force. Enjoy the fruits of your labor and let the benefits accrue, moving forward to master every realization of your achievements to know "How Great Thou Art".

20-20-20-20-20-20-20-20
DAY TWENTY
20-20-20-20-20-20-20

Not overly ambitious for your own desires, you are more concerned and sensitive about the desires of others. You have a knack to make other people look important, and this will be helpful to you in achieving your own status and success.

Living graciously in a peaceful and harmonious environment is what you strive for, yet circumstances beyond your control seem to force you into conflicting life conditions. Problems of conflict can be threatening to you because you want to live in a world of tranquility. Learn to compromise and be more tolerant of others without trying to force your will on them. You are not so much a leader as you are a joiner and a team player. Even though you go out of your way to please others, you must always strive to maintain your own center. Sometimes it is difficult to distinguish when your ideas are your own or when your ideas are strongly influenced by others. Your life requires a lot of outside interests or creative hobbies to reduce daily tension and to calm your nervous energy.

In your attempts to be all things to all people, avoid sacrificing your own needs for the needs of others. Your sensitive nature and strong emotions require a lot of attention and understanding. You do not do well as a single person and will be devastated easily by rejection of any sort. In your need for love and affection be careful that you are not led into unhealthy or meaningless relationships which are non-loving and destructive. You need strong emotional support from others and a loving partner to provide happiness and to maintain a peaceful environment.

To be most effective work with a mate or in a partnership with someone you respect. Control your possessive nature and do not become a slave to your feelings or to another person's wishes. When you are blessed with a cherished love that is respected and nurturing, it will be the source of your abundant energy and give you the confidence to be productive in reaching your potential.

With your strong communication skills, and your camaraderie in social functions, many blessings will be bestowed upon you through your associations. In your lifetime you will be blessed with many wonderful friendships and acquaintances, and to many of these people you will always be their hero even though you may not be the "Leader of the Band".

21-21-21-21-21-21-21-21-21-21-21
DAY TWENTY-ONE
21-21-21-21-21-21-21-21-21-21-21

"If Tomorrow Never Comes" your day-to-day experiences will provide you with a beautiful and full life. You are capable of reaching your goals with little effort and will certainly make the most of life. Like a butterfly, your sociable and outgoing personality makes it easy for you to gain favors in affluent social circles. Mingling with people is first nature to you, and in your lifetime you will be blessed with many faithful and long-lasting friends. You have an optimistic and fun-loving persona which makes you fun to be with and the life of the party at any social gathering.

Fearless in your approach to most problems, you are not afraid to take risks. Even in the face of adversity or when you err in judgment, you will always come out on top. Your unshakable self-esteem, charm and numerous talents will advance your cause for you to reach your goals.

You have an intriguing personality with a wide range of interests. You will never be at a loss for words and your exuberant vitality will be helpful in accomplishing your goals. Sports and physical activities are important to you, whether your interest is as a participant or just an observer. You can be quite accomplished in sports due to your dexterity, limber physique, endless energy and your competitive nature.

Your curious nature will never leave you bored. You are definitely an extroverted individual who is always looking for excitement or entertainment to keep life interesting. Intellectually you are knowledgeable and well-informed on many subjects, making you an interesting companion. One weakness you have is your vacillating moods. In your need to be stimulated you can be led from the beaten path to search for new and interesting accomplishments. Learn to focus and finish one project at a time before you set out to seek new achievements. Success and fulfillment only come when you allow yourself to perfect one objective at a time. When you hop around like a rabbit from one goal to another, you could miss important opportunities.

Being in professions where you have freedom to make independent choices will be intellectually challenging for you. Nothing stifles you faster than boredom. One thing for sure, you will always have a life full of exciting friends, and you will seldom be in want of affection or passion. Do not allow your charmed life to keep you from reality or your true success in life. Your journey in life will certainly bring you more than you bargained for, and you will feel gratitude for all the "Magic Moments".

22-22-22-22-22-22-22-22-22-22-22
DAY TWENTY-TWO
22-22-22-22-22-22-22-22-22-22-22

You are an individual who needs to interact with others. Although you love people and enjoy socializing, you do take your professional responsibilities seriously. While you will have many friends in your lifetime, you will not allow these friendships to distract you from your obligations. In you, people feel a strong ally upon whom they can rely. Many will respect your mature outlook and practical logic and will seek your help with their problems.

Although you may be challenged with seemingly insurmountable difficulties in your lifetime you must never get discouraged or give up as a result of your defeats. Life for you will always be full of movement and activity because of your power and vibrancy. You pride yourself on maintaining a balanced lifestyle giving quality time to everything you do, whether it is your family, friends or profession.

Working with the public, using your leadership and managerial skills is definitely what you should seek to do to become most effective. Community positions, international undertakings, government offices, world-wide corporations or being involved in your own personal business are other ways to achieve the most satisfaction from your career. Your professional opportunities will depend on how you express your potential.

Twenty-two is considered a master number, capable of bringing individual prominence through a profession, or by being able to leave your footprints of success in the world. Hall of Fame, Nobel Prize winner, diplomat, statesman, judge, scientist, inventor, professor or business magnate are a few of the accomplishments the number 22 can attain to attract recognition.

This number has unique insight and awareness into understanding others and knows how to promote good will. You will often throw yourself into questionable endeavors without thinking of the obstacles or the outcome. You seldom lose your balance, despite the adversity you endure because of your strong self-confidence and persistence. In your dedication and perseverance you will successfully build a secure foundation to enjoy all the comforts of life. Learn to master your intellectual and social skills to acquire all the necessary credentials to reach your goals and to benefit the human race.

Number 22 represents strength with idealism. You are able to be the mediator in your community because of your competence and ability and you must not to be confused or misled by the opinions of others. Do not allow material comforts or personal success trap you in the vision of your purpose. Go into your journey and have a beautiful experience singing your song "Life Is Just A Bowl Of Cherries".

23-23-23-23-23-23-23-23-23-23-23-23
DAY TWENTY-THREE
23-23-23-23-23-23-23-23-23-23-23-23

This number is looked upon as the "Royal Star of the Lion" and is considered an auspicious number associated with major power. Day twenty-three is looked upon as fortunate and people born on this day generally have a reasonably easy life. You can have a life of advancement and personal benefits in both your personal and professional life. Many gratifying opportunities will be gained in your lifetime that will benefit you in having a successful career.

Avoid becoming Indulgent to food, alcohol and drugs. These are vices that need to be controlled or these negative habits could lead to undesirable compulsions. Promiscuity should be a concern to your reputation since there will be many opportunities for sexual encounters. Your sensual appeal is strong and certainly a twin to your sexual appetite. Allow yourself to feast and enjoy, but do not let your weakness for this physical delight detour you from the ultimate goal of your life. Do not be blinded by your indulgence or let the unpredictable side of your nature obscure your vision.

Born with a gift to communicate it will be easy for you to strike up a conversation with anyone. Your easy manner and magnetic appeal will be your key to success and you will be fortunate to have plenty of helpful support to achieve your goals. Your entertaining personality will be most effective in the cultural or creative fields. Being in the limelight and receiving public adulation is easy for you to enjoy because you crave that type of attention. In fact, a vocation as a public speaker or lecturer would be excellent. You will be able to hold your audience captive on whatever subject you present. When you find it appropriate you will undertake any topic in which you are not knowledgeable, making it appear that you are.

Arrange your life to be orderly. It is important not to let outside distractions keep you from performing your mission. In your own positive and happy way you will bring much joy and laughter to many people while you get to enjoy "The Wonder of You".

24-24-24-24-24-24-24-24-24-24-24-24
DAY TWENTY-FOUR
24-24-24-24-24-24-24-24-24-24-24-24

Sincerity, helpfulness and gentleness are some of the virtues that will be helpful to you in your spiritual awareness. You are a dedicated individual and passionate in whatever you set out to accomplish. Your enthusiasm along with your steadfast nature will help you in your professional goals to achieve the success you seek.

Willingly, you will make many sacrifices in your personal and professional life as long as you feel it will benefit those you help. Though you can be quite gracious when you want to, there is also a vein of stubbornness within you that can be difficult to deal with when you cannot have your own way. The 4 in your birthday brings out insecurities in your nature that you must learn to deal with, especially when you get depressed or in one of your mood swings. Do no allow your emotions or disappointments to get in the way of your ideals or your goals.

Working with flowers, gardening or any type of arts and crafts can help you to work through stress. Blessed with many talents you will always find life interesting and stimulating. Through your sixth sense and your natural instincts in human understandings, you will be effective in dealing with both children and animals. Your feelings for both humans and animals is compassionate, sincere and has a healing effect on them. You believe in extending yourself for the purpose of nurturing others and you will do it through your helpful advice and your human love. Working in a profession as a psychologist, social worker, fields of medicine, in service to people or with animals will benefit you in your self-fulfillment.

Your good deeds and capacity to love unconditionally are your greatest strengths to help gain success in any profession.   It is through your healing love that you can reinforce positive thinking in people during their difficult times. It is important for you to always project a positive image to empower others who seek your advice.

Home and family are very, very important to you. You are a protective and nurturing provider always looking after the needs of your children, spouse and parents. This number also contributes many excellent cooks, chefs and bakers, due to these natural skills that are inherent in this number value. In your sympathetic nature and understanding ways, your sound advice and unshakable faith will always be helpful to family and friends. Even though your life is burdened with many difficulties you always find time for others.

It is easy for you to attract friendships and opportunities for success because the people with whom you come in contact will have confidence in the belief that "You Can Do Magic".

25-25-25-25-25-25-25-25-25-25-25
DAY TWENTY-FIVE
25-25-25-25-25-25-25-25-25-25-25

Not only are you gifted with intelligence, but also with the skills of communications.   You project a charming, diplomatic and vivacious personality yet, in your interactions with others you always maintain a certain mystique. When you set your mind to achieve your desired goal you will obtain the needed accomplishments you desire to succeed regardless of the obstructions in your life.

Be careful of your changeable moods because your personality can be easily influenced by your temperament. Because of these mood changes, you will experience disturbances of the mind and body, making it easy to lose your center or to isolate yourself from the real world.

You are good at concealing your innermost thoughts and feelings making it difficult for others to understand you. Do not allow yourself to get entangled in a web of loneliness or to feed destructive behavior thoughts through vengeful deeds. This behavior can only lead to constant unhappiness for you provoking a dismal and a unfulfilled life. Your actions could produce your own personal battleground, leaving you angry and in turmoil. Avoid turning your suppressed feelings inward, only to eventually turn that anger outward expressing hostility towards others. Cultivate an attitude of cheerfulness to gain a peaceful state of mind. Until you have peace in your heart you will not find it in the material, physical or spiritual world.

One of the many things you are good at is your ability to size up a situation and be able to use it to your own benefit. Twenty-nine is a number that should avoid risky ventures or speculative enterprises unless well informed. You love to work with your mind, so choose a career or profession that allows you that opportunity. With your philosophical outlook on life and penetrating insight, your intuition will guide you to your true purpose in life. Trust your inner voice when there is doubt. You have the capacity to achieve anything you strive for when you call on your impersonal self. It is important for you to focus on fields of science, philosophy, teaching and psychology to bring out the best of your intellectual talents.

Be independent, do your own thing, and life will provide you with the assistance of friendships and circumstances to help you achieve your ultimate goals. With your inspirational and idealistic approach to life, you will be able to motivate others to help you in achieving your aspirations. There will be many blessings and opportunities in your life to enable you to perfect all the flaws in the fabric of your destiny, so be sure to "Always Look On the Bright Side of Life".

26-26-26-26-26-26-26-26-26-26
DAY TWENTY-SIX
26-26-26-26-26-26-26-26-26-26

"What A Wonderful World This Can Be" as you attempt to attain the impossible dream with your eloquent persona and strong humanistic qualities. You require freedom to capitalize on your intellectual skills and your soft touch in all business and social affairs. You will always exude authority through your responsible and mature judgment Blessed with vital talents necessary to achieve material advantages, you will be allowed to travel first-class and enjoy a secure financial life.

This destiny number makes it easy to aspire to any professional achievement for which you set your goals. You will always be triumphant and fortunate regardless of the setbacks or discouragements you meet in life. Two, six and eight (2+6=8) are all even numbers and are in harmony with each other, working together as a team. Although you enjoy being a team player when it is necessary, you will never like being in a subordinate role. Born on a powerful day, you have the ability to gain status and merit from your achievements giving you a very special place in this world, which may make you enviable to others.

Connections with others will be profitable because of your enduring loyalty and heartfelt compassion. These assets make it possible to gain positive recognition in your chosen profession. Your career could be connected with family members, relatives, or a spouse. At times your personality could appear impersonal in your effort to achieve material success as well as personal recognition.

You can be heartless and uncompromising in relationships, especially if they affect your ambitions. Gaining mastery over yourself will be your identification to success; however, you manipulate others by attempting to gain mastery over them. You will not settle for second best, not even in close relationships. When you meet the person of your dreams and this person shows understanding to your spirit, it will then be very easy for you to be faithful. You know what you want and how to keep it. In marriage your partners may sacrifice many interests of their own for your benefit. But through your inflated ambitions, your family's life will be enriched, and they will never be without material comforts.

The first half of your life will be quite demanding. Much of your time and energy will be spent on your relentless ambitions-- the second half of life will be more pleasurable as you take time to enjoy that which you have worked so hard for. Underneath all your power is a tender-hearted soul. Blessed with the potential to develop your own boundaries, you will gain in self-respect, fulfillment of goals and a life of material bliss.

27-27-27-27-27-27-27-27-27-27-27-27
DAY TWENTY-SEVEN
27-27-27-27-27-27-27-27-27-27-27-27

"Something Happened On The Way To Heaven" and in this incarnation you somehow feel a need to be involved in the human race, universal brotherhood or in a vocation where you will benefit humanity.

Maintain an objective viewpoint even though to others you appear unusual and unconventional. You thrive on eccentricity because it makes you more difficult to know and understand. When people accept you and love you unconditionally as the lighthearted being you are, then they will accept and appreciate your mysterious qualities as well. Neither your lack of knowledge nor the insensitivity of others to see you for who you are will keep you from inspiring others in your philosophical pursuit.

You are a very candid person with a colorful and eccentric personality. You are talented, intellectual, self-assured, buoyant and interesting, with ideas unlike anyone else's. For you, life will be lived through learning, talking, writing and interacting. Avoid becoming personally attached to too many people or overly concerned with material comforts or it will detract from your true mission.

You have a sense of drama and humor that attracts others to you. As a humanitarian hungry for knowledge, you will be centered in your intellect and nothing in the world can shake that craving. You have open and objective viewpoints with the ability to communicate to people from all walks of life. Your unprejudiced views and your positive qualities will propel you to achieve success in powerful positions. Always be open to seeing both sides of a story without making judgments or taking sides.

You will be viewed by others as a diplomatic and accommodating mediator that people will greatly respect.

It is important in your early years to obtain strong academic skills. In your yearning to study, attain a good educational background to help you shape your future and eventually that of society's. You were born to be able to attain the highest ideal. Material comforts will be important in shaping your life, but it is your intellectual skills that will bring you the most rewards.

For yourself and others you have a vision to help improve existing conditions on this planet for liberty, equality and social justice. You are not a person who is concerned about the past, you are an idealistic person who looks forward to the future.

28-28-28-28-28-28-28-28-28-28-28-28
DAY TWENTY-EIGHT
28-28-28-28-28-28-28-28-28-28-28-28

Truly an individual with unusual wisdom and awareness, you will always present yourself with class. There is a silent, iron-clad will within you that gives you strength of character and self assurance. Your social graces are second to none, and in this lifetime you will have exposure to many different experiences with a wide circle of acquaintances.

Because of your magnetic charm and your strong sense of justice, you will be able to achieve popularity and public success. With your colorful and dramatic personality you are a natural ham and quite entertaining in social functions. There is a part of you that enjoys public exposure, and yet a part of you which is very private.

Your spirit loves charging into new adventures and in your unshakable optimism you do it with the kind of courage and superior attitude that makes you successful, despite the odds or obstacles you encounter. Good luck will always seem to be on your side benefitting both your emotional and professional life.

Strong leadership qualities make it easy for you to manage and direct groups of people to new frontiers. Once you commit to any endeavor you will become forceful in your thrust and determined to succeed despite the uncertainty. Although you listen to other viewpoints, making any kind of compromise for you is difficult because you have the tenacity of a bull. Your flamboyance and charm allow you to get away with your mischievous deeds. In your humanness you never expect anything more from anyone else than you yourself are willing to give. It is these qualities that will make most people overlook your shortcomings. You know how to turn a negative into a positive.

In fact, the people who respect your power will show allegiance to you even if they do not agree with you. Many sacrifices will be made in your personal life for career, status and control. Because of these sacrifices you will achieve great financial growth enjoying many of the comforts in life. Your credentials will be influential in the realm of society. Use your power and competence to make this world a better place in which to live.

As you come into maturity you will understand and respect the realities of life. Your path will not be easy, and you do not learn from strict discipline or restrictions imposed upon you. You are a seasoned individual who learns from experience. You will be admired for your generous heart and expansive mind--and much of your life will be full of travel, material comforts and sophisticated pleasures. For the many people in life whom you will inspire and help, they will be grateful to you for being "The Wind Beneath My Wings".

29-29-29-29-29-29-29-29-29-29-29
DAY TWENTY-NINE
29-29-29-29-29-29-29-29-29-29-29

"Cast Your Fate To The Wind" because your spirit of friendliness and great communication skills make it easy for you to communicate to large groups of people. Your eloquent style and gift of charm will be the redeeming qualities to help you achieve honorable success. You are both warm-hearted and intellectual, adding magnetism to your expression.

In your restless nature and in your need for diversity you can appear impulsive and unreliable. Your day to day existence is sometimes all that concerns you and your erratic lifestyle needs to have freedom at any cost. Avoid making long range goals or you may set yourself up for disappointment in reaching those goals. Goals and projects have importance to you as long as they do not restrict you from having a carefree lifestyle.

Even though you are blessed with a fine mind, in many situations you will be led by the inspiration of your intuition rather than practicality or logical reasoning. Your sixth sense knows where you are heading even when it appears to others that you seem to be drifting without a goal. Because of your strong faith in destiny, you will appreciate all life experiences knowing they are part of your fate.

It is important that you center your career around the public in some way, because interaction with others is as important to you as the sun is to daylight. You will benefit throughout life from your talents and from your many friends in their dedicated loyalty to you, although it may be only after the age of forty. Much of your life's work will be as an arbitrator for others.

As you gain success in life it will be possible for your friends to reap advantages from your accomplishments and blessings. You always look after people in a fraternal way, wanting them to also benefit from your good luck. There is a certain element of sacrifice and loneliness that will be experienced in your life at different intervals due to the harmonics of the number 9. The depression and insecurity you encounter will be necessary to help your soul discover the true meaning of your life here on earth. Your fundamental skills will help you to triumph from all obstacles in life and to reconcile them into spiritual wisdom.

When your life is at low ebb or when despondency puts you in low spirits, you are still able to see the light and find order in confusion. In the determination to succeed your strong leadership qualities and judicious behavior will strengthen your character to achieve the success you strive for and deserve. Although you will be a late bloomer, avoid becoming frustrated due to the slow-moving progress in your early years.

If the seed of a fruit tree is planted properly and nurtured patiently, the tree will grow to full maturity and will yield abundant fruit. A good tree will always bear good fruit, even though it may take many years of growth.

30-30-30-30-30-30-30-30
DAY THIRTY
30-30-30-30-30-30-30-30

No one should ever try to figure you out. Born on the 30th you have a moody disposition that is hidden by your charm and unusual friendliness. The opposite sex will always be attracted to you because of your mystique and sensuality. Your sexual energy is strong which makes your powers of attraction even more compelling and inviting. There will be many acquaintances in and out of your life always seeking your free-spirited nature and making it difficult for you to take life seriously. Having a committed relationship is not difficult for you as long as it does not prevent you from enjoying your social life. You have an aversion to marriage because of the responsibility that is attached with it, and for your spirit that responsibility is a scary thought.

Your playful disposition and irresponsible behavior make it difficult for you to take life seriously until you reach your mid-thirties. Good times and unrestricted freedom are important to you. In the first half of life you will find it difficult to be disciplined. Much for you time is spent being sociable and carefree because it is important for you to be popular. As outgoing and friendly that you are, there is a side of you that is quite touchy and subject to moods of despondency. Remember a dysfunctional lifestyle can be corrected when you are ready to take on responsibility and maturity as part of your independence. You have considerable potential to meet with success when you utilize your talents where they are most appreciated.

It is necessary for you to develop discipline and focus on important goals early in your life. If you exclude this fundamental practice, midway in life you will find you have wasted your time on frivolous interests. The mastery of your whole life is your true mission and your first duty to yourself, not just pleasure seeking. Use discernment in the choices you

114

make in life so you do not lose out on opportunities because of careless decision-making. You are your worst enemy and must be careful not to undermine yourself by getting lost in delusions of grandeur.

You make a wonderful salesperson or promoter due to your charismatic charm and non-threatening friendliness. But remember, it is also important to use discipline in your career to gain mastery over goals. Career and job positions best suited for you are those working with the public where you have exposure without limiting restrictions. You do not like punching a clock, and you are not a nine-to-five individual, so avoid careers that are restrictive and structured. Gratifying vocations could be in fields where you have a lot of versatility such as the entertainment world, modeling, photography, tourism, travel, sales, or professions where you can be in the limelight. Remember a rolling stone gathers no moss, even though you were born to be "Footloose and Fancy Free".

31-31-31-31-31-31-31-31-31-31-31
DAY THIRTY-ONE
31-31-31-31-31-31-31-31-31-31-31

With everything we do in life we always "Save The Best For The Last". Last but not least of the numbers, you are definitely an individual with strong leadership qualities and initiative. Tradition with old fashioned values will provide you with stability in your both your career and personal life and your leadership qualities will never go unnoticed or unrewarded.

You have certain standards and opinions that make you set in your ways and rigid in your thinking. Flexibility is necessary in your viewpoints to work cooperatively with others to win friends and influence people. A sense of superiority makes it easy for you to impose your authority on others, even those who display a strong superiority ego. Inwardly you are a person with a strong inferiority complex, consumed by the fear of not getting what you want. In corporate management and large institutions your organizational skills make you a competent and capable leader. You enjoy being in charge of others but take your role too seriously, becoming dictatorial and unreasonable.

There will be many sudden changes in your life up to the age of forty-five that could lead to frustration and limitations, keeping you from realizing your ultimate objective. Tenacious in your goals, you will constantly drive yourself to achieve them. You want to be outstanding in what you do and to be a leader in a chosen field, never accepting less than the best in life. Whatever it takes to reach success, you will attempt to do it. Your nature is hardworking, resilient and independent. When these strong qualities are used in a positive way it helps to remove all the obstacles in your path. Once you thrust yourself into a project wholeheartedly, you give it your all.

You are not always trusting of other's decisions and will usually trust your own intuition about situations, especially if they involve you or the people close to you. Even when you are not under pressure you can appear militant and quarrelsome, but underneath that hard shell you have a heart of gold that cannot be matched.

Many times you are not understood by others, yet somehow you always get the help and cooperation needed to achieve your goals. Do not allow complications, setbacks or failures to interfere with your projects. When you realize your path you will be able to conquer all obstacles with your strong faith and optimism. Develop faith and trust in others as well as cultivating objectivity to be open-minded.

With the energy and steadfastness of a dragon you never lack in courage, you just need constant reassurance. Take life one step at a time and you will avoid tripping over your own two feet.

You have the capability to gain merit in athletics and it is important to involve yourself in competitive sports to use your high energy. Once your life becomes balanced you will eliminate many of the blocks in your path. Allow time and credibility to be your teacher guiding you to become effective in the unfoldment of growth and success. And remember there is only "One In A Million, You".

DIRECTIONAL NUMBER
TIME OF BIRTH

Each time division consists of (2 hrs. + 40 min.) and the 24-hour period is divided by 9 divisions, indicating the time designated by the numeric timetable, (2 hrs. + 40 min. x 9 = 24 hours in time)

Use the table below with your birth time to calculate your directional number only.

NUMEROLOGY TIME TABLE :: DIRECTIONAL NUMBER

12:00 am -- 2:40 am	1
2:41 am -- 5:20 am	2
5:21 am -- 8:00 am	3
8:01 am -- 10:00 am	4
10:01 am -- 1:20 pm	5
1:21 pm -- 4:00 pm	6
4:01 pm -- 6:40 pm	7
6:41 pm -- 9:20 pm	8
9:21 pm -- 11:59 pm	9

Persons who share the same birthday will always have the same destiny number, possibly even the same psychic number; however if the individuals are not born within the two-and-a-half-hour time table, their directional number will differ. The birthtime is important but not crucial to the reading. You can absorb volumes of information from the date of birth; however, the time of birth acts as a weather vane indicating the manner to which the destiny number should focus its movement. The directional number can signify intensity and be the energizing force that motivates you to put up a fight to resolve your problems.

The directional number indicates how you will actively pursue your destiny for success, money or personal fulfillment. The directional number is similar to a powerful magnet or gravity pulling at you and forcing you into a specific direction. For example; imagine that you are going to take a long journey. If you are driving a car in good condition and the weather is pleasant you should arrive with few probems. If you are driving a car that is not in the best driving condition, you could experience having one problem after another. The frustration, extra time and money that could be spent on car repairs might be some of the limitations that could affect you before you arrive at your destination. The car is the vessel that determines whether the trip will be miserable, full of problems or full of enjoyment. Life is a journey, enjoy the ride.

The directional number is the vessel of expression for the destiny and psychic number Together, the three numbers need to be analyzed as separate entities and as an assembly of numbers to understand the effects and influence of their combined strength. Keep in mind that life in general will always have its difficulties, even when all the numbers are harmonious. However, it is a lot easier to take a trip in a car that is in excellent driving condition than traveling in one that is a hazard to begin with. It certainly is a lot easier coming into this world with good equipment than it is with impediments. This last sentence refers to the old saying, "All individuals are created equal, but all are not born equal". There is a certain measure of fate to your destiny, and there are certain things you have no control of once you take your first breath. Step out of your physical limitations and develop your potential as much as you can within the mold of your apparatus to build character.

The numbers in your birthdate show where your capabilities and talents lie, but the molding of your personality springs though your childhood experiences and how you navigate your vessel in the ocean of life. Just because you go into water over your head does not mean you have to drown. You must learn survival skills that keep you confident in your abilities and keep you maneuvering to achieve understanding of right action. I like what Edward Henry Harriman once said, "It is never safe to look into the future with eyes of fear." Learn to accept the laws of nature with strong convictions to develop and strengthen your inherent qualities of survival. To live is not merely to exist or survive. Life is also meant to be appreciated and enjoyed. You cannot allow a car with problems to keep you from your journey. You must make every effort to fix the car to get it in good driving condition or find a way to get a safer automobile as ways to improve your journey; the effort must be made. In order to find happiness you must connect your mind, body and spirit to your external world and your spiritual self. Rid your life of darkness by moving into the light.

Lessons in life are not intended to deprive you of your goals, but to strengthen the personality through your struggles toward personal growth. When the directional and destiny numbers are not in harmony with each other at birth, it is symbolic of a karmic discontent from a previous life. In this life you may have to strive continually to overcome obstacles, but must remain positive and keep faith. There may be times when you feel like life is punishing you and you may become bitter, even resentful, when you fail to make something positive of those encounters. The challenge and the discord that come from conflicting numbers needs to be understood to discover the fault of the conflict. You need to overcome any despair and not concentrate on the obstacle; instead, strengthen the forces that will help you to find solutions to transform your life. No negative circumstance or condition will be able to ruffle your tranquillity if you accept your life's journey with confidence and understanding. Remember, in any storm you encounter you must steer your own vessel as you navigate across the ocean of life.

Each number has either a masculine or feminine vibration, whether it is the destiny, psychic or directional. The odd numbers which are masculine numbers are active, extroverted and impatient. The even numbers which are feminine numbers are passive, receptive and tolerant. When the masculine and feminine numbers interface, they add tension to the personality because of their dual nature. A great deal of give and take must be used by the individual to have a conversion of the numbers. Birthcharts that have several numbers or a 0--the stronger your soul is from past incarnations. By many numbers I mean a birthdate that has two numbers in both the day and the month; for example, 1937-11-11 compared to 1937-1-1. In the first example there are two extra numbers in the birthdate.

The directional number determines how you can deal successfully with the events in your life. The destiny number is how you will evolve through the events of your life. The destiny and psychic numbers direct their focus to the directional number. The directional number is the point of tension forcing the person to grow. Regardless of the combination of numbers, it is important to use all the numbers constructively with logic and practicality. Take nothing for granted, because there will be cycles that create external and internal conflicts. Allow part of your destiny to be guided by fate and faith.

The directional number can indicate success, dependency, difficulties and happiness. It can also create obstacles, demand attention and work against the destiny number. When the directional number is at odds with the destiny number, the negative energy produces difficulties forcing you to build character and to infuse life with balance. This conflict is indicative of a past life lesson that was not perfected. When the directional number is positive with the destiny number, the benefits will come easily to you with little or no effort on your part. Numbers in harmony to each other will help you to respond more openly and lovingly to life.

DIRECTIONAL NUMBERS AND THEIR MEANINGS:

ONE————*Needs to seize opportunities.* In your aggressive approach and without limitations, you must have plenty of free reign to conquer your objective. You always rely upon yourself, seldom accepting help from anyone. One is a powerful number that promises success with any destiny number with which it is associated because it is neutral in leadership. Goals are ambitious, forceful and aggressive in actions. You endlessly strive to accomplish your objective no matter how difficult the task. This directional number has little patience for weak or passive behavior. Your ambivalence towards others can lead to impatience and arguments. You are a diehard, who accepts only your own judgments. You operate best when you are independent and that helps you to avoid struggles with others. Learn to tone down your extremes of behavior, especially in personal issues, or you could destroy the stability of relationships. It is easy for you to think only of number one because that is who you are. Live valiantly in your individuality because you are the seed of life. The power of spiritual and physical energy flows through you to bring mastery to your quest.

TWO————*Needs to rely on others.* Two is the number of teamwork. In your efforts to be a team player you need to be willing to cooperate with others. Usually diplomatic in interactions with others, you like to be the peacemaker or the bridge between opposing forces to keep the environment balanced. You do not like to stand alone and feel comfortable when supported by others. You will take a passive position when you want to have a peaceful environment and will aim to please everyone to keep relationships on a friendly basis. Personal pleasures will come from socializing and being in a meaningful relationship that is loving. You enjoy being in a relationship and when you are not you become anxious because you dread being alone. Rather than working in a solitary position seek vocations where you interact with other people or try to succeed through your creative abilities. Do not allow the need to have friendships outweigh your potential for success by placing more importance on friends. Connected to the pulse of society, you are the vine of life that unites people bringing them together. You understand the meaning of cooperation and diplomacy and because of this you will be granted many boons through your associations.

THREE------------*Needs to be the networker.* Fortunate in life you acquire opportunities for success that will lead to fulfillment through your extroverted nature You are versatile in your abilities, interests and activities and your youthfulness will never desert you. Benefits always comes to you through good luck. All these special privileges help to create a healthy environment for a strong professional identity. Not content to be idle, you want to be where the action is especially if it is a social gathering. Your focus gets easily scattered, so use discipline in your goals and try to complete all projects. Strive to be well-versed in many subjects for you will meet with people from all walks of life. Three is the communicator and the source of connections in life. Your smile is worth a thousand words but that is not good enough; you want to communicate those thousand words through your speech and writings. Always approach life through your sense of humor and in a friendly way to attain life's achievements and financial power. You are the umbrella of happiness bringing joy to benefit others who are dealing with unpleasant situations.

FOUR------------*Needs to establish security* through practicality and dedication. For you a home, family and security are paramount to your happiness and you easily assume the responsibility as caretaker of the family. Seek happiness and satisfaction through your work as a means to self-fulfillment. Working hard to reach your goals is important, but do not deny yourself worldly pleasures. In your passion to have security and success, be careful that you do not box yourself into a workaholic syndrome, becoming a lone-wolf, isolating yourself from friendships. Love of family and friends is necessary for your well-being, but it should not become the only source of happiness. Your frugal and stubborn ways can make it difficult to attain happiness until you learn to be more considerate and less selfish. Flexibility is important in your daily living to avoid losing opportunities When you realize that life is more than responsibility, work and security, you will then find hidden inside of you a person waiting to enjoy life and to have fun. Make a genuine contribution of your personal love to others to gain respect, not only from the love of family but also from associates. Do not pay homage to the sacrifices of the four corners of the cross, instead let your life be seasoned by the winds of the four seasons to illuminate your life.

FIVE------------*Needs to experience life passionately* through all the five senses. Personal freedom is demanded from you at all levels of expression. You like to express yourself in a sensual, dramatic and intelligent way, enjoying the attention you get from it. Your aim is to have your own way in life both professionally and personally. You become difficult to deal with when not in control. With such personal power within your personality, it is possible for you to reach any goal you desire and to accomplish anything to which you set your mind. Five is symbolic of the magical five-pointed star, no matter which direction the star is facing the foundation on which you stand will always look balanced. Aware of your powerful five senses and fascinated by all intellectual subjects, you know how to use this strength to commensurate with your abilities. Because you constantly want to open new doors, avoid having too many choices just for the adventure and not the treasure of the accomplishment. Be whatever you want in life, but overlooked you will never be. Allow your star to shine.

SIX------------*Needs to experience love.* You function best on both the psychic and intellectual plane. Do not allow your feelings to get trapped in the emotional webs of your personality. When you blend your psychic ability with your intellectual skills you will have the best of both worlds. Because of your aesthetic nature you seek your fantasies through romance and living a life of luxury. You have a constant need for love, praise, and approval which keeps you in bondage and unable to balance your life. Even though you have loving and gentle ways, when provoked your stubborn temperament will respond with a gutsy and headstrong force. Avoid procrastination hoping things will change, or wasting time in complacency. You can achieve any goal you set for yourself when you set your mind to it. Perseverance and tough discipline is needed to perform your duties in serving the needs of humanity. Your loyalty, devotion, and compassion is second to none and is greatly appreciated by others. Six is the path toward perfection and needs a harmonious environment to sustain a warm and gentle spirit. Six is the ornament of love and the link of unity which nurtures through unselfishness and inspiration, bringing happiness to many people.

SEVEN------------*Needs to be mysterious.* With a mysterious aura surrounding your personality and a tendency to be secretive you enjoy being difficult to understand. People never see you the way you see yourself. Skeptical about most things in life, you are not always receptive to new ideas requiring more faith in yourself and in others. Your mental reasoning can pull you in a wayward direction unless you prepare yourself to be skilled and dedicated in your professional world. You have the ability to be broad-minded when you gather knowledge by watching and listening to the people you respect. Until you specialize in a chosen field or become inspired by your creativity there will be dissatisfaction with your life. Even though you prefer to spend a lot of time alone, you also display a gregarious posture when you are in the mood which makes you fun to be with when you are in the mood. You enjoy having friends and will attract people of many backgrounds, especially those that could take advantage of you. Commit to an important person in your life who can accept your independence. Integrate balance to find happiness in your independent lifestyle for a healthier environment. When dealing with people do not allow conventional values to override your human feelings or you will find yourself being alone. Do not allow your life to become obscure, just mysterious and visionary. When enlightened, you are the spiritual mind and the spiritual heart that will serve mankind's needs.

EIGHT------------*Needs to have power and self-mastery.*   In your evolution you will be captivated by worldly success, material comforts and professional status. Your foresight can be used in any profession where plans and ideas can be executed with free expression. You know how to play the game in the corporate world and will use that advantage to achieve your ultimate desires. You radiate power even in your stillness and will always walk with confidence. The need for material wealth and power is so great within you that you unconsciously neglect the true understanding of real happiness. Your hunger for self-importance and external fulfillment drives you to be irrational and overbearing in your efforts to reach your pinnacle. Many compromises will have to be made in life until you gain the wisdom of compassion with your family and associates. It comes naturally to you to manipulate and use force to get to the top, and you are not always sensitive to the feelings or opinions of others. When you use power prudently you will demonstrate brilliance in your ability to accomplish great things on the physical plane for you are the eternal motion to evolution. When your actions and ambitions are honorable you will be the winner in all ways and always.

NINE------------*Needs a life of greater purpose and freedom.* To achieve altruistic goals you must be willing to raise the mass consciousness. Your spirit, intelligence and persuasive skills make you a natural teacher of life who can help to shape a better place for all to live. You have a flair for the dramatic in everything you do in life, whether it is in your style of dress or actions. Because of your mood swings you will experience highs and lows in temperament with unrealistic viewpoints--not always accepting life for what it is. Do not get lost on your journey through pettiness or resentments. Your goal needs to be universal not controversial. You are the humanitarian and the philanthropist who can help solve the problems of society and of this land. Strive to raise the vision of this world through your social aspirations, group associations and humanitarian service. Your wisdom and perception will be helpful in stimulating spiritual growth. Stay in the mainstream of the life force, committing yourself to a purpose to reach your mission in life. A commitment to helping the world represents a phenomenon which you cannot fully imagine; yet it is very essential to your internal happiness and the betterment of all mankind.

THE DESTINY AND DIRECTIONAL NUMBERS

Once you become familiar with your numbers, they will assist you in your strengths and weaknesses. Numbers provide a valuable source of information to the signature of your personality. The numbers themselves uncover desires inherited from past lives that disclose the decisions made about them in the combinations of your numbers--for good or bad. These combinations of numbers will lead you to understand your destiny and life's lessons. There will be experiences of pain and of pleasure that will affect your actions and your attitude. Lessons in life are necessary for personal development, for without encounters, there will be no motivation to transform. Lessons are the cause of existent energy coming from the strength of numbers in the birthdate.

When reading the combinations of the destiny and directional numbers, please bear in mind that the numbers are not always representative of your individual personality or your life. The interpretations are just symbolic of what the numbers represent together as energy. All your primary numbers, plus the wheels, must be taken into consideration when observing your profile. The directional number will add proportionate value to the effects of your destiny and psychic numbers and also to the cyclic 9-year challenge.

Nothing about life or your personality is written in stone. You have free will to alter the energies and to unravel the mysteries within your numbers. When you exert positive influence over the negative energies of two numbers, you repel the negative combination giving strength to your own free will.

Think of the numbers as strings on a violin. If one of the strings begins to vibrate or becomes too tight or too loose it will cause adverse vibrations in the corresponding strings. This is one of the reasons why violinists constantly tune their instrument, assuring that all the strings are in harmony to get the proper effect of balance. The harmonic theory also works for human beings. When your numbers are weak or inharmonious, you must fine-tune them and bring balance to all the numbers to stimulate positive vibrations.

The combination of the directional and destiny numbers indicates an emphasis of two qualities symbolizing unresolved issues of past life. The challenge is to make it right in this lifetime, working to harmonize one number with the other. The destiny number is the crucial foundation of your soul's purpose for this life and the directional number points to the path to provide that development.

NUMBERS	1	3	5	7	ARE HARMONIC BLENDS
NUMBERS	1	2	4	8	ARE HARMONIC BLENDS
NUMBERS	1	3	6	9	ARE HARMONIC BLENDS
NUMBER	1				IS NEUTRAL TO ALL THE NUMBERS
NUMBERS	3	5	7		ARE BEST FRIENDS TO NUMBER 1
NUMBERS	1	5	8		ARE AGGRESSIVE NUMBERS
NUMBERS	2	6	4		ARE NON-AGGRESSIVE
NUMBERS	3	7	9		ARE PASSIVE / AGGRESSIVE
NUMBERS	3	6	9		HAVE SPECIAL RELATIONSHIP WITH EACH OTHER

DIRECTIONAL AND DESTINY COMBINATIONS

The first column is the directional number.
The second column is the destiny number.

Directional ----- Destiny

1--------------1   Born leader, headstrong, achiever of success and aware of personal wants. Single-minded in thoughts and listens to no one. Temperamental and moody. Does not like to lose, whether it is in love or work. Not always physically coordinated.

1--------------2   Conflict between wanting to be independent and needing to be cooperative. Loves peace and harmony, yet is strongly confrontational Highly unconventional with a driving need to achieve. Torn between wanting to please self and others. Will hide their needs but never their emotions.

1--------------3   Much success in professional life. Able to achieve through talent and intellect. Spontaneous and idealistic. Highly persuasive and it takes a lot to discourage them. Fun to be with and always sees the positive in life.

1--------------4   Independent mind that resents interference. Does best in own business. Likes to be in charge. Hard worker who knows how to make money. Appears cold and aloof, making closeness seem difficult. Can be impersonal but never dispassionate.

1--------------5   Responsible and dedicated worker with strong self-esteem. Rebels against limitations. Super achiever, great salesman and effective promoter. Extroverted and enjoys being center stage. Exaggerates situations and is known to fabricate facts.

1--------------6   Torn between need for independence and emotional dependence. Can be stubborn, listening to no one, yet competent in obligations. Affectionate and emotionally vibrant demanding the same in return. Loves to live in luxury and can be lazy.

1---------------7   Fixed mind. Does not always work well with others. Likes freedom to think independently. Wants to achieve on own abilities and will avoid help from others. Learn to be more compromising and less analytical in relationships.

1---------------8   Strong, powerful personality with overblown ego.   A born leader. Takes many risks in life for sake of money and power. Appears cold and insensitive to others feelings, but not intentionally. Capable of manipulation to get way. Passionate nature.

1---------------9   Strong political leader, pioneer, rebel, great writer, but needs to serve humanity without thought of self-importance. Concerned with reforms. Must work toward the advancement of human welfare and abolition of oppression.

2---------------1   Likes to work as a team member, but does not always take suggestions easily. Good in administrative positions or as an effective leader. Erratic in emotions just like a seesaw, fluctuating from passive to aggressive behavior.

2---------------2   People pleaser.   Emotional and sensitive. Works cooperatively and harmoniously in partnerships.   Does well in counseling and teaching positions.   Excellent as a speaker. Needs to be in public realm. Great artistic abilities. Emotional and sensitive.

2---------------3   Strong emotional needs. Loves good times. Tendency to overindulge the sensual appetite.   Lacks practicality and logic in thinking.   Disappointments in love.   Takes people and situations for granted because of free-flowing nature.

2---------------4   Excellent business person. Works favorably with the public. Success and benefits rewarded because of disciplined and sincere nature. Sentimental about home and family. Will enjoy a lovely life. Appreciates gardening, flowers and plants.

2---------------5   Overly sensitive to criticism. Weakness for drugs and alcohol. A strong appetite for multiple sexual partners. Lacks willpower. Loves being sociable and outgoing. Artistically inclined with strong aptitude for details and perfection.

2---------------6   Warm individual. Passive in nature yet stubborn in willpower and thinking. Not overly ambitious but desires the comforts of life. Excellent counselor or social worker. Extremely cultured. Works best in spiritual and creative aspirations..

2---------------7   Losses through circumstances beyond your control. Tormented by sexual fantasies and temptations. Dissatisfaction in love and career if life is not balanced emotionally, mentally and spiritually. Day dreamer. Physically sensitive to environment.

2---------------8   Life is built around material comforts. Blessed with many loyal friends. A lot of travel for both business and pleasure. Business skills in financing. Logic and diplomacy help to achieve dreams. Loves to socialize. Can be an overbearing mate.

2---------------9   A lot of travel in life. Enjoys working with groups, institutions, corporations or government. Intelligence, friendliness and diplomacy in approach helps to achieve recognition. Actions not always sensible. Advances toward goals with faith.

3---------------1   Outgoing, friendly and energetic, constantly on the go. A strong need for variety in life. Enjoys the center stage always being the life of a party. Always working toward a greater goal. Needs patience and to avoid stubbornness and arguments.

3---------------2   Very talented. Many opportunities through friends, yet friends are a disappointment. Makes great actors and actresses. Nature is loving and outgoing and requires a lot of physical affection. Loves people and is a good judge of character.

3----------------3   Extremely fortunate in knowing how to win friends and influence people. Exciting and interesting lifestyles filled with variety, fun and success. Can be reckless. Avoid scattering focus for excitement. Follow instincts to achieve success.

3----------------4   Worries too much about security. Works diligently for success instead of happiness or ends up in positions they do not enjoy. Focus on practicality with variety with less concern on material achievements. Examine values and philosophy carefully.

3----------------5   A lot of enthusiasm and talent. Extremely fortunate, enjoying the fruits of life. Weakness for sexual pleasures and a variety of partners can create personal problems. Profits greatly from intellectual ideologies and creating new realities.

3----------------6   Easy-going individual with charming childlike ways. Youthful energy that never seems to age. Attracts many friends in life. Achieves comfortable lifestyle. Willing listener but can be too self-righteous. Open minded and will profit from a positive attitude.

3----------------7   Concerned with intellectual achievements. Inspirational and gifted in the arts as a writer, reporter or journalist. Knows how to act on dreams. Deep thinker with unusual insight and intuitive powers. Open to religious and spiritual philosophies.

3----------------8   Super achiever torn between a militant attitude and wanting a carefree lifestyle. Good moneymakers. Successful through lecturing or public speaking, . Likes to think big, with ability to instantly evaluate environment. Craves success and prosperity.

3----------------9   Can be highly successful in political arenas or scientific endeavors. Will travel worldwide. Rejects domestic responsibility in lieu of intellectual and spiritual expansion. Not always practical. Excellent writers, journalists and problem solvers.

4---------------1   Security conscious and aggressive in desire for status and material comforts.   Workaholics and unreasonable in self-driven ambitions. Needs emotional depth or will constantly be challenged by other people. Must be guided not forced.

4---------------2   Attracts abundance of power through successful vocations. Makes a great mate. Responsible to home and loved ones. Domestic and loving, yet disciplined and orderly. Good sense of balance and confidence helpful in personal ambitions.

4---------------3   Goals   not always realistic. Can lack success or fulfillment in life due to obstacles along the path. Hope and faith is never lost which preserves unflagging determination Maturity brings greater benefits as understanding and perspective broaden..

4---------------4   "Salt of the Earth" personality with strong ethics and beliefs.   Conservative and traditional homebodies with little interest in social life. Businesslike. Works exhaustively at success.   Too rigid and serious in attitude. Learn to operate from heart.

4---------------5   Difficult emotional life.   Unexpected money losses and difficulties in   reaching success when careless. Superficial.   Feels misunderstood, restricting ability to communicate.   Handles life in a purposeful way, but not always rationally.

4---------------6   Able to reach financial success through service to others. Loyal and sincere with loved ones. Benefits through others in personal and professional life. Makes a loving and stable parent. Gifted teacher of life. Appreciates music, art and culture.

4---------------7   Stress and losses due to bad luck. Mental worries over finances, security and health cause nervousness. Needs to have spiritual or religious reinforcement. Loner-type individual. Not concerned with happiness but with success. Add humor to life.

4---------------8   Aims for high standards and succeeds. Fortunate in career and finances. Spends a lot of time away from home. Roots and tradition hold importance despite ambitious drive. Materialism and conservatism strong. Understands reality of life. Stubborn mind.

4---------------9   Makes improvements and attains security through experimental approach to life. Needs a vocation that is independent and yet with stable finances. Philosophical mind with a logical vision for life. Needs to be more loving and considerate of others.

5---------------1   A go-getter who forges ahead to achieve goals. Many skilled and creative people have this combination.   Outspoken and independent, especially in relationships. Direct in action and will fight for principles. Makes dreams come true.

5---------------2   Ambitious individual who allows relationships to get in the way of success. Many friends in life.   Lots of travel and opportunities for success. Excessive sexual energy with many opportunities for passionate or friendly relationships.

5---------------3   Charismatic charmer. Can manipulate with personality. Attains success through shrewd imagination and quick wit.   Dislikes regularity. Restless mentally and physically. Lacks patience. Educational pursuits are favored. Humorous personality.

5---------------4   Many fluctuations in life make it difficult to achieve success. A lot of outside interference and hardship in environment. Hard worker who takes nothing for granted. Attachment to home and family. Busy with hobbies and interests.

5---------------5   Mind and body moves with lightening speed. Alert most of the day because of restless energy and finds relaxing very difficult. There will always be a lot of activity in life so be careful not to abuse physical and mental resources.

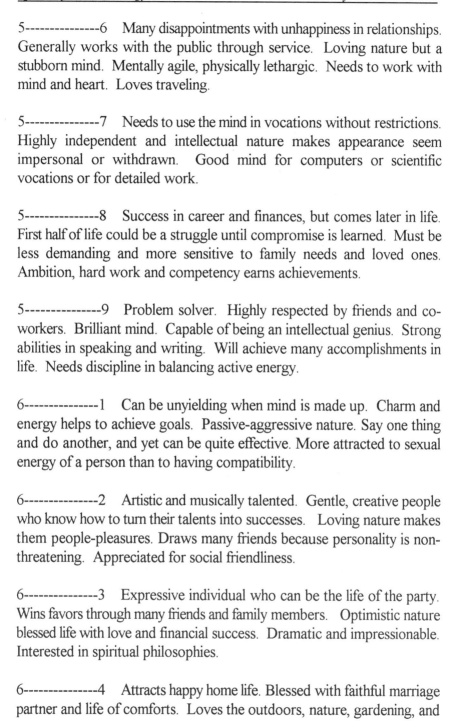

5---------------6   Many disappointments with unhappiness in relationships. Generally works with the public through service. Loving nature but a stubborn mind. Mentally agile, physically lethargic. Needs to work with mind and heart. Loves traveling.

5---------------7   Needs to use the mind in vocations without restrictions. Highly independent and intellectual nature makes appearance seem impersonal or withdrawn. Good mind for computers or scientific vocations or for detailed work.

5---------------8   Success in career and finances, but comes later in life. First half of life could be a struggle until compromise is learned. Must be less demanding and more sensitive to family needs and loved ones. Ambition, hard work and competency earns achievements.

5---------------9   Problem solver. Highly respected by friends and co-workers. Brilliant mind. Capable of being an intellectual genius. Strong abilities in speaking and writing. Will achieve many accomplishments in life. Needs discipline in balancing active energy.

6---------------1   Can be unyielding when mind is made up. Charm and energy helps to achieve goals. Passive-aggressive nature. Say one thing and do another, and yet can be quite effective. More attracted to sexual energy of a person than to having compatibility.

6---------------2   Artistic and musically talented. Gentle, creative people who know how to turn their talents into successes. Loving nature makes them people-pleasures. Draws many friends because personality is non-threatening. Appreciated for social friendliness.

6---------------3   Expressive individual who can be the life of the party. Wins favors through many friends and family members. Optimistic nature blessed life with love and financial success. Dramatic and impressionable. Interested in spiritual philosophies.

6---------------4   Attracts happy home life. Blessed with faithful marriage partner and life of comforts. Loves the outdoors, nature, gardening, and arranging flowers. Not afraid to work long hours for success but does not like constant change. Modest, helpful and kind.

6---------------5   Many career changes. Falls in love easily but finds contentment difficult in relationships. Extremely creative with an eye for beauty. Restless and inconsistent nature. Not always honest or open with feelings. View of reality not always practical.

6---------------6   Service-oriented individuals, always sacrificing for others. Loving sentimentalists with extremely romantic nature. Unhappiness in love comes from expecting perfection. Loves to cook and bake. Playful spirit always ready for fun.

6---------------7   Disappointment in relationships through lack of ability to discern between fantasy and true love. Use integrity in relationships and business dealings. Lack of educational skills will hold success back. See the reality of life, not the illusion.

6---------------8   Mature and responsible individuals Happiness in both career and domestic situations. Fortunate with many blessings in professional and personal life. Loving, but demanding of mate and children.. Pursues success and material comforts..

6---------------9   Success in fields of counseling, teaching, philosophy, religious careers or government positions. Travel in life both for business and pleasure. Service to mankind is required through vocation. Foreign countries and cultures will have appeal.

7---------------1   Intellectual who carries out plans but has difficulty attaining financial security.   Loner-type individual, yet has many acquaintances. Good public orators. Mind is intelligent but impractical. Too self-centered and picky. Driven by altruistic motivations.

7---------------2   Torn between wanting friends and wanting to be alone. Lacks self-assertiveness, missing opportunities. Financial setbacks through indulgences and carelessness. Too generous without practicality. Works best under supervision.

7---------------3   Communicator. Knows a lot about many subjects and loves to converse.   Rewards in life through   vocation and public achievements.   Inclined to be competitive in intellectual pursuits. Inspirational and perceptive but mind can become bewildered.

7---------------4   Difficulties in life because of lack of opportunities. Knows a lot and yet works hard for little compensation.   Loneliness leads to   isolation and moodiness.   Needs to have affection.   Dissolve vindictive or destructive behavior patterns to get satisfaction.

7---------------5   Gifted with intelligence and constantly searching to gain new knowledge. An eternal student. Will do well in educational pursuits for career or public achievements. Person has a happy life. Adventurous and free-spirited but sensitive to worry and stress.

7---------------6   Difficulties in relationships and work situations. Gains through dishonest dealings. Prone to addictive behavior.   Self-sacrifice through relationships. Insecure, wants closeness, yet keeps a certain distance which only makes matters worse.

7---------------7   Spiritual achiever or religious fanatic. Philosopher and researcher of truth, dedicated to beliefs. Excessive desire to be educated. Not overly sociable.   Enjoys solitude.   Prone to fantasies due to impractical thinking. Daydreamers.

7---------------8   Torn between spirituality and materialism. Discrepancy in idealism and ambitions leads to disappointment and frustration. Strong intuition with practical insight, but lacks stability. Mind is challenging and vitality stimulating. Excessive willpower.

7---------------9   Idealistic mind. Seekers of truth dedicated to mankind and high principles. Independent and progressive native but not always down-to-earth in the quest. Connect to practical basics. Will have many prophetic dreams and psychic experiences.

8---------------1   Powerful and active leader ambitious for status and material gains. Success comes through constant struggle with the will and ego. Unyielding attitude. Lack of patience. Competitiveness for self-interest motivates individual towards goal.

8---------------2   Lucky in love. Successful with goals and the comforts of life. Diplomatic approach will to gain public acceptance and opportunities through influential friends. Passionate nature yet disciplined in pursuit of goals. Flexibility helps achievements.

8---------------3   Dynamic and popular individual. Stands out in a crowd. Intense energy. Influential and powerful friends help in attaining objectives. Friendly appearance hides ambitious nature. Applying positive principles will enhance effectiveness.

8---------------4   Compelled to discipline, responsibility and progress through perseverance and power. Rigid and materialistic in hunger for success. Insecurity and hardship in early years. Happiness and tranquillity in later years. Financially successful.

8---------------5   Power driven. Will step on toes to get what is wanted. Can soar to great heights and succeeds through persistence. Cannot always be trusted. Enjoys sexual compatibility but may have trouble with commitment because of eager ambition.

8---------------6   Blessed with good life. Compassionate individual. Soft on the outside, tough on the inside. Generous with loved ones. Motivated by security, material comforts, and pleasures of life. Wisdom gained through knowledge of life.

8---------------7   Hollow combination unless ability is used to influence the world. Strong need for power. Does not always use intellectual skills. Confused attitude about desires creates trouble between spiritual and material integration.

8----------------8   Compulsive and obsessive toward achieving power and success. Main objective is to have status symbols for the strong ego. Manipulator. Highly competitive and extremely resourceful.   Great success is assured both financially and professionally.

8----------------9   Have much to contribute to the world. Cannot work to stroke the ego or self-fulfillment. Must work for unselfish aspirations through service. Constant struggle with inner and outer conflicts. Torn between self-discipline and freedom.

9----------------1   The sublime to the ridiculous, a tough combination. Nine is selfless, one is self-centered.   Constant pull between idealistic and realistic. Needs to become balanced to find perfection. Unconventional and rebellious but willpower serves well.

9----------------2   Progressive in ideas with a strong interest toward universal advancement. Works well with groups of people. Well mannered and diplomatic nature . Must focus on decisive objectives to avoid frustration Affected by the opinions of others.

9----------------3   Knows no mental boundaries. Independent thinker that puts ideas into action. Strong need to travel and have freedom. Hard to catch or hold onto.   Intellectual and inspirational communicator. Spontaneous and engaging. Able to attain dreams.

9----------------4 Wants liberation but gets caught up in practical discipline and materialism.   Likes personal independence yet needs a nesting place where friends can enjoy gathering.   Torn between the idealistic mind and the realistic ideals.

9----------------5   Tendency to reform everyone but self.   Views and principals need structure to be successful   Loves travel, adventure, aviation and constant challenges More idealistic than conventional in attitude. Mind and body constantly in action. Highly Intellectual.

9-----------------6   Self-sacrificing nature that must definitely serve mankind. Idealism is humanized by sensitivity. Disappointments in love due to expectations of partner. Extremely psychic. Must be more objective. Life is never a normal routine.

9-----------------7   Lives through the mind and even skeptical of own beliefs. Problem solver. Active subconscious mind. Strong intuition. Gets confused and needs to be practical. Tendency to worry or become high-strung. Spiritually and philosophically inclined.

9---------------8   Highly creative and resourceful individual. Inventive thinker. Many obstacles to overcome. Has the endurance needed to succeed. Not easily understood and likes it that way. Respect is desired and demanded from others. Not understanding.

9---------------9   A karmic indicator of extreme individualism. Magnetic personality but it is unpredictable. An intellectual genius or artist. A master planner who is open-minded. Communicative and interesting companion. Life of considerable karmic influences.

UNIVERSAL MONTH AND YEAR

The universal month and year are looked upon as the higher octave of energy because they work in a collective way, singular in force yet generational in consciousness. They are not primary numbers to the numeric profile. This universal energy is shared by a collective group of people born in the same year or the same month and can be included when interpreting the primary numbers. The universal month and year are secondary numbers and do not have the same importance as the destiny, psychic or directional numbers. The vibration of the universal numbers are not personal in nature due to the karmic influences shared by all other people born in the same months or years.

You will find that you attract people into your life whose destiny or directional number is the same as the final depositor number of your birthyear or your psychic number. For example, if you were born in 1975, you add all these numbers together for a final digit (1+9+7+5=4). The final digit is the number 4 and is called the final depositor. The number 4 is the universal number for anyone born in the year 1975. Individuals who have a destiny or a psychic number of 4 will be attracted to people with a universal number of 4.

This method works in the same way for the month of April, which is a 4 because it is the fourth month. The more connections two people have together through their numbers, the stronger the relationship (this does not necessarily mean intimate relationships). The universal year and month can also reveal your preference in determining your career or the type of mate you attract. We are all conditioned by the complete spiral of numbers that are relative to our numeric value. People born in the same month and year, but on a different day, will respond differently and yet will have a similar outlook on life.

The directional number which is the time of your birth, is the vessel which channels the direction of the destiny and psychic numbers. Two separate individuals born in the same month will have similar characteristics, yet different personalities, because their destiny and psychic numbers will differ. It is similar to a family tree with several children in one family-- each individual will have a unique look and personality. There will be varying features in each child, yet there will be certain features which make it easy to see a family resemblance. The background of the family comes from the same weave of fabric, but the cut will be different in design. For example, if you divide a yard of fabric and make one part of it a shirt and the other part of it a dress, there will be two different garments from the same fabric--and so it is with the numbers. When looking at your natal month or year, remember, you are looking at a generational movement of energy. Individuals sharing the same month or year will be affected in similar ways, yet each individual will have a different personal reaction to the effects of that number.

The number of the universal month and year in the natal profile do not have the same self-expression as the numbers of the orbital personal month and year. The universal natal numbers of your profile rule the personality. The universal orbital number of the year and month rule the urges or the impulses. That is why people born in the same year, or even in the same month but on a different day, will have different responses to the same stimuli.

The universal numbers when transiting in orbit as challenge numbers work at different frequencies than those of the natal universal numbers. Universal orbital numbers rotate every year and change in sequence. Universal natal numbers never change or rotate. The natal universal numbers reveal how you are attuned to the energy within the vibration of that generation. The orbital universal transits show how the effect of rotation changes you as an individual but not necessarily the environment.

* Two people born in January have a natal universal 1 month.
* Two people born in 1990 have a natal universal 1 year.
* The year 1990 adds up to 19. Nine plus 1 equals 10, so 10 is the final depositor of 1990, because when the final depositor has a 0 with it you never drop the 0. (for example, 10 is 10, not 1; 20 is 20, not 2)

People who are born in the same year or the same month share the same universal number. If their day and time of birth is different both individuals will have two different numbers, thus changing the design of the fabric. The only common characteristic you share with individuals born in your same year or month is the natal universal number. That is why it is important to have the complete value of all the numbers in a profile and to weave them all together to complete the masterpiece that you are. The assemblage of numbers is not as complex as it appears; it just takes time to understand the complete spectrum and when you do, you can learn to master your destiny.

Listed below are behavior patterns for the universal numbers 1 through 9. These tendencies are described in a broad sense and can be restricted or limited, in their expression. The definitions stated below are tendencies for both the year and the month, since they are similar in doctrine. The universal month and year represent the attitudes of a collective generation rather than a single attitude.

1--------- Tendency to make snap judgments. Self-projection and self-reliance makes one extremely competitive and independent in nature. Consciously directed toward personal desires in principle and actions. Needs to satisfy physical excitement because of strong sexual urges. Control how the mind is spoken. Ones take great risks to meet goals or attain desires. One needs to express itself not prove itself.

2--------- Desirous of having emotional connections in friendships or emotional relationships. Subject to unexpected mood changes. Persuasive, but not forceful in seeking support from others. Excellent memories that retain everything that is heard or read. Loving nature with strong emotional urges for self-gratification. Many opportunities for romance. Emotional well-being is primarily dependent.

3--------- Enjoys the pursuit of intellectual, physical and social growth through versatility and expansiveness. Strong self-confidence. Ability to expand and seek many horizons but can become scattered in the ever-changing need for excitement and variety. Lucky regarding money, love and success. Overachievers. Needs attention and recognition.

4--------- Security conscious to build status and material resources to have a secure lifestyle. Primitive and conservative in traditional values. Lack of faith and trust can lead to inhibition and narrow-mindedness. Experiences of pain in life may reflect in a serious personality. Never satisfied in life regardless of how much is attained. Personal well being or suffering depends on mental outlook.

5--------- Eloquent with excellent writing skills and an intense intellectual pride. Ability to be mobile. A sensualist and an adventurer. Concerned with detail, precision and accuracy. Must keep nervous mind and energy restrained to feel peacefulness. Can handle most crisis and actually works best when under pressure. Constantly searches for experiences to contribute to personal growth.

6--------- Appreciates and desires the finer things of life, the personal enjoyment of friendships and worldly pleasures. Prefers mental work to manual labor. Sensitive to the needs of others. Mate and children will be important source of happiness in life. Does not like to be burdened by responsibility, yet will never shirk from it. Self-esteem is based on love and material acquisitions.

7--------- Expression is served through a compassionate and intellectual nature. Must understand life and people to emerge from aloneness to wholeness. Lives life through receptivity and intellectual capability. Capable of deep spirituality. Practicality and patience required in life-force to achieve objective. Easily addicted to drugs, alcohol or obsessive behavior patterns. Does not judge based upon the opinions of others. Loves to live near water.

8--------- Powerful essence and presence. Projects self-expression with authority. Requires financial prosperity because it is a sign of power. Must balance life through integrity and peaceful conciliation. Family life can be inharmonious until goals are reached. An 8 is are similar to still water, it has a powerful undercurrent. Onward and upward is your motto. Be humble to become the beloved master.

9--------- Progressive and universal mind requires independence in thought, action and spirit. A number of freedom and completeness. Universal souls with important message to share with mankind. Must share self universally but in a supportive environment. Nine represents that the initiation of life has been reached and now the soul must complete the lessons of the past, the present and the future.

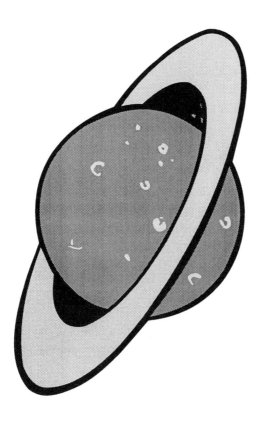

"Lord Shiva"

The silent teacher of all power and force who has burnt all his evil desires. Lord Shiva represents the complete cyclical process of generation, destruction and regeneration.

RELATIONSHIPS AND
HARMONICS OF NUMBERS

Every person emits vibrations that are electromagnetic in nature and can be detected by an especially designed apparatus. The vibrations of a destiny number 1 will be similar to any individual born on the same day.

When two different numbers blend together they form vibrations that combine wave lengths. These wave lengths exert mutual or adverse conditions which can influence each other. When a number is in harmony with another number it is supportive and sympathetic; when they are disharmonious they become antagonistic, creating an enemy that produces opposing results.

You have to know your enemy before you can attempt to achieve victory. You cannot heal your fears, anxieties, faults and addictions until you distinguish the numbers that oppose each other. When you become aware of the numbers that are disharmonious to each other you will learn to bring them into harmony, releasing yourself from the effects of the negative strain and opposition.

Opposing energy from numbers can be reconciled. Positive action is needed to offset it. Look for the positive number in your profile that will give you the self-discipline and strength to see you through your greatest obstacles to overcome the negative influence.

Outside circumstances are rarely the cause of your problems. The static within your own character creates the struggle until you become aware of the contradictory focal point of the tension. You need to eliminate the deficiencies in your character, and replace them with virtues to find real peace of mind.

NUMBER 1 is friendly with all the numbers, but has the best friendship with	3	5	7
NUMBERS IN HARMONIC BLENDS	1	3	5	7
NUMBERS IN HARMONIC BLENDS	1	2	4	8
NUMBERS IN HARMONIC BLENDS	1	3	6	9
NUMBERS THAT ARE AGGRESSIVE	1	3	5	8
NUMBERS NON AGGRESSIVE	2	4	6	7
NUMBERS THAT ARE NEUTRAL	1	6	9
NUMBERS THAT ARE MATERIAL	1	4	8
NUMBERS THAT ARE EMOTIONAL	2	5	7
NUMBERS THAT ARE INTELLECTUAL	3	6	9
NUMBERS THAT ARE SPIRITUAL	7	9

(I believe all the numbers are spiritual, but 7 and 9 are more philosophical, inspirational and intuitive in their consciousness because of their mystical and mysterious nature.)

* Number 1 is friendly and immune to the other numbers.
* 1 seems to favor 3 5 7 as far as relationships are concerned.
* The numbers 2 4 8 cannot always rely on the 1 and will find that 1 can easily deceive them
* 1 will always join forces with 3 5 7, because it has the best rapport with them, especially when 1 gets to the parallel point of opposition with 2 4 8.
* 1 will never bring harm to 2 4 8, yet it will not join forces with them.
* 1 has an exceptional relationship with number 9. 1 will always aid 9 and be friendly with it.
* 1 is numero uno and is a hermaphroditic number; whichever number it is added to, it produces an opposite effect.
  For example:
  -When 1 is added to an even number the total becomes odd. (1+ 2 = 3)
  -When 1 is added to an odd number the total becomes even. (1+ 3 = 4)
  1 is the most independent in nature of all the numbers.
* 1 will trigger the 0 to challenge all the other numbers while it takes control to gain in power and strength and deliver 0 to enormous achievements.

2---5---7 EMOTIONAL VIBRATIONS OF CHARACTER

2---BALANCER, *The Polarity of Life*

The goddess supported on the back of the man. Warm in affections. Can be more imitative of others than original in own character.   Two is passive in nature and if not careful will be absorbed by the influences of other numbers. Two will not fight but will not give in either. Mostly attracted to numbers 2, 4, 6 and 8, but is open to a relationship with all the numbers. Enjoys having mutual interactions with all the numbers, so 2 allows the other numbers to take charge;   yet 2 will subtly try to control every situation. Two will only be overruled and controlled if the numbers are stronger to avoid friction.

5---EXPERIMENTER, *The Five Senses of Life*

It is the five-pointed star, interested in experiencing all the five senses. Number of strong mental, physical and romantic feelings. Five seeks active sexual partners because of strong physical feelings. Needs a mate who is exciting and sensual. Attracted to numbers 1, 3, 7 and 9. Carries a strong faith and a burning desire to sense all of life.   Five has to feel important and will clash with numbers that try to stand in the way. Will give in to no one unless it is for sensual pleasures and sometimes the hunt is more important than the conquest. Five awakens mankind to the awareness that they are both human and divine.

7---MYSTIFIER, *The Mystery of Life.*

It is the number of the Sabbath day, the most sacred of all numbers. Seven has a temperament with many mood swings and will fight to the death for their beliefs. Can get self-absorbed in idealism; subject to depression, losses and gains throughout life. Although 7s can be difficult to understand, their intellectual powers will be the root of happiness for them. The nature of 7 is drawn to numbers 3, 5 and 7, although 7 is not always compatible with another 7. Sevens lack in trust and feel unfairly judged by the other numbers. Avoid personal confrontations by stating your opinions, not challenging other's opinions. Do not live a life of isolation to be concealed from visibility or the mainstream of life.

1---4---8---MATERIAL VIBRATIONS OF CHARACTER

1---INITIATOR, *The flame of life.*

Oneness in autonomy. Strongest number in dynamic force. This number is unrelenting. Strong pride. Gets along well emotionally with any number, as long as 1 is in charge. Prefers numbers 3, 5, and 7 for personal relationships. Number 9 is the favorite for 1. One is very demanding and will fight to get what is desired, even in a relationship. An individual with too many 1s in a profile can be unreasonable and impossible to deal with. Ones always face life boldly but not necessary rationally. The personality must be lived with authority and vitality.

4---CARETAKER, *The Foundation of Life.*

The guardian of the four corners of the earth-- North, South, East and West. The provider of security and home. Not very inspirational or romantic, but has a good pulse for bargains and material gain. Good in physical strength and endurance. Four can be stubborn and will give in, but not easily. Attracted to numbers 4, 2, 6 and 8. The brooding and sobriety of a 4 alienates the extroverted numbers. Even though the 4 is inhibited and reserved it adds depth and dependability to the inconsistency of the odd numbers.

8---TRANSFORMER, *The Evolution of Life.*

The evolution from the lower realm of the circle 8 to the higher realm. Interested in progress, advancement, success and status. Strong love for home, children and luxuries and very protective of them. Eight must be the governing power in a relationship and is attracted to weaker numbers like 2 and 6. Their obsessive desires will fester resentment from 1, 3, and 5 for control. Eight will give in only to a number 1 or 9 in double strength. Regardless of the obstacles 8 has in life, success is rewarded through strong character and determination. Eight has the ability to rise like the Phoenix with hope for the future.

3----6----9 SPIRITUAL VIBRATIONS OF CHARACTER

3---INSPIRATOR , *The Trinity of Life.*

Triangle of mental, physical and spiritual manifestation. Congenial and lighthearted. Likes to bring joy into all situations and relationships. Will not control another number nor will it be controlled. Will avoid relationships with numbers 4 and 8 because of their somber and businesslike ways, especially the 4. Seeker of adventure and excitement. Three will avoid monotonous routine. Even though 3 is indifferent and independent in attitude, socially it is very easy to get along with. Extravagance is its weakness because of over-indulgent desires.

6---HEALER, *The Nurturer of Life.*

The perfectionist that seeks spiritual and physical aspiration. The ultimate giver in love and compassion. Easily obsessed by love. Important for a 6 to have love in order to freely give love, but when hurt can turn to avengefulness. Gives unselfishly without expectations. Sensitive to the plights of others with a compassionate heart and a healing nature. Attracted to numbers 3, 6, 8 and 9. Can have conflicts with numbers 1 and 7. Six will try to appease all numbers until pushed to the limit. Six always comes to the rescue of those in need and will try to inspire others to see the best in themselves.

9---TEACHER *The Spiritual Foundation of Life.*

Number of unity and realization. Strong intuition. Dedicated to higher causes. Understands the vision of universal unity and strives to seek it for all. Nine has the ability to reach the masses and transform society because of 9s genuine interest in mankind. Nobility of spirit attracts all of the numbers, except 4 and 8. Nine tries to have meaningful interactions with all numbers. Nine is the only number that you can multiply by any other number and it always remains a 9, coming up with the depositor of number 9. For example: 9x1=9 9x2=18=9, 9x3=27=9, 9x4=36=9. 9x5=45=9,etc.

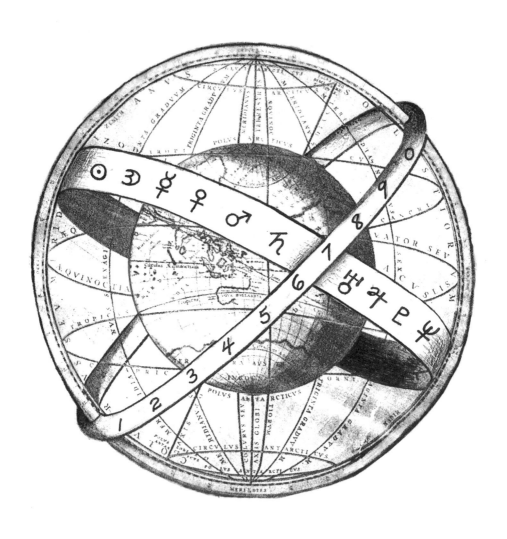

Numerology and the Planets
Universal Friends

NUMEROLOGY AND THE PLANETS

Life is surrounded by many mysteries in life. No one has ever been able to explain all these mysteries. The entire physical structure of the human body and its functions is still a profound mystery we are trying to unravel. Numerology and astrology are mysteries of mystical sciences, both based upon the principle of Divine Order. Numerology and astrology believe that everything on earth has its agreement in the heavens and everything in the heavens has its purpose on earth. In their own independent application both sciences have a phenomenal correlation to each other.

Numerology and astrology are universal friends; they have a special union with each other and both partake in the cosmic journey of mortal and eternal life. Both can show where abilities lie and what you entered this world with; however, they cannot define the exact pattern of your life in advance. Through mathematical laws, the planets and numbers will direct your soul's movements.

In numerology or astrology individuals born at a particular place on a given day will have certain characteristics but different potentials when born at a different time. Astrology is more precise and exact in its predictions than numerology, based upon the principle of "Divine Order".

One science cannot disassociate from the other because both give a greater understanding of human behavior and insight into future events. Even though astrology is more precise in interpretation it cannot be stated that it is more valid than numerology. Both sciences have their own language dealing with behavioral modification. You need to accept the laws of nature without reservation in your search for inner peace. The planets and numbers are only the screens on which certain conditions are focused, but it is the whole of the Heavens that influence the world we live in.

When you recognize and understand your personality and behavior patterns, you can alter your attitude to control your reactions to the personal events that take place in your life. As of this date, astrology has 10 known planets that basic astrology works with and numerology has 10 numbers. Why 10 when there are only 9 numbers in the numeric assemblance? I consider 0 as part of the assemblage of numbers because it influences life through the numbers. Zero is an important figure in numerology and has a lot of energy and power. Although it is not a number like 1 to 9, it is used as a power to direct energy to the other numbers. Zero multiplied by any number manifests that number, but when multiplied by itself it is infinite. All life comes from the eternal and all life returns to the eternal. Zero similar to the sun is infinity.

In eastern numerology people are influenced by the destiny number (all the numbers in your birthdate), psychic number (particular day of birth) and directional number (time of birth).

In astrology the three most important influences are the sun, moon and ascendant. There are several more planets to consider, and all have a very important place in the analysis of your birthchart. The position of the sun, moon, and the ascendant gives much information about an individual.

In numerology there are cycles; in astrology there are transits. Both systems have orbital rotations that revolve around the birth patterns. Cycles have nothing to do with the personal analysis of a chart. They affect each chart through an indirect involvement in bringing life experiences into the destiny number.

In numerology there are major and minor cycles that affect the numbers in the natal day of birth. Astrology has major and minor transits that affect the planets and houses in the natal horoscope.

Cycles in numerology or transits in astrology are movements of energy pointing to trends and issues in life. Certain cycles and transits are learning experiences stirring up energy to stimulate self-development. The effects of transiting energies depend upon the compatibility between the transit numbers in motion and the destiny number.

Astrology is definitely more fundamental and complex than numerology. There are numerous levels of knowledge, comparable to a measureless ocean. This section is not a course in astrology, so I want to keep it simple. I just want to open your awareness to the synastry of both sciences, how they each affect your date of birth and the basic principles involved.

Astrology is one of the "para" sciences that was used during the ancient Mesopotamian World (7th Century). Seven pertains to spirituality, scientific knowledge and mastery of skills. St. Thomas Aquinas endorsed astrology in the year 1225-1274. Numerology was also used as an ancient reference for the Koran, Kabbalah and the Hebrew alphabet.

Numerology has many variations and is a science that can be found in the Judeo-Christian faith dating back at least 7,000 years, including passages in the Old Testament. In the East, these sciences were used traditionally by the upper castes. The stars, planets and numbers were regarded as deities because of their important mystical value which goes back about 15,000 years to the era of the Prophet Rama.

Numerology and astrology give a microscopic look into the mysterious being. These sciences can help you to assess your weaknesses and teach ways to use your strengths. The combination of both numerology and astrology produces a cosmic rhythm. Both subjects are intrinsic in their mathematical accuracy. Both are profound sciences and need to be respected.

This book offers valuable esoteric knowledge to help you gain awareness in the use of numbers. Proper study is necessary to determine the magnitude of human behavior. It is not always easy to interpret the profile of an individual. It is helpful to have an understanding of the individual's character before the age of seven and to know their spiritual evolution at the time the reading takes place.

This book is to be used as a tool to supply the numeric principles necessary for individuals to develop constructive qualities and to understand the analysis of the 9-year, 9-month and personal year cycles. The study of numerology is a fascinating subject that you can use as reinforcement in your mental, material and spiritual growth.

The principles of this science can help improve and transform inherent attributes. When using the techniques offered in this book, you learn to deal more compassionately and with an open mind toward others. Numerology is a complete science and is very fascinating and intriguing.

There are complexities and variables in numerology and astrology, just as there are in the respected fields of medicine and law. The esoteric sciences speak in the terms of facts. Man speaks through the principles of the sciences according to his knowledge, abilities and beliefs.

Numerology and astrology are ancient aspects of eastern philosophy. Both sciences are based on the concept of Divine Order through reincarnation and karma. It is not the planets or the numbers in destiny that impels the soul, it is the result of past lives. Numbers and planets are symbols of divine realities to evolution both spiritually and physically.

The mystics from the East say that destiny prevails, and all you can do is exercise free will within the orbit of your fate. The mystics also affirm that through spiritual disciplines you can achieve great success, and fate will be less challenging during adverse periods. Their belief is that you should never be handicapped by inharmonious conditions; instead you must use the spiritual practices of daily prayers, mantras, or affirmations to help ease the conflicts of daily living.

It is important when delineating numerical or astrological profiles to understand that these are profiles of the personality and not of the spirit or the soul. When you have the power to create, you will have the power power to redeem. Life from infancy to maturity is governed by the characteristics of your environment.

Spiritual practices, prayers and daily mantras do influence our thoughts and life to help remove negative thought patterns and to successfully change the direction of life. Many different fears and mental anxieties are precipitated through discordant astrological transits and numerical cycles. Through meditation and spiritual practices you can eliminate negative principles that provoke havoc within you to receive help to remove the veil of ignorance that prevents you from having a balanced and happy life.

After many years of research in both subjects, I recognize that numbers and the planets have similar characteristics that bind them together. Numerologists do not always agree on what a number represents or its rulership to the planets. It is not a question of who is right or wrong. Today's advanced thinking recognizes the correlative attributes (that are presented in this book) between the planets and the numbers. A number is abstract and has no physical existence; however, it does have defined characteristics that determine its power and purpose.

154

Just as astrology must give recognition and meaning to new planets as they are discovered, so must numerology give new meaning to a different energy in symbolism for the new millennium. The earlier ways of presenting numbers have changed significantly and will change even more in the year 2000 because the numbers will react differently under a new vibration. The meaning of numbers and planets is expressed in simple terms of orderliness and has infinite possibilities.

NUMBER	PLANET
0	Sun
1	Mars
2	Moon
3	Jupiter
4	Saturn
5	Mercury
6	Venus
7	Neptune
8	Pluto
9	Uranus

In numerology the destiny number is the most important number; in astrology the sun sign is the most important planet. Above are the numbers and their planetary rulerships. The purpose of the combined qualities show how the energies of each are similar in relationship and in their behavioral qualities. For example, a number 1 individual and an Aries sun person have similar personalities and so their thrust in life will be similar. Their manifestation will always work through the rulership of the sun sign.

A destiny number never functions alone because there are other numbers to consider. Just like the sun is not a planet all to itself, other planets must be given consideration. The other numbers in your numeric profile work with the destiny number. The numbers influenced by their planetary position will affect the balance and the circumstances of those forces. Different combinations of numbers and their rulership creates the ease or the tension produced from the dispositions of the combined energies and all are important.

According to the accepted principles of numerology and astrology, the compatibility of the numbers that I have given to the respective planets may not be agreeable to all who understand the sciences, but it is my truth as I have experienced it. The value given to the interpretations of the combined energies will be difficult to diminish-- especially entering the new millennium of the 2 vibration. Exhaustive research and deductions were made based upon basic numerology and the sun signs to present this astonishing revolution.

After careful research, I chose the Sun to have rulership with the 0. Today's school of numerologists believe that the number 1 has rulership with the Sun; I respectfully disagree. One is a number that is aggressive and is considered a warrior, similar to that of the planet Mars. The Sun is not a warrior, rather it is the most powerful center of the solar system. The Sun is a heavenly body which is the source of life and energy, not the defender of life. The Sun is royal, to be respected, not to be feared--representing the soul. It is similar to the outdated thinking of Catholicism--that God is to be feared while being revered. How can you love someone of whom you are afraid. Fear does not always mean respect; it creates misconceptions.

My belief is that the Sun has rulership with the 0, and planet Mars has rulership over the number 1. The number 1 is energetic in nature, but also challenging, symbolic of a warrior. The Sun and the planet Mars have similar energy; both are fire planets, but working at different levels of expression and not outwardly agreeable. The Sun is the power of vitality on the spiritual level and the passion desired of the soul. Mars is the power of vitality on the physical level and the passion desired of the body.

Zero and the Sun are eternal circles--both have absolute flow of life energy, representing the place of man within the cosmic life. The last 1000 years have been a period of strife, struggles, individualism, strength, constant wars and activist movements. It was a period when the world was exploited by dictators, lawlessness, reckless disrespect for life, sensuality, materialism, ambitious drives and egocentric leadership.

Parents pushed and encouraged children to become leaders, to be bold, to have strong characters, to move forward, to be competitive and to reach for the impossible dream. These are not characteristics of the Sun; but represents the behavior of planet Mars and the number 1?

I have given meaning of the Sun, a luminary with rulership to the 0. I view Mars to be synonymous with number 1. The Sun and 0 both represent the soul, not the ego, providing equal expression. They are like heaven and earth, the Sun working through the spirit of heaven (the higher octave) and the 0 working through the spirit of earth (the lower octave).

After researching hundreds of chart combinations of astrology with numerology, I have uncovered significant similarities and differences in the rhythms of the planets and numbers. This research helped me become more astute in the pursuit of the technique which I use to correspond the numbers to the planets. Intense study was done to carefully examine the pros and cons of the concept used in this book; the results of these studies have supported my hypothesis.

Certain numbers and planets have consistently shared similar characteristics. In looking at the numbers in terms of the four elements, air, fire, earth and water, I have been able to project the recurrence of certain elements to certain numbers. In my research the destiny, psychic and directional numbers were the primary numbers used to provide synastry with the planets because they are the most significant in the natal profile.

I also used the combination of numbers of the birthdays, without the year and month. For example, if a birthday fell on the 25th day, I used the numbers 2, 5 and 7 (7 as the total of 2+5), along with the other vital findings of the destiny and the directional number.

On page 162 is a calculated mathematical formula of percentages based on research I have done. I based my extrapolation on my own expertise and what I learned from my clients' charts. Using numbers from 1 to 9, I divided them into the four elements of air, fire, water and earth.

The ratio of percentages is used to indicate the basis of the four elements and the quality of their strength associated with the numbers. The percentages are just indicators of the elements and numbers that I found to be consistent in the charts. There were some charts that varied in opposition to my findings, but 75% of the charts investigated had parallel or repeated patterns of similar characteristics.

The percentages were determined by using the destiny, psychic and directional numbers of an individual's profile and comparing them to the planets and house placements of their astrological chart.

The destiny number in numerology is equal in expression of the Sun in astrology. The psychic number is equal to the ascendant and the directional number with the Moon. Other repetitive patterns are too involved to explain within the scope of this book.

The highest percentages relate to the high frequency of the appearance of certain numbers with certain elements. The lower percentages had minimal activation between certain numbers and the four elements.

For example: A destiny 1 in many profiles had a lot of fire planets in the astrological charts. A destiny number 2 had a high percentage of air planets and the number 9 destiny had both air and water elements prominent.

In numerous astrological charts, combined with the numerology profiles of my clients I have found significant similarities. The individuals with 0 in their birthdates have significant aspects in astrology to their Sun sign. The Sun either had a conjunction, inconjunct, opposition or square to the Moon, ascendant, Saturn or Pluto. Uranus and Neptune were also included, but not as frequently as the others. It appears as if the personal journey of the ego was the focal point in the past life holding life in suspension.

NUMBERS WITH	AIR	FIRE	WATER	EARTH
ONE	24%	155%	11%	12%
TWO	43%	5%	28%	24%
THREE	28%	49%	7%	18%
FOUR	11%	6%	46%	36%
FIVE	33%	16%	10%	40%
SIX	12%	8%	42%	38%
SEVEN	19%	5%	54%	21%
EIGHT	17%	10%	41%	33%
NINE	36%	19%	31%	11%

GEMS, COLORS, FLOWERS AND SPICES, CHARACTERISTICS AND PERSONAL NEEDS ASSOCIATED WITH THE NUMBERS AND THE PLANETS

0 AND THE SUN

GEMS   Diamond, king of all gems. India was considered the first source of diamonds in the world. Some Eastern Indian traditions in past history believed that a person's soul had to be purified before joining the "Universal Soul". The diamond is rated as the most precious of all gems, and is considered to have many mystical powers, especially as a powerful healing cure. A diamond is made of pure carbon, an element that is the foundation of life. It was believed in ancient times that if you swallowed the powder of a flawless diamond, it could provide good health, prevent illness, give energy or a long life. Diamonds can be used to protect the individual wearing it by warding off phantoms, demons and black magic. Majestic and awesome diamonds symbolize wealth and power. Other metals and stones associated with the sun are: *silver, gold, crystal, quartz, peridot.*

COLORS	White (like pure sunlight), silver and gold
FLOWERS	White lotus (Divine Consciousness), white rose (divine love), gardenia (flower of purity), sunflower (consciousness turned toward the light of the Sun to receive pure energy), red lotus (Supreme Avatar of flowers)
SPICE	Tumeric (used in Sun worship)

The sun is a luminary (not a planet) and the closest star to the earth. The sun is a rotating mass of volcanic gases and dust which alters the color of the sunlight. This is why at times the sun appears to be golden yellow or red and sometimes even bluish. The white sunlight contains all the colors of the rays of the sun and of the rainbow. The atmosphere and weather conditions affect the brightness and reflection of the colors.

The 0 without a companion number is similar to the Sun. Neither has an effect unless another energy aligns with it. Both are reflectors of positive and negative energy. The 0 or the Sun can only focus when related to another energy or element. The Sun and 0 are significant because both will affect every area of life and are destined to play an important part in the life of the individual.

I have associated the colors white and crystal to 0 and the Sun because 0 is neutral or colorless, and sunlight is white. The Moon is also white because it is the reflection of the sun. White is appropriate as a color for the 0, because 0 does not have energy of its own and picks up energy from the number with which it is associated.

The sun is white, containing all the colors in the rainbow. Zero is abstract, containing all the numbers from 1 to 9. Both the Sun and 0 are pure in form and shape.

CHARACTERISTICS
individualistic, infinite, eternal, absolute, boundless, sustainer, prideful, noble-minded, authoritative, fortifying, enthusiastic, dramatic, integrative, unlimited strength, worldly, eternal, magnificent, divine, evolved, enduring, power to do or be, omnipresent, without beginning, without end

PERSONAL NEEDS
Needs a sense of purpose and effectiveness to do something important, to be recognized or achieve prominence. With a strong Sun or 0 you want to make significant contributions to society. The source of life for both is to have power and status. Needs to have freedom to make choices because of strong self-image. Can either draw energy from the world or draw away from the world seeking isolation. Happiness and success only comes after redemption of the soul.

NUMBER 1 AND PLANET MARS

GEMS	Red ruby, red coral, garnet, fire opal, red sapphire, red spinel, red jasper
COLORS	Red tones, reddish orange
FLOWERS	Snapdragon (power of assertion), azalea (flame red), red rose (physical love), zinnia (for physical endurance), daisy (for frankness), red hot poker lily, peacock
SPICES	Peppercorn (energizes the body), pepper (a zingy spice), garlic (pungent and flavorful)

CHARACTERISTICS

strong will power, initiator, leader, courageous, independent, determined, forceful, uncompromising, quarrelsome, impatient, competitive, energetic, passionate, masculine, feisty, aggressive, motivator, achiever, enthusiastic, mover and shaker, resourceful

PERSONAL NEEDS

Needs to be a channel of energy. A strong desire to be first. Dislikes routine. Actions are courageous and have to be independent. Radical in behavior. Enjoys living life in the fast lane always seeking the adventure of the moment. Impatient and impulsive with a short fuse. Difficult to reason with. Never hides from responsibility but finds it difficult to be devoted to long term goals due to a short attention span. Personality is never timid in approach and does not like be told what to do. Warriors with a strong self-confidence and courage in endless supply.

Strong passions with strong sexual desires. Use this intense energy through physical workouts or aggression or it will work against you. Planet Mars and the number 1 are willing to take risks for the purpose of achievement and adventure. Both possess a dominant temperament, always wanting control of the environment. Mars and the number 1 give strong character with fiery energy and self-assertion. When energy is used favorably a strong Mars or 1 can be the pioneer that springs new frontiers for others to succeed.

NUMBER 2 AND PLANET MOON

GEMS   Pearl, ivory, white agate, white opal (queen of gems), moonstone (spiritual gem), aventurine

COLORS   White, cream, ivory

FLOWERS Moonflower (self-giving), carnation (cooperation), carambola (congeniality), moonflower, gladioli (receptivity), forget me not (lasting remembrance), white rose (purity), moonflower (emotions)

SPICES   Ginger (keeps the heart warm), paprika (adds zing and glitz to light or colorless dishes)

CHARACTERISTICS
feminine, sensitive, receptive, changeable, psychic, passive, gentle, duality, demonstrative, thoughtful, nurturing, sluggish, supportive, vacillating, moody, unpredictable, loving, gullible, understanding, sensual and sexual in nature, emotional, maternal, charismatic

PERSONAL NEEDS
Needs to find the balance of duality between the feminine and masculine union. Conductors of human nature, moody in emotion, intuitive; passive personality, always wanting to keep peace. Instinct is to love and nurture and does not do well living alone or in hostile environments. Friendly rapport with the public. Will gain through women or be of service to women through a vocation. Cooperative team player. Physically affectionate with strong romantic feelings. Loves to travel. Easily meets new acquaintances because of non-threatening personality; however, will always try to have own way. Restless nature finds it difficult to be satisfied with life. Does not surrender easily and will fight for a cause until satisfied with the results. Rebels against constitutional authority, always striving to establish own center. The Moon and 2s are receptive to all human instincts, feelings, the sub-conscious and the conscious memory bank. Their nature requires sympathy and acceptance of loved ones to feel secure. When that security is established the waves of emotions will bring number the 2 and the planet Moon safely to shore.

NUMBER 3 AND PLANET JUPITER

GEMS   Yellow sapphire, golden beryl or morganite, amber, "heliodor" (loom of the Sun), yellow topaz, citrine

COLORS   Yellow, orange, gold, honey

FLOWERS   Yellow champa (divine smile), grandiflora (desires), poppy (spirited joy), yellow rose (mental joy), daffodil (vibrance), water lily (wealth), hibiscus (eternal youth)

SPICES   Sage (perks up dishes). oregano (versatile in its use), Vanilla beans, (used in custards, savory dishes).

CHARACTERISTICS

friendly, outgoing, sociable, pleasurable, adventurous, indulgent, expansive, visionary, extravagant, appreciative, charming, optimistic, stimulating, generous, energetic, athletic, confident, exaggerative, jovial, philosophical, open-minded, extroverted, masculine, playful, gullible, benevolent, fortunate

PERSONAL NEEDS

Motivation is to expand through communications, knowledge and travel. Restless natures constantly in motion. Jupiter and 3 are the gamblers of life. Both love pleasures and the easy life. Never satisfied with life--always moving forward. Generally fortunate with a comfortable and happy life. Seldom worries and never expects the worse no matter what the situation. Winners that always comes out on top. Broad circle of friends and acquaintances. Magnetic and charming personality. Engaging charisma. Seeks the attention of the opposite sex because the conquest is greater than the win. The planet Jupiter and the number 3 want a lifestyle of many rewards, rich experiences, spectacular achievements and to be in the limelight. Enjoys nobility and will have good fortune in lifetime because Jupiter is a strong source of radiation, reflecting light from the sun. Three is the trinity full of a bountiful nature. Both are dynamic and prosperous energies that achieve emotional, intellectual and financial contentment. Jupiter and 3 are optimistic in nature, broad in outlook and liberal in views.

NUMBER 4 AND PLANET SATURN

GEMS   Blue sapphire, amethyst, carnelian (brownish red), indicolite (dark blue), hematite (grayish black), jade (bluish-gray), melanite (blackish brown), lapis luzulli (deep royal blue), malachite (used for healing)

COLORS   Dark blue, brown, copper, black, grey

FLOWERS   Tobacco flower (common sense), chrysanthemum (life energy), zinnia (endurance), bougainvillaea (protection), phlox (skill in physical work), crocus (continuity), lilacs (steadfastness), salmon rose (sacrifice)

SPICES   Yellow and black mustard seed (a good preservative), salt (traditional seasoning)

CHARACTERISTICS
responsible, disciplined, truthful, dignified, puritanical, mature, economical, conservative, phobic, cold, suspicious, selfish, taskmaster, thrifty, traditional, introverted, shrewd, dependable, emotionless, hardworking, ambitious, limited, serious, faithful, depressive, wise, elderly, pessimistic

PERSONAL NEEDS
Structure a solid base in life and strength will come from patience, endurance and faith.   Establish functional guidelines for balance and realistic values. Use staying power and personal growth to achieve status and success. Self-centeredness and selfishness can come from too much emphasis on financial accomplishments. Everything gained in life will come from devotion, dedication and a crystallization of negative thought patterns.   Age brings blessings of wisdom, happiness and character. Maturity helps to appreciate the beauty and quality of life. The planet Saturn and number 4 reflect a dispassionate nature that reflects fears and insecurity. Four and Saturn are considered the taskmasters or the "Gods of Harvest", because life will always seem to be filled with discipline, control and limitations involving great sacrifices in life.   The first half of life will feel limited; but the second half of life reaps all that was sown. Many individuals achieve glowing tributes in later years, even after death.

NUMBER 5 AND PLANET MERCURY

GEMS   Emerald, green jade, green topaz, green grossular, green beryl, green sapphire

COLORS   Deep yellow, green, turquoise, shades of green

FLOWERS Marigold (advancement or progress), yellow rose (mentality), poppy (mental constancy), begonia (perfect mental balance), petunia (physical passion)

SPICES   Star anise (five-pointed star shaped seed used as a diuretic), oregano (flavorful and interesting in taste)

CHARACTERISTICS

articulate, informative, dexterous, clever, dynamic, restless, inconsistent, talkative, flexible, nervous, reasoner, enterprising, intelligent, easily bored, judgmental, inquisitive, broad-minded, youthful, mind games, traveler of mind or body, masculine, extremely sexual, deceitful, temperamental, scholar, communicator

PERSONAL NEEDS

Needs to communicate and experience life on all levels. Possesses intense mental energy, has physical restlessness and a tendency to worry a lot. Becomes bored easily and does not like to be in a rut regardless of the situation. Mercury and 5 need intellectual stimulation and a lot of mental interest to constantly provide challenging learning experiences. Must learn to relax. Impatient and restless in desire to be successful. Venturesome curiosity needs to be more grounded. Superficial in eagerness to please just to be socially accepted. Use friendly persuasion to achieve the desired objective because the goal will be easier to attain. Youthful nature stays long into life and always makes 5 and Mercury alluring to the opposite sex. Generally lucky in life regardless of the obstacles. The planet Mercury and 5s are responsible for intelligence, learning skills, education, travel and both are quite articulate and impressive in communication skills. Both the planet Mercury and 5 are known as the messengers of the gods and the keepers of records that preside over all communications.

NUMBER 6 AND PLANET VENUS

GEMS   Pink sapphire, rose quartz, pink topaz, pink beryl, rhodonite, diamond microline, benitoite (rare and beautiful gem, colorless and pink), pink tourmaline

COLORS   Shades of pink, rose, white

FLOWERS   Mistletoe (kissing flower), pink rose (true love under the spiritual influence), jasmine (purity and beauty), sweet pea & baby's breath, (gentleness), shell flower (eloquence), impatiens (generosity)

SPICES   Cardamon (most beautiful of all spices) mace and vanilla beans (used in desserts and sauces).

CHARACTERISTICS
idealistic, diplomatic, affectionate, romantic, graceful, devotional, sensitive, psychic, virtuous, domesticated, complacent, creative, artistic, charming, lazy, obstinate, indulgent, friendly, compassionate, honorable, feminine, sensual, vain, nurturing

PERSONAL NEEDS
Typically, nature is meant to give love and pleasure, but soul also needs to feel appreciated. There is a power of attraction that makes Venus and 6 fortunate with people and with opportunities. Having a natural talent for entertaining, cooking and social graces benefits the nature to be service-oriented, to provide happiness and make to people comfortable at home or at social functions. Planet Venus and 6 love comfortable lives and love to indulge in sweets. Their loving dispositions and shyness opens them to vulnerability-- but inside the velvet glove is an iron hand. Seek out vocations that are service-oriented or fields of creativity with more aesthetic accomplishments. Physical labor or mundane tasks are not suitable for refined nature. Romantic as lovers because of the strong physical pleasures inherent in both. Travels, a busy lifestyle with friends, and happiness in love life is necessary to keep contented. Both number 6 and Venus are considered the goddesses of love ruling marriage, beauty, intuition, romance and creativity. Both have the beauty and delicate nature of the rose within the nature as well as the prickly thorns. Their unique and precious natures contributes to the love and the well being of others. Inner spiritual beauty and their loving natures will be the gifts that bring pleasure to all their friendships and relationships.

NUMBER 7 AND PLANET NEPTUNE

GEMS   Amethyst, chrysolite, tanzanite (lavender blue), aquamarine almondine (deep violet red), violet sapphire

COLORS   Pastel blues, pastel greens, purple, violet

FLOWER   Smargosa, (spiritual environment and emotional strength), oleander (peaceful mind), gardenia (loves the water), African violets, bael (known as wood apple, devotional purposes), lavender or mauve rose (humility, and benevolence)

SPICES   Sage (aromatic spice), cumin (mysterious flavor)

CHARACTERISTICS
imaginative, inspirational, impressionable, visionary, devotional, clairvoyant, mystical, knowledgeable, eccentric, secretive, artistic, studious, mysterious, pessimistic, unusual, self-sacrificing, fanatical, solitary, addictive, healer, vulnerable, intellectual

PERSONAL NEEDS
Inspirational and spiritual. Many sacrifices must be made in life so it is important to keep grounded and focused to maintain equilibrium. Can be deceptive, with a hidden agenda, or can be easily deceived. Involved in obsessions and emotionalism taking things for granted in life that others would question. Life is not always centered around material security and this could lead into a constant financial crises. Personality is easily addicted to vices, especially alcohol and drugs, and must be completely avoided . Not always understood by others because of the mysterious and obscure nature Prone to despondency and worry. Neptune and 7 are never overlooked even though the natures are to stay in the background. Inquisitive minds constantly searching for the ideal in the mental, emotional and intellectual--yet, have tendencies of absentmindedness and inattentiveness. Sex appeal is strong but it must not distract from pursuits and goals. Planet Neptune and the number 7 do not like to face reality or see life the way it is and could end up dreaming through life instead of acting it out through realiistic goals. Both are considered sacred and mystical. Both influence the psychic with changeable natures. Neptune and 7 are viewed as nebulous in nature. Attracted to bodies of water.

NUMBER 8 AND PLANET PLUTO

GEMS   Black pearl, black onyx, zircon, labriadocite (dark gray),
            tourmaline, black opal, tigers-eye
COLORS   Black, magenta, maroon, deep red, charcoal gray
FLOWERS   Dahlia (dignity), Indian cork tree (transformation), peony
            (material expansion), crown imperial flower (nobility),
            hibiscus (magnetic power)
SPICES   Basil (means royal, one of the most important culinary
            herbs), clove (adds richness to taste)

CHARACTERISTICS
superior force, power, rebellious, driving ambition, dictator, corporate world, confident, secretive, manipulative, challenging,, strong ego-temperament, greedy, statuesque, leader commanding, transformational, healer, pressure, builder, influential, dominant, dynamic, confident, materialistic

PERSONAL NEEDS
Needs to be balanced to be peace-loving. Difficult to understand because of dual natures. Both number 8 and Pluto rule over power, corporate institutions, organizations, operations, businesses, underworld and outer world and deals with big money. Must be of integrity or involvement in subversive activities can create problems and scandals. Negative or corrupt behavior in ambitions or activities must be dissolved to achieve spiritual evolution. Both are capable of dealing with the masses but needs to handle people with compassion and diplomacy to influence others in a positive way. Avoid imperious and forceful behavior with others. Build to protect not destroy. The planet Pluto and the number 8 can be troublesome energy and will destroy anyone who stands in the way. Both are altruistic in desires to rebuild or reconstruct. Number 8 is two 0s connected to each other by one line; representing heaven and earth. Pluto is the line of strength and independence enclosing itself at the center ending in a 0. Pluto and 8 must work to build harmony of the spiritual and the material spirit to unite mass consciousness through transformation.

NUMBER 9 AND PLANET URANUS

GEMS   Lapis lazuli, cat's eye, pyrope, golden beryl, spessartine
          (red-orange), fire opal
COLORS   Reds, oranges, hot pinks, bright yellows, purples
FLOWERS   Crossandra (realization), day lily (mental sincerity),
          canna (affinity with the divine), orange rose (blissful
          love of the divine), bicolored roses (unique and graceful)
SPICES   Cinnamon, cassia, caraway, (universal in use)

CHARACTERISTICS
*liberated, unconventional, unique, erratic, rebellious, humanitarian,
detached, impersonal, spiritual, intellectual, progressive,
enlightened, intuitive, unstable, benevolent, undisciplined,
dramatic, cosmic, imaginative, unpredictable, eccentric*

PERSONAL NEEDS
Seeks to be universal in idealism to reform society and to improve
conditions for all of mankind and womankind. Nine is humanitarian
in principle, but not always in action. The sparklers of society with
enormous ambitions to push forward to greater possibilities. There
is an immense need to hold life loosely and still enjoy the drama. Be
practical in actions because of idealistic and extremist nature.
Rebels of revolutions who are able to awaken awareness in all to
cultivate a sense of brotherhood. Scattering too much of energy
accomplishes nothing. Focus vision on helping to build a society
based on love, caring and spiritual development. Planet Uranus and
number 9 are fanatical, extremely independent and progressive; both
are difficult to control, yet both are teachers of wisdom and
experience. Uranus is tilted on a rotational axis compared with the
rest of the planets resembling a wheel spinning on its side and can
trigger sudden occurrences. The number 9 has a straight line and
needs to be independent, but the circle of the 9 wants unity. The 9
projects eccentric behavior due to that duality. Nine and Uranus are
like the hush before a storm knowing events are about to get out of
control, helpless in the hand of fate.

MANTRA HEALING

Karma and destiny are governed by the influences of the numbers and planetary positions. The power of prayer and daily mantras can help to overcome negative influences. There are several healing mantras to choose from, even personal ones for each of the planets and their numbers. The syllables and words have specific vibrations and sounds that require distinct pronunciation. Unless the sounds and words of the mantra are spoken with articulate perfection the mantra is meaningless. A mantra should be translated to an individual through a qualified mystic or spiritual teacher. There are tapes and books to help you learn the proper method of pronouncement. It is worth the effort, if you so desire, to attain and learn the high spiritual chanting that comes from the mantras.

Following are three mantras that can be chanted by every individual to receive special salutations. The first is for prosperity, the second is for memory and education and the third is for wisdom and power. You can purchase books or tapes with the chants from most Eastern temples, Eastern Indian specialty shops, or metaphysical book stores.

The Sacred "Om"

PROSPERITY

OM SRIM MAHALAKSHMY AI NAMAHA
I propitiate Mahalakshmi, the Goddess of Wealth, to bless me with prosperity.

MEMORY AND EDUCATION

OM EIM SARASWATYAI SVAHA
I propitiate Goddess Saraswathi to bless me with memory and education.

WISDOM AND POWER

OM EIM HREEM KLEEM CHAMUNDAYAI VICHHE
Salutations to Shakti, who showers blessings of wisdom and power

The above Mantras come from the book *Healing Techniques Of The Holy East* by the most beloved and respected Satgru Sant Keshavadas.

"*Lakshmi*"

She is the consort of Vishnu and and is worshiped as the Goddess of Wealth & Prosperity.

"*Brahma*"

His consort is Sarasvati who is worshiped as the Goddess of learning and education

MATHEMATICS

Name _____

Address _____

_____

Phone _____

Birth Date _____

Time _____

Place of Birth _____

Friend's Birth Date _____

Time _____

Name : Hirindra Singh
Time : 6:37 p.m.

Destiny Number: 6
Directional Number: 7
Psychic Number: 18
Personal Year Number: for 1997 is (3)

18 DAY — 1 · 2 · 4 · 8 — 1-4-5 MATERIAL
4 MONTH — 7 — 2-5-7 EMOTIONAL
1937 YEAR — 3 · 6 · 9 — 3-6-9 INTELLECTUAL

Destiny	6	6	6	6	6	6	6	6	6	6	6	6	6	6	6	6	6	6
9 yr. challenge	1	1	1	1	1	1	1	1	1	9	9	9	9	9	9	9	3	3
9 mo. cycle	1	9	7	4	1	1	1	8	9	3	1	9	4	7	1	1	8	7
Dates Cycles Are In Effect	4/37	1/38	8/39	4/40	10/41	8/42	4/43	10/44	8/45	4/46	10/47	8/48	4/49	10/50	8/51	4/52	10/53	4/54

Destiny	6	6	6	6	6	6	6	6	6	6	6	6	6	6	6	6	6	6	6
9 yr. challenge	8	1	4	3	3	3	3	3	3	1	1	1	1	7	7	7	7	3	3
9 mo. cycle	4	8	1	3	7	4	1	1	1	7	3	1	1	3	7	4	1	8	1
Dates Cycles Are In Effect	10/56	8/57	4/58	1/59	8/60	4/61	1/62	8/63	4/64	10/65	8/66	4/67	10/68	4/70	10/71	8/72	4/73	10/74	8/75

Destiny	6	6	6	6	6	6	6	6	6	6	6	6	6	6	6	6	6	6	6
9 yr. challenge	4	4	8	4	4	4	1	1	1	1	1	1	1	1	1	8	8	8	8
9 mo. cycle	7	4	8	1	9	7	4	1	9	3	1	1	7	8	9	3	7	1	1
Dates Cycles Are In Effect	4/76	1/77	8/78	4/79	8/80	8/81	4/82	4/83	4/84	4/85	1/86	1/87	4/88	1/89	8/90	4/91	1/92	8/93	4/94

Destiny	6	6	6	6	6	6	6	6	6	6	6	6	6	6	6	6	6	6	6
9 yr. challenge	9	3	7	1	8	1	6	6	7	1	6	6	1	1	7	7	7	7	7
9 mo. cycle	9	3	7	1	8	1	9	3	7	1	1	3	7	1	8	9	3	7	4
Dates Cycles Are In Effect	10/95	8/96	4/97	1/98	8/99	4/2000	1/2001	8/2002	4/2003	10/2004	8/05	4/06	10/07	8/08	4/09	1/2010	8/11	4/12	1/13

8/14

MATHEMATICS

MATHEMATICAL CALENDAR
FOR A BIRTHDAY PROFILE

The page on the left side is a calendar to assist you in setting up a birthday profile. Information should be filled in across the top of the calendar before you begin to construct the bottom portion. On the back of that page is more information that should be filled in before you proceed into the actual calendar profile. Make sure all your information is accurate. It is very easy to make mistakes because of errors made in the birthdate or time. Fill in all the information so you have it for future reference (a good habit to establish).

*   <u>Front Page</u>:

*   In the upper portion on the left hand side of the calendar fill in the person's name and phone number.

*   In the middle portion of the calendar in the appropriate spaces fill in the year, month and day

*   In the upper portion on the right side of the calendar, fill in the appropriate lines for the destiny number, psychic number, directional number and the personal year number.

*   The **destiny number;** the final "depositor" of all the numbers in your birthdate after they are all added together.

Birthday Example: April 18, 1937, change April (the 4th month) to a 4.

Place the year first, month second, and day last adding all the numbers of 1937 4 18.
Add all the numbers to get a final depositor.
$1 + 9 + 3 + 7 + 4 + 1 + 8 = 33$ (3+3) = 6 as final depositor.
Place the final depositor on the line next to the word Destiny <u>6.</u>

*   **Psychic number;** day of birth, is entered in the line next to the word Psychic <u>18</u>.   *(Do not reduce the psychic number, for example it is the 18th.)*

175

*   **Directional number;** time of birth, is placed on the line next to it, for example it is <u>7</u> .

(To find the correct number for your time of birth, refer to the timetable on page 119 using the number that is associated with the hour of your birth)

*   **Personal year number and universal year number**.

To find the **universal year** number, add the numbers of the year in question. *For example:* The year is 1997, so add   1+9+9+7 = 26   or (2+6 = 8).   <u>8 becomes the universal number for the year of 1997.</u>

You then add the universal number of 8 to your own personal month and day of birth numbers to get your personal year number.

To find the **personal year** of the example birthday of (Month) 4, (day) 18, add the personal year number of 8 to the 4 and the 18.   (8 + 4 + 1 + 8 = 30 = 3) <u>3 is the personal year number for this individual for 1997</u> .

To calculate for the year of 1998, add 1 + 9 + 9 + 8 = 27 (2+7 = 9) 9 is the personal number for the year 1998. Add 9 to the 4 plus 18 to find the personal year number.   9 + 4 + 1 + 8 = 22 or (2 + 2 = 4). <u>4 is the personal year number for 1998 for the example chart.</u>

IMPORTANT TO REMEMBER: *The year in question is added to find the personal year number, not the individual's birthyear.*

*   After you have filled all the numbers in their respective underlined spaces; place the birthyear, month, day and destiny numbers into the three chariot wheels, (as explained in next chapter).   Each wheel is divided into three separate segments and has three designated numbers that will go into each of these segments.

*   In the first wheel place the numbers, 3   6   9.

*   In the second wheel place the numbers, 2   5   7.

*   In the third wheel place the numbers, 1   4   8.

* The 0 goes into the same wheel with the number to its left. If that wheel is full place it into the wheel of the number to its right.

Always keep a uniform pattern when placing numbers into the wheel segments.

* First wheel: 3 in the left---6 in the right---9 in the bottom

* Second wheel: 2 in the left---5 in the right---7 in the bottom

* Third wheel: 1 in the left---4 in the right---8 in the bottom

1937	4	18	=	6
year	month	day		destiny

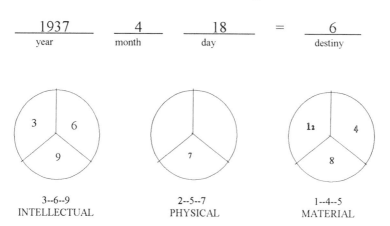

3--6--9	2--5--7	1--4--5
INTELLECTUAL	PHYSICAL	MATERIAL

ELEMENT OF ZERO---------The element of 0 is energy and not considered a number. It needs to be plugged into a number to be effective. Zero should be placed in the same wheel as the number to the left of it. If that wheel is filled with numbers, the 0 should then be placed into the wheel with the number to its right. (See the next section for more information and examples).

When there is more then one 0 in the profile, keep them in the same wheel that the number to its left is placed in. If you have two 0s in your birthdate they could be placed in separate wheels if they are associated with different numbers. The 0 should always be interpreted with the number to its left, even if the 0 cannot be placed in the same wheel as its sponsor when the chariot is full of numbers. The 0 is flexible and can make adjustments.

When you have completed the upper portion of the calendar fill in the lower portion. *Use all the numbers except the directional and personal year numbers.*

LOWER PORTION OF CALENDAR

The lower portion of the calendar has four columns and four concepts of importance, followed by a row of small boxes across the sheet. These boxes continuously follow the same format throughout the page. The necessary numbers and years can be filled in depending on the age of the individual's profile needed. The example calendar contains the birth information of April 18, 1937. Remember, when placing the birthdate numbers into the calendar, put the year first, the month second and the day of birth last. This birthdate is used in all the examples.

Destiny	6	6	6	6	6	6	6	6	6	6	6	6	6	6	6	6	6	6	6
9-yr Challenge	1	1	1	1	1	1	1	1	1	1	1	1	9	9	9	9	9	9	9
9-mo Cycle	4	1	8	1	9	3	7	4	1	8	1	9	3	7	4	1	8	1	9
Dates Cycles Are in Effect	4 37	1	10 38	7 39	4 40	1	10 41	7 42	4 43	1	10 44	7 45	4 46	1	10 47	7 48	4 49	1	10 51

DESTINY BOX--------The very first row of the four sections is for the destiny number of the birthdate and is the same throughout all the boxes in the destiny columns. If you do not want to fill in all the boxes then just fill in the spaces that are needed for the required number of years. For example, if the profile is for a 40th birthday then you would fill the destiny number in the spaces of the destiny columns at least 40 times. I like to look to the future as well as the present so I add 5 to 10 more years to the profile.

Destiny	6	6	6	6	6	6	6	6	6	6	6	6	6	6	6	6	6	6

9-YEAR CHALLENGE BOX---------The second row of boxes is used to fill in the challenge number. Nine years is the time element of the challenge cycle; however, when the numbers are put into the spaces the number has to be filled in 12 times, not 9, for each cycle. This number of times may sound incorrect, or confusing, but is correct. There are twelve 9-month cycles within each 9 year period; therefore, it is necessary to use twelve spaces for every 9 years in order to have the correct series of the 9-month cycles.

The calendar works out accurately. The numbers used for the challenge cycles are your **birthyear, month, day and destiny** in chronological order. The example birthdate I use throughout this book of April 18, 1937, is of Prince Hirindra Singh. His age is 59 at the time I am writing this book. In looking at the 9-year challenge box you will find the spaces completely filled. Your psychic will be aroused when you personally fill in all the numbers in a calendar for an individual.

*(**1**) of birthyear (**1**937) is the *first number* to be placed 12 times in the spaces.

*(**9**) the *second number* (1**9**37) is placed 12 times in the spaces

*(**3**) the *third number* (19**3**7) is placed 12 times in the spaces.

*(**7**) the *fourth number* (193**7**) is placed 12 times in the spaces.

*(**4**) month of birth is the *fifth number* to be placed 12 times in the spaces

*(**1**) the 1 of the **1**8, day of birth is the *sixth number* to be placed 12 times in the spaces

*(**8**) the 8 of the 1**8**, day of birth is the *seventh number* to be placed 12 times in the spaces

*(**6**) destiny number is the *eighth number* to be placed 12 times in the spaces

*(**7**) directional number, time of birth is the *ninth number* to be placed 12 times in the spaces

After all the numbers are used, the sequence is repeated. (Hirindra will be 81 years old at the end of his number sequence.)

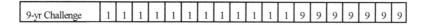

| 9-yr Challenge | 1 | 1 | 1 | 1 | 1 | 1 | 1 | 1 | 1 | 1 | 1 | 1 | 9 | 9 | 9 | 9 | 9 | 9 | 9 |

9-MONTH SUB-CHALLENGE ----------The third row of the calendar is for the 9-month sub-challenge cycle. Using the **year, month and day only,** fill in the consecutive spaces using one number in each space until all the numbers are used; repeat the series of numbers until you come to the year in question you have completed in the destiny and in the 9-year challenge rows.

9-mo Cycle	1	9	3	7	4	1	8	1	9	3	7	4	1	8	1	9	3	7	4

DATES THE CYCLES ARE IN EFFECT---------In the fourth row longer boxes are used to fill in the 9-month groupings. There are four series of months that are used when filling in the boxes. The series of the four months are used in consecutive order starting with the month of birth. The month of the individuals birthday is the first of the 4 month series, followed by the three succeeding months of the same series.

The following table outlines the four consistent series of months to be used corresponding to your birthmonth series. The month of your birthday is the group of months and numbers that you will use as your teammates.

JANUARY, OCTOBER, JULY, APRIL team together:
   1   10   7   4

FEBRUARY, NOVEMBER, AUGUST, MAY team together:
   2   11   8   5

MARCH, DECEMBER, SEPTEMBER, JUNE team together:
   3   12   9   6

The months that are teamed together will always be the same four months and numbers of that series. If your birthday falls in the four month category of 1, 10, 7, 4, you will never use any of the other numbers. Similarly, if your birthday falls in the second category of the four numbers 2, 11, 8, 5, you do not use the rest of the numbers as part of that series. This holds true of the third category also.

* When filling numbers in this deeper row keep in mind it is to be used in two portions. Placed in the upper half of the box will be the four

month categories of numbers. In the bottom half of the box leave space for each chronological year starting from your birth to the desired placement.

* In the first box, place the first of the four series starting with your birth month.

* In the second box, place the second number of the four series

* In the third box, place the third number of the four series

* In the fourth box, place the last number of the four series

* Continually repeat this sequence of the four numbers until you have come to the desired age in question.

In the **bottom half of the spaces,** place the years in chronological order, beginning with the year of birth. The first box will be filled in with the year of 1937, the next box will have 1938, continuing thereafter with each following year.

* When two of the months fall in the same year use only one year for both months. Regardless of the sequence of the four numbers you use, whenever two months fall in the same year only one progressed year is used for both numbers of that same year.

* This system is the same throughout the entire calendar. This is very important to remember. Always check for errors because a year spaced incorrectly will put the orbit of prediction out of sequence and will then be an error in the analysis of the cycles and interpretation. See example below.

Dates	4	1	10	7	4	1	10	7	4	1	10	7	4	1	10	7	4	1	10
Cycles																			
Are in Effect	37		38	39	40		41	42	43		44	45	46		47	48	49		51

PINNACLES

The pinnacles of life have universal meaning and affect every individual in the same way; however, they do not have any relationship with the 9-year challenge cycle. The stages are developmental growth patterns in everyone's life to identify certain time periods of normal development.

UNIVERSAL PINNACLES FOR ALL INDIVIDUALS

Pinnacle	Age	Meaning
First	1 thru 9	First beginnings, first movements, first actions, first learning
Second	9 thru 18	Learning to interact and get educated, interest in relationships
Third	18 thru 27	Higher education, socialization, enjoying adulthood
Fourth	27 thru 36	Period of hard work, domestic duties, ambitions, raising children.
Fifth	36 thru 45	Restlessness, wanting to make changes, expansion period
Sixth	45 thru 56	Grandparenting, reaping rewards of success, menopause
Seventh	56 thru 64	Reflection period, preparing for retirement, more melancholy
Eighth	64 thru 73	Retirement, end of life, period of letting go and letting God
Ninth	73 thru ??	Congratulations, you are living on God's good graces

The pinnacles in the above table are age/growth patterns for all individuals.

TO ORDER CALENDAR CHARTS
FOR BIRTHDAY PROFILES PLEASE CONTACT :

Joice Ashly
P.O. Box 44126
Phoenix, AZ 85064
602/996-9887

Chariots

Wheels of Infinity

Pretzangle
© 1995
Kells Manuscript Publishing (DT)2

Illustrated
by
Mary Jo Willis

CHARIOTS--WHEEL CONCEPTION

The wheels are chariots of combined energies that focus on three separate wheels, each indicative of a categoric application. The wheels are indicators expressing the intellectual, emotional and material environment in which you operate. Each wheel is aligned to the other wheels through actions in daily life. Each wheel has three separate divisions within the wheel. These wheels uncover the human attitude, actions and expressions of the life force. When the numbers are integrated they polarize all the threads linking all your potentials to gain mastery of your life force. Each wheel contributes a mode of expression to your evolution and is significant to view yourself in mind, body and spirit.

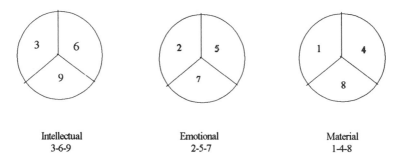

Intellectual
3-6-9

Emotional
2-5-7

Material
1-4-8

Within the three wheels are three divided sections. In all, there is a division of nine sections. There are a total of nine numbers and a zero. The numbers are divided into three separate sets, each set having its own significant wheel of fate. The three wheels determine the achievements in that particular area of life. The combination of numbers in the wheels indicate the person's accumulative tendencies and desires.

The wheel that is most occupied reveals the area of life which is really important to the individual or where there will be the most activity. No one wheel should be taken by itself as defining one's character, temperament or fate, because this is not the way to assess psychological and spiritual progress. The need to express or fulfill that wheel results from one's collective experiences.

The wheels along with the destiny, psychic and directional numbers are all necessary to determine the effects of the combined energies. To fully understand and appreciate the source of one's potential, all energies must be analyzed to decide the strongest force to motivate one's activities and psychological needs.

INTELLECTUAL WHEEL

The intellectual wheel governs the head through the numbers 3--6--9. These numbers deal with the mental and intellectual focus having an idealistic attitude.   This wheel is the collective foundation of one's intellectual activities of the conscious and subconscious expression. It is symbolic of scholarly achievements. These individuals are concerned with public approval and the need to express their intellectual abilities in the outer world.   When the wheel is complete, or two of the three sections have numbers in double or triple strength,   the person will have many cerebral opportunities to make a significant contribution to society.   They will use a subjective basis in their reasoning and decision making.   The mental objective of this wheel is to serve society through philosophical, idealistic and intellectual stimulation.

NUMBER 3--- Associates with unusual mental abilities. A wheel with two or more 3s is extremely mental in approach. It signifies the union of reason with intuition. You will be drawn to vocations such as, teachers, reporters, writers, lecturers newscasters, or a vocation that represents opportunities for growth and expansion through knowledge. Use your natural gifts of expression through speaking, writing, acting or sales. Your versatility and your creative mind will be your contribution for golden opportunities.

NUMBER 6--- Operates through determination, will power and the emotions. The mental reasoning is more on the intuitive thought form. Generous and compassionate, you give counsel through wisdom and wise advice to serve humanity. Six is less aggressive than the numbers 3 or 9, identifying with the body, feelings, and sensations. As your personality becomes more visible and expansive you will also find your popularity will prosper in an upward direction, and you will have a strong influence with humanity. Your resolve is strong and thoughtful; your treasure is your heart.

NUMBER 9--- Contributes to society through scientific aptitudes and wisdom. The mind integrates internal and external awareness of the environment to direct political, economical and social transformation. More than one number 9 needs and respects freedom of thoughts and actions. Must be willing to perform all actions lovingly and selflessly for the benefit of mankind and womankind to find fulfillment. Service should be the ruler of your life with devotion to the pure spirit. You are like luminous lightening, redeeming while reforming.

EMOTIONAL WHEEL

This wheel holds dominion with one's affections, emotions, domestic happiness and concerns itself with relationships. When the wheel is full life seems to be reflected through the concerns of family and friends. It is the wheel of security and the shelter for the soul. Life is built around associations with siblings, neighbors, relatives, personal friends and love relationships. This wheel involves friendships also earned in past lives. Individuals will project themselves into the environment in an extroverted manner. It is the spiritual, physical and sensual identity of the personality. When the emotional wheel is full or in double strength the native is passionate and can be obsessed with pleasures of the flesh. It can also turn the energy inward into spiritual prowess. This wheel deals more with the unconscious mind and as a result of this the individual is able to turn the energy into spiritual enlightenment. A full or active wheel is indicative of a fated life affecting the individual through the affairs of other people.

NUMBER 2--- Number 2 is emotions within emotions. It demonstrates unreliability because of changeable moods. The spirit needs to express itself through outlets of creativity and through interaction with others. Too many 2s become dependent on others because they need to feel close to someone, seeking their happiness through love and friendships. Within the 2 is the goddess of fertility and the protector of mother earth.

NUMBER 5--- Five is passion within emotion. A lot of emphasis is put on physical activity and appearance. There can be unrestrained sexual energy due to compulsive desires. Attention and awareness must be focused to master skills. Learn to rationalize and serve your higher ideals through perfection, compromise and objective understanding. You are the bridge between the conscious and the unconscious needing to serve mankind's every desire.

NUMBER 7--- Seven is intellect with emotion. It is the balance of the numbers 2 and 5 manifested through inspiration, vulnerability, compassion and oneness. It is the spirit of self-sacrifice and morality. More than one 7 can be extreme in moods and overly sensitive; must strive to become spiritually enlightened. The awakened vision is like a bright halo that brings awareness to spiritual enlightenment.

MATERIAL WHEEL

This individual assumes command through the power of wealth and the material assets achieved. A strong wheel indicates obsessive desires and issues with authority and ambition. There is a compulsion to have money and recognition. The need for security and power is intense if the wheel is full, if there are several numbers to the power of 2, or two full segments within the wheel. It is the wheel of endurance and single-mindedness always trying to mold the environment to the will. Numbers to the power of 2 or a full wheel has constant struggles and obsessions with materialism. If the wheel is weak, the individual struggles to maintain an appropriate lifestyle needing to be practical in seeking goals. A weak material wheel with a strong intellectual wheel is helpful to the individual attracting recognition and wealth. If the material wheel is weak, with a strong emotional wheel. Financial success is more often through good luck or inheritance. When individuals can rise above the self and use their power to serve others, they will find true fulfillment of success. An individual with a complete or strong wheel, especially with an 8 in it, will have an above-average job or salary and is generally financially comfortable in life.

NUMBER 1--- Assumes command through power of leadership. A wheel with several 1s makes a strong natured individual who is extremely independent and very single-minded in ideas which can bring on stress in daily life. Number 1 represents the ego, the I am, and will fight against those who will try to oppress it. The self-serving ego is motivated by power and pride. One is like fireworks on the 4th of July, full of brilliance, color and noise.

NUMBER   **4---** Relates to hard work, responsibility, structure and security. In 4s we have the salt of the earth people setting standards in perfection, humility and survival. Being too rigid in standards and self-reliance can affect your happiness. It is important to learn to be flexible. Success will come through faith, steadfastness, hard labor and patience. Progress in life is similar to an obscure rock, giving shape through time while crystallizing into a dignified diamond.

NUMBER 8--- Propels toward one ideal--financial and material success. A strong 8 in the wheel is indicative of influential leadership and a resourceful life. Obsession to have it all or to constantly win if there is more than one 8. Eight can be ruthless and manipulative to achieve its purpose. An 8 is capable of earning high wages and attaining leadership positions. Seldom lacks in focus, and always makes own decisions. Eight is like the imperial eagle that can evolve mankind through the flight of its wings.

WHEEL COMBINATIONS

Complete intellectual and material wheels can represent dignitaries or high-powered individuals. There is a personal determination to get ideals accomplished.   A complete intellectual and emotional wheel can be indicative of spiritual leaders or yogis who have no need for material wealth making sacrifices for others, or giving away their money to others. When the emotional wheel is complete and more powerful than the other two wheels, individuals will be more governed by the heart. Capable of making many sacrifices for the people you love to maintain domestic happiness and security. With this combination the meaning of life is not just on the intellectual plane but also found in the material realm. Most of life is driven to fulfill the desire for recognition.

When the **intellectual and emotional wheels are complete** individuals are regarded as intelligent and interesting conversationalists. Able to attract the masses to their way of thinking and will work hard to become a master of numerous subjects. Always willing to share knowledge with others. Desires and outlooks stimulate others to seek new ideas to improve cultural development. Full intellectual wheels indicate an ability to attain wealth through others, even when material wheel is weak. When the material wheel is weak but the partner's is strong both can aspire toward the ideal to achieve financial success and personal fulfillment. A lot of emphasis is put on serving the physical senses and playing out fantasies through lovemaking especially if the principal numbers are 5s or 2s. Thoughts and reasoning are easily agitated by the emotional nature eliciting emotional responses.

With **complete emotional wheels** manifest strength through interactive powers and in any business or profession working with the public. Personal contact and networking with people helps to attract people who can help to achieve desired goals. The traveler, sales person, journalist, artist and service-oriented individual with a unique touch to produce results. In a full emotional wheel there is a harmonious flow that is created through all three segments in the wheel. Because this energy has tremendous force to deal effectively with many personalities a lot of luck is obtained through the help of others and personable nature--but a large part of life can also be tied up with others because of the strong hold they have on your emotions. A lot of loyalty is shown to the people who assist in success and happiness. True nature cultivates a loving and kind human being always willing to be of service.

The **intellectual wheel** is a universal type who is concerned with and spiritual aspirations. It has to do with expanding consciousness into truth, meaning and educational pursuits. Usually quite self-contained, with a lot of pride in beliefs and ideas. Able to create order from confusion. Although qualified to excel intellectually, never satisfied with mental achievements--always aspiring to do better. There is a single pointed desire to constantly expand mind and goals. When the energy is used positively one is capable of unique achievements in most professions or careers to enrich worldly experiences. The teacher of teachers as a result of life's experiences in mental accomplishments. A full wheel or a wheel with number 3s or 9 to the power of 3 can produce a genius. Opinions are undeviating, but also able to back them up with facts.

A **full material wheel** always predominates over the other two wheels of fate. The desire to have material wealth is a primary preference and rules over the head and the heart of matters. Earning power has more influence than intellectual achievements or sentiment. When a material wheel is weak but the destiny number is an 8, there is still a materialistic drive to attain wealth at all costs to be comfortable in life. Eight has a powerful presence and will use this influence through either the intellectual or emotional wheels, depending on which is the strongest   With a full material wheel it is important to know what is necessary to achieve goals and how to attain desires in life. There is an impersonal determination to achieve material desires especially to build status. Always operates in a positive and direct manner. Basic instinct is to project whole-heartedly in projects and to have complete control. Security and fulfillment is sought to have self-recognition and to establish authority over the environment.

After you have determined the wheel that has the most influence in your life, you will have a good idea of the kind of forces you are dealing with and what those needs represent. When judging a profile take into account the gender of the individual because it makes a difference whether male or female. The nature of the individual should not make a difference, but it does to some degree, because of society and beliefs. Although the female has made great achievements in the material and physical world, at the time of this publication the female and male still do not have fair distinctions of equality.   A male continues to have greater influence for financial status than a female and also has better opportunities to achieve more high-powered positions.

As I have stated before in the beginning chapters, complete emphasis of a numerical profile can never be interpreted just from the wheels alone or from just the destiny significator.   A complete profile is achieved through the integration of each wheel and each significant number in the birthdate. When you are able to perceive your strengths and weakness you will be able to develop a healthy self-preservation.   The wheels are just a quick glimpse of the psychological needs, like looking through a window into the personality.   The wheels show a fraction of the makeup--not a complete blueprint.   When the characteristics of all the numbers and wheels are considered, you can then apply that information to the external approach to life, as well as to the inner motivations of your human development.

ZERO IN THE WHEEL

The presence of a 0 in the birthdate is powerful and compensates for the absence of any one number, especially in the wheel it occupies. The power of the 0 is used in compatibility with the number to its left. Whatever wheel that number is placed into, the 0 should also be placed in it. If the 0 is associated with a number 1, 4 or 8 it goes into the material wheel. If the 0 is with a 2, 5 or 7 it goes into the emotional wheel; if the 0 is associated with a 3, 6 or 9 it goes into the intellectual wheel.

When there is a 0 with the destiny number it should go in the same wheel into which the destiny number is placed. When the wheels are full with the paternal numbers and there is no room for the 0, then it should be placed into the intellectual wheel. If that wheel is complete with numbers, then place it into the material wheel using the emotional wheel as the last wheel of placement. Whatever wheel the 0 is placed into it adds strength and wisdom to that wheel, for it becomes a circle within a circle. The nature of the 0 can be limited or limitless. Energy of the 0 is activated by its associated number and gives power to the wheel in which the 0 is placed. Zero does not think of what to do, 0 responds to a number like a child would to the authority of the parent.

Two or more 0s in the intellectual wheel can be an intellectual genius or a scholar of an incredible nature. Individuals who have one or more 0s are definitely old souls and have come into this life to fortify the personality. The mature nature of the individual with a 0 is due to past incarnations, and the many learning experiences with which these individuals had to deal with in their previous lifetimes and in their childhood years in this lifetime. Individuals with a 0 will be blessed with wisdom and benevolence especially in their elder years.

Natives who have one or more 0s in the numbers profile usually have a strong planet, Saturn, Uranus or Pluto influence in their astrological chart; these planets are usually adversely aspected with their natal sun. I have also observed strong Aquarian or Uranus energy with the people who have one or more 0s. When the 0 is placed in a particular wheel, the wheel will have a force of energy that will initiate many obstacles and uncontrollable events. However, it can also propel the individual to impressive heights of achievement. It is the responsibility of each individual with a 0 to develop a meaningful life meeting with occasional failure and frustration and yet aspiring to be the very best that you can be.

BELOW ARE SAMPLES OF ZERO IN THE BIRTHDATES TO HELP YOU IN YOUR UNDERSTANDING OF THE PLACEMENTS OF NUMBERS WITHIN THE CHARIOTS.

> 3 6 9 are always placed in the intellectual wheel.
> 2 5 7 are always placed in the emotional wheel.
> 1 4 8 are always placed in the material wheel.

Zero always goes into the wheel in which the number to its left is placed; if that wheel is full, it should then go into the wheel to the number on its right side, but still be interpreted with the number to its left. If both of the those wheels are full, the 0 should then go into the remaining wheel.

EXAMPLE: Birthday of January 9, 1940, is shown as 1940 1 9 = 6 destiny number. Place numbers 1, 9, 4, 0, 1, 9, 6 in the wheels as shown below:

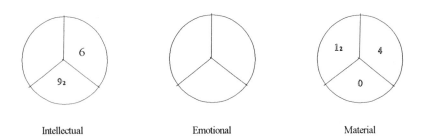

| Intellectual | Emotional | Material |

With over half the numbers missing in this birthdate this female will experience many frustrations in her social and mental expression. Because of those missing numbers a lot of emphasis will be placed on the physical self and spiritual growth. This individual will be constantly pushed into situations with powerful personalities that will either challenge her or push her to her potential. Domestic and family situations will put enormous demands upon her. There will be difficulty enjoying life wholeheartedly because of so many missing numbers which keep her from being realistic instead of idealistic. Mastery and unfoldment in life will come through her universal outlook or in metaphysical accomplishments. Being born on the 9th day contributes to her universal outlook on problems, the 4 for her responsible behavior, and the 6 for her sensitive and generous ways.

EXAMPLE: Birthday of April 10, 1942 is shown as 1942 4 20 = 20. The destiny number is a 2, but placed in the wheel as 20.
Use numbers 1, 9, 4, 2, 4, 2, 0, 2, 0

When the destiny number has a 0 in it, never reduce it to a single digit number as you would with singular numbers, yet interpret it as a single digit number. In the above situation the destiny would be interpreted as a 2 destiny, but in double force, placing the destiny 0 in the chariot wheel with the 2.

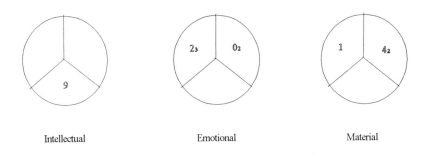

Intellectual   Emotional   Material

A powerful need for the male with this birthdate to master the vibration of the 2 and not exploit it by crossing his desires with his passions, or by abusing the spiritual force of creativeness. He has a strong need for warmth and love, and yet can treat his affections lightly until he experiences true love   There is an unusual desire for him to live on the evolved plane and to seek enlightenment. Endowed with creative talents, it is important he gets involved in undertakings that are inspirational, or of an international scope.   This individual should not dominate or be dominated; yet he must also be prepared for confrontational situations in partnerships or relationships, which is the duality and lesson of experience for a destiny number 20.   He can be narrow-minded in his focus because he lacks a 3, 5 or 7.   With so much energy of the 2s and 4s, including the 0s picking up more intensely on those numbers his energy can lack focus restricting his nature.   His endeavors need a solid base and he must use good judgement to retain a responsible attitude in his affairs. The 4s make him responsible but also impractical. The 2s aid him in his friendships to work in a persuasive way with others. The coming millennium of 2000 will be very important to this individual to assist others toward a universal path.

EXAMPLE: Birthday of September 30, 1966
shown as 1966 9 30 = 7 as the destiny number.
Use the numbers 1, 9, 6, 6, 9, 3, 0, 7

In this profile you will find there is no room for the 0 to be placed in the wheel with its partner the number 3, so it will go into the emotional wheel with the number 7, the number to its right. It will still be interpreted with the number 3 even though it has to be placed in another wheel.

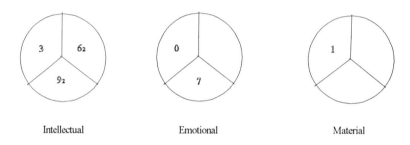

Intellectual   Emotional   Material

There is a strong need for the female with this birthdate to unite her mind with her emotions. Because of the strong emotional hunger in this individual (two 6s with a 0) that has to be nurtured, suffering could be linked to dysfunctional relationships. Until she finds her emotional satisfaction there could be a lack of direction of her aspirations, hopes and dreams. At present she is a bi-sexual finding it difficult to be straight She does not have strong primary numbers, however she has a strong intellectual wheel. She lacks numbers that would give her a stabilizing influence to maintain reality. Her quest is to fulfill her desires through her intellectual abilities. She is also working to attain mastery of her independence and of her need for emotional attachments. In this life, the male half and the female half of her personality must become androgynous. She needs to find one expression in the manifestation of the physical, mental and spiritual to experience the thrill of oneness. This profile is that of an extremely creative and intellectual genius.

EXAMPLE: Birthday of October 25, 1935 is shown as 1935 10 25 = 8 destiny number. Use the numbers 1, 9, 3, 5, 1, 0, 2, 5, 8.

The only numbers missing in this birthdate are the numbers 4 and 6. The day of the 25th becomes a 7 when added together so the number 7 is not missing; it is just invisible--operating through the energy of the day of birth.

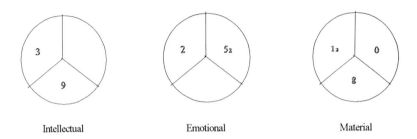

Intellectual   Emotional   Material

This female will find that her physical health in life may require constant attention. Due to the 7 energy of her birthday (2+5), it will be necessary that she become socially interactive to avoid isolation and loneliness. The challenge of the missing 4 and 6 will force her to become independent and self-reliant by adjusting to circumstances at work and in her domestic domain. To achieve what she wants she will have to be flexible to other personalities and learn to respect individuals who differ from her standards and beliefs. In life, she will have to shoulder her fair share of obligations and live with people who constantly confront her ideals. Mastery of her expression will come when she becomes a surface personality and open to spiritual growth. When the sting of the serpent within her is healed, her knowledge, not money, will be the healing power that introduces happiness and success to her. She has all the numbers necessary to enjoy success and the two 5s will be beneficial for her in whatever vocation she chooses. Because of her destiny 8 she will be fortunate in careers associated with institutions and large corporations. Her 7 and 5 make her a perfectionist in the English language and should use these skills as a teacher an editor, or journalist.

EXAMPLE: Birthday of June 30th, 1971 is shown as 1971 6 30 = 7 destiny number. Use the numbers 1, 9, 7, 1, 6, 3, 0, 7.

With this birthdate the 0 should be placed in the wheel with the 3, the number to its left, but since that wheel is full it will be placed into the wheel with the number 7, the number to its right.

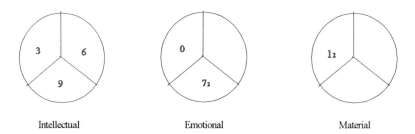

Intellectual   Emotional   Material

All the numbers in this birthdate are odd except for the number 6. This male uses his charm to succeed in life and he will always use his luck to improvise for his lack of responsibility. The 0 in his birthdate intensifies his 3 so he will constantly search for a more colorful and social level of existence. Intellectually and physically he is quite adaptable, but lacks perseverance and staying power putting too much emphasis on his social life, friendships, good looks and strong sexual drive. He is reckless with his financial affairs, has trouble with punctuality and allows his emotions to devour his creative abilities because he lacks a grounded number and wheel. His mastery will come after the age of 40 and will become effective in using his creative abilities. Until then he will have many obstacles to overcome. Discipline is necessary in his life and he needs to focus on his vocational accomplishments. He is extremely sensitive to advice and will seldom ask for others opinions. The indulgent lifestyle he prefers will never bring him happiness unless he tightens the bands of responsibility to his personality.

Prediction

PREDICTION

Truly spiritual practitioners of mystical sciences or parapsychology seldom speak publicly of their own spiritual achievements nor look for the light to shine on them. Rather, they look to be the light that shines for others. Practitioners must be guided by an unselfish desire to help others to glorify the true art of mysticism, which is sacred, and to awaken the spiritual instincts of the seeker to attain realization of their inner search.

The strength of practitioners is dependent upon their souls growth and the realization of their wisdom and compassion. The art of prediction is a science without a formula that is of the unseen and cannot be understood because it is not visible, tangible, or learned in a book.

Prediction comes through the mastery and the receptivity of the practitioners instincts and unfolding inner powers which cannot be grasped or understood. Within all people is an inner intuition called the third eye. It is up to each individual as to how they attune to that inner kingdom. The third eye is like a light bulb that works through watts--you can have either a 20 watt or a 150 watt, depending upon how much light you desire. Some people just like to keep a night-light glowing, not wanting to commune with the inner divinities. Others actually seek the higher frequency of a brighter light. Acknowledge your own divine potential through your intuition and allow it to become a part of your inner being.

People who use intuition or hunches, work through the higher self. Wisdom comes from a higher wattage of light connecting to the inner awareness; however, some people may not always be cognizant of it. Each individual has the capacity to have whatever light is desired, but a change of bulbs (awareness) might be necessary to give added spiritual light to your journey. Awareness of intuition does not mean you have to live in a constant state of higher consciousness. To use your intuition means to become more aware of the inner signals you receive from within as you use it in your daily life.

As you enter the Aquarian Age, give full attention to your intuition, perception, hunches, dreams and flashes; and know that this part of your nature is instinctive.   Replace the light within you to a higher watt and tune to the frequency you desire. Your third eye can be the stream of light that brings you to your ultimate union with the Higher Self.

Numerology is not meant to be a predictive science. It is a mystical link that identifies cycles and trends for the developmental growth needed for your evolution. In this unique system of numbers, the orbital cycle of the revolution of numbers is used to predict only possibilities for the future, not promises. Numerology is not a philosophy although the principles can be applied philosophically. The fundamental purpose of prediction is for classification and greater insight to find a sense of order and balance for a deeper and more fulfilled life.

Through the awareness of cycles, predictions can be made from a rotation of numbers that orbit the natal profile. The rotating numbers are cycles called the 9-year challenge, the 9-month challenge and the personal year cycle.   It is an individual calendar formed by numbers through the date of birth, using those numbers as the orbit of revolution.

A practitioner must consider several factors when doing predictive analysis. The environment of the individual, occupation, status, condition of life, religious preference, skills, and spiritual evolvement are all affected. Predictions are meant to be like flashlights in the dark--not the main source of light, but a tool to shed light in temporary darkness.

Many people possess the human curiosity of wanting to know the future so they can understand what lies ahead and what to look forward to at a given time. No practitioner has the answers to all fundamental questions. Adults are like children, learning through experience, sometimes making mistakes through choices. Trust that through your experiences you will be led to the awareness that awakens your spiritual knowledge, enabling you to find your way in the dark and to your true purpose of that number experience.

It is difficult to teach another person to interpret a numerical profile. Craftsmanship is based upon the philosophical intuition of each individual, your love for others, your compassion and knowledge. One may have a head for knowledge; but, without using the heart or intuition it is difficult to be the spiritual teacher.   Intelligent people write books on esoteric subjects, but that does not guarantee they will be wholly effective as a predictive counselor on the subject. I have been to professionals who are worldly and reputable; yet I have had disappointing sessions with many of their predictions never coming to pass. Some practitioners claim 90% accuracy. From my extensive research and experience, not I, nor anyone else, can or should make such a claim.

Prediction is looking into the future to make known beforehand the best times to make decisions and when to take action.   It is a process of divination that is by no means completely accurate in principle.   Use predictions as a basis of theory, or a guide, to assess the strength and the compatibility of the cycle in which you are presently in, or which you will be entering.

The greatest tragedy of not knowing the trends or cycles of prediction is that when the numbers battle with each other you do not always see where the fault lies or what your weaknesses and strengths are. Consultants can give clients an indication of the future, but it is up to each individual to make their own decisions about the opportunities that are offered.

Numbers not only foretell future events but influence your emotional and spiritual feelings as well. All numbers derived from a birthdate are interpreted within the cycles of numbers, especially in predictions. Cycles have a special importance to facilitate the interpretation of future forecasting. There are many variations of numeric systems in numerology and most are based on the theories of the Greek mathematician and philosopher, Pythagoras, on the Kabbalah.

The power of numbers is very important. Nothing could exist without numbers. Numbers are used every day of our life. They are used for days of the week, to tell time, for money exchange, social security, licenses, the phone, driving or flying, buying groceries, clothes sizes, banking, the TV, sports and especially for birthdays.

Predicting a numerical profile is an art and it is not an easy task. Knowing the facts and information about numerology and being able to memorize the characteristics is very important, but it does not determine a practitioner's skill or sophistication of prediction. Expertise and mastery comes from working with hundreds of personal charts to become proficient in the art of interpreting the maze of numbers. Every experience is unique, every individual is special, and every situation is different.

Consultants must shed their personal beliefs and become emotionally detached regarding the fundamentals of any hypothesis. Hence, it is important to state to a client that whatever comes through in a reading may not always be accurate and will not always reflect what will take place in the future. A reading can be changed through free will or your desire to change the outcome within your ability.

Your destiny may be predetermined through your birth, but an esoteric prediction is not. Miscalculations or misinterpretations in predictions occur, and events or situations that are predicted may not always come to pass. A professional advisor can only reveal what is channeled to them through their higher power. When you go to a professional consultant, go with an open mind, knowing everyone is fallible.

A client should be guided by the knowledge received in a reading, but should not live life dependent on the outcome of any reading. If you are not happy with the results of your session, accept only the information that is helpful to you and let destiny lead you. People must respect the fact that life is not only pleasant experiences but also unpleasant, and a consultant cannot change that reality. Life is a school of positive and negative adventures to produce and stimulate growth. Readings are tools to reinforce direction when periods of struggles or anxieties about the future concern you.

Life is a cycle of peaks and valleys, and when you are aware of these periods, you can then make the necessary adjustments in your environment to become the master of your fate rather than a victim of circumstance.

A consultant of any esoteric science cannot allow their joys, fears or personal problems to reflect on the client's reading. The consultant must emerge into the light of truth and knowledge, becoming focused only with the individual who has sought counseling at that particular moment.

Consultants must understand the client's joy, pain and problems and guide them to their being of perfection without judgment.

Through the help of spiritual knowledge, understanding, love and compassion, a counselor must help to vanish the darkness of despair their client may be experiencing and move them into the light. Clients who seek professional help are coming for guidance regarding their lives and future, because they are feeling blocked or helpless in their present situation.

A consultant assumes great responsibility for their client's welfare. Everything you do must represent integrity and professionalism, from your behavior to the apparel you wear. It is the mission of the practitioner to acknowledge the truth, to give hope, to define the client's choices and to give a basic understanding with inspiration of what can be expected from the future, or the problems that may occur.

The consultant's personality must be controlled in order to meet the needs of the client. All the attention and focus should be on the client's to benefit their session. By applying that process, you will become more effective in using your esoteric wisdom wisely and with value. It is important as a professional consultant to concentrate on your experimental knowledge more than the historical information.

I am distrustful of practitioners who will not tape their readings. They claim it disturbs their concentration or their spirit guides. When a professional does a reading the concentration should be on the spiritual energy of the client. A small tape recorder should not interfere with a reading unless the counselor is insecure, insincere, or without credibility. When a practitioner meditates on another individual in a reading or if a chart is used to forecast an individual's profile, a recorder is insignificant as a disturbance, as the tape is imperative for future reference.

A client should refuse to pay or reject the reading unless it can be recorded. The mind cannot remember every detail of a half hour or more consultation. The only time you can remember information is when one or two things are significant to your present situation. Information is not stored, as these "prophets" claim, and you will not always have recall to everything you heard. Many practitioners state that the client only hears and remembers what they need to know. Rubbish! Not true. I have had numerous clients testify to the accuracy of my predictions concerning things which they had forgotten. Clients even had predictions come to pass several years after the reading, and if it were not for the tape, neither my client nor I could have appreciated the value of the recorded session.

Avoid any advisor who wants to burn candles for you for a costly fee to remove obstacles in your life or to change your luck. In the back of this book, there is a section on candle burning that will be helpful for you. Candle burning can be done by any individuals for their own intentions, and no one should ever be paid a fee to do it for you. I always share information on candle burning with my clients if they request it or if I feel sharing it will be helpful to their circumstances or attitude.

No one except the Higher Power has greater powers to help you than you have to help yourself. The power of prayers, mantras and affirmations will heal you faster and more completely than any *magic* which another practitioner, or so-called spiritualist, can perform for you. Between the Higher Power and the mortal man are intercessors such as angels and spirit guides and they should be called upon when all else prevails.

When you decide to seek the guidance of an esoteric counselor, or teacher, take your time selecting one. Get references on their background, conduct, credibility, how long they have been established and who can recommend them. As counselors, we share one common spiritual heritage and that is to use our gifts and knowledge in a trustworthy approach--to suggest ways and ideas to enable a client to reach a higher level of understanding.

A vast majority of people spend a lot of time shopping for clothes, furniture, food, alcohol, or vitamins that go into the body. Little time is spent choosing advisors who can affect the mind. Minds are more vulnerable than bodies, and negative advice computed in the mind also affects the body. People shop carefully for mundane items; yet give little value to who taps into their mental consciousness where one is most vulnerable. Be conscious of what you put into your mind as well as your body.

People are searching for cosmic order, the Divine, and to embrace their natural power. Going to the cheapest or the most expensive practitioner is not the correct way to seek advice. Be practical in what you do and do not give form to your frustration or an impulsive reaction. Today, society is inundated with a multitude of psychics who feel they have powerful abilities--and some do. Having the ability to be psychic is not enough of a basis for an individual to give counseling, nor does it make one a professional. Many people become hopeless, especially under stress, and in desperate circumstances seek out psychic counseling without carefully choosing a reputable reader.

Remember, just as you choose a certain physician for quality and experience, look for these same qualities when choosing a reputable counselor. When you look to someone for guidance, do not always seek the person who claims 90% to 100% accuracy, but one who is skilled in the art of counseling. Percentages about accuracy are ambiguous and have never been proven at any level of observation. As a professional for the past thirty years, I have never made any claims, except that my skills are attached to the threads of a higher power within me. With spiritual training, sensitivity, and the skill of knowledge, I am capable of using my natural psychic gifts. When I do readings, I just wish to prepare the soil for your garden to help you plant the seeds that will be necessary for your growth.

Remember, a physician cannot always accurately diagnose a problem without you giving him the symptoms you are experiencing, which is also true of a psychic. When a client gives helpful details of a situation you help the psychic to channel more effectively to help achieve more productive results. The stages of developmental growth with each individual varies and the reactions to these stages also vary in each person. Every circumstance is different for each individual, according to their bio-rhythm of energies. Through the cycle of numbers, a professional numerologist will be able to foretell the circumstance a client may experience. The numbers of your birthdate give a broad analysis into your inner nature. Please be advised, there is no *proven* method of predicting the future. However, through the revolution of the numerical cycles, a professional numerologist is able to accurately observe a positive or difficult period.

How you use your potential cannot be predetermined. Learn to understand your position within your environment through your needs, motivations and anticipations. Through the cycles of numerology and astrology a practitioner can predict what *could happen in your life*, not what *will happen*. Specific events are not always predictable. Trends and cycles stimulate a certain activity that produces certain effects. These trends are recognized and understood by a professional practitioner's knowledge, along with the intervention of their psychic intuition. Allow the higher forces to reach into your inner-self to weave the formulation of perfection and wholeness in achieving a greater wisdom to spiritual guidance.

The sciences of prediction vary, but the language spoken is universal. Regardless of the science offered, as a consultant you must be responsible to the individual involved and the integrity of the science. A consultant must retain a flexible mind and be of assistance to a client seeking help; thus aiding the client to see the positive aspects of his or her profile.

Predictions help to focus and explore new dimensions, expand personal growth and to express the creative powers during a certain cycle. To become a master craftsman of numerology it is important you love helping people, are compassionate, desire to be of service to mankind and be dedicated to human spiritual development. A well-guided reading can be the healing of your past, present, and future.

MANTRA FOR DIVINE WISDOM AND POWER
(Chant this before doing a reading)

OM EIM HREEM KLEEM CHAMUNDAYAI VICHHE NAMAHA
Salvations to Shakti, who showers blessings of wisdom and power.

MAJOR 9-YEAR CHALLENGE

The foundation of any stationary number in numerology is to have movement or a progression to activate it. Through orbital velocity in numerology, there are cycles that orbit to invigorate and provoke motion. This motion is called an orbit. It stimulates currents of energy to project an individual into different stages of development. It is revolutions of 9-year cycles taken from the sequence of numbers in your birthdate which take a 9-year period to rotate for each number. This rotation is called the major 9-year challenge.

The 9-year challenge begins from the time of birth until we pass from this earth. These numbers are not taken from a numeric order of 1 to 9 or used randomly to fill space. The sequence of the numbers used are from year, month, day, destiny and directional. The 9-year challenges are called a major challenge because it has a 9-year effect on your destiny number. These 9-year cycles also affect the psychic (day of birth) and the directional (time of birth) numbers but in lesser proportions.

I like to compare all the numbers in a birthdate to a home with a family tree. The owner of the home or the power behind the throne, is the destiny number. The destiny number is the most important number to consider in the relationship of the 9-year challenge orbital number. It is like having a different guest come to stay with you every nine years. Each guest number has its own personality and will have a different effect on you, your home life and lifestyle.

There are certain combinations of numbers that are compatible and others which are discordant. The 9-year challenge cycle can either complement or contradict your destiny number during that cycle of your life, depending on the elements of the two numbers. If your destiny number is an even number and your 9-year challenge is an odd number, they will trigger contention in each other, each wanting to maintain its own individuality.

You have a commitment to the challenge number because it is a guest in your domain, and you must take responsibility for the result of its action. It can become a period that is pleasant and enjoyable or a period that is challenging and conflicting.

The odd numbers are male in energy and extroverted in nature. The even numbers are feminine in energy and introverted in nature. An odd number in a 9-year cycle with an even number can agitate that 9-year period, adding frustration and problems to your life because the energies find compatibility troublesome.

Every number is defined differently, and with all the variables it is hard to anticipate where the fault lies or from where the apprehension comes. For certain combinations of numbers, the stress is related to relationships; for others, it could be career related, health or attitudes.

There are certain combinations of numbers or vibrations, whether they are odd or even, that are less stressful than others--even in conflicting circumstances. This combination is especially true of a 2 challenge, even when it is in dispute with an odd number. Two is not negative by nature and will concede under stressful conditions, just to keep peace. Two will always compromise itself to the strength of the odd number, unless the 2 is to the power of a 2; it can then be more resistant.

When a favored cycle begins, it is considered fortunate and can recharge your energy. The long-range effects are powerful in producing general prosperity, wealth, prestige, happiness and the blessings of life in general. These blessings do not suggest that when you are in a favorable cycle you will never have problems; however, the overall effect will produce a positive period of growth.

There are also major 9-month cycles you have to consider during the 9-year period. If there is a negative number for 9-months transiting the challenge or the destiny numbers, this negative number will create tension for that 9-month period of time whether it is to the destiny or the challenge number. This basis holds true when an odd or even challenge number are in conflict with the destiny number.

The 9-month challenge can bring balance to a 9-year period of conflict creating a harmonious situation for 9 months, even when the destiny and the 9-year cycle numbers are in conflict. The 9-month cycle during a 9-year challenge is similar to having a migraine headache that lasts for days. It is like taking medication to get some relief. The headache does not immediately disappear, but the effect of the medication gives temporary relief. You have to work patiently and therapeutically with a migraine during the crisis to give it relief, and it is the same with an adverse 9-year period and a 9-month positive cycle. To minimize an adverse period therapeutically, sort out the difficulties from the unreal or distorted viewpoints to have fewer complications. Although the 9-year period is subject to adjustment because of the shorter cycles of duration that continue to orbit within that period, the activity of the 9-year period remains unchanged.

When there are two matching numbers in the birthdate next to each other then the 9-year challenge lasts 18 years. For example, the year 1988 has two 8s together, so each 8 has to go through a 9-year challenge period.

Another factor that has to be considered in the revolution of cycles is the personal year number. This number has a psychological influence lasting from one birthday year to the next. This number does not follow a sequence of numbers as in the birthdate of the challenge 9-year and 9-month cycles. The personal year numbers are followed in sequence from the natural numbering of 1 to 9. This number is calculated from the total numbers of the day and the month of your birthday added to the total numbers of the universal year in question.

The personal year number changes every birthday and is always proceeded by the next number in succession of 1 through 9. It is the universal rhythm cycle representing the value of the year in question and the energy that is needed by the individual to move in the right direction. The personal year affects your life, but its influence is felt more internally than externally.

The personal year number does not involve itself personally with the destiny number as the 9-year challenge does. Instead, it influences the activity that will be of concern to the individual in that particular year. The activity that is activated will show itself through the quality of the personal year number. The personal year numbers are neither constructive nor destructive. They are the messengers of a higher octave energy, advising you of what to expect from the universe or from your environment in that particular year.

Conflicting revolutions between the 9-year challenge, the 9-month challenge and the personal year are not meant to inhibit you or your life's situation, but to encourage growth in a certain direction. Because of the tenure of any cycle, establishing a foundation to prepare yourself and to have awareness of these cycles can be quite helpful. When there are triple numbers in your birthdate it is significant that the forces of your past life have extended into this life to complete the necessary circumstances that control your destiny.

The directional and psychic numbers play an important role in the cycles of the 9-year challenge. Hours of the AM or PM births are also significant factors to be considered. The birth time is referred to as the directional number and is considered a *spiritual number*. It strengthens the soul force by directing the inner vision of what you came here to accomplish. The directional number is like a weather vein, pointing to the direction of how the numbers will need to conform to meet the cycle of the challenge. When the destiny and directional numbers are harmonious; they will add strength and significance to the challenge number. The psychic number, which is the day of birth, influences the type of profession or career you are drawn to. or the type of mate to whom you will be attracted.

This combination is similar to a family tree where different personalities live under one roof. Everyone must learn to cooperate to create harmony, learning to live with each other and their faults. All home situations have a purpose to maintain balance, behave idealistically and deal with the different personalities. In order to achieve mastery in the universe, you must first achieve mastery over yourself and your environment. You cannot deal with outside influences successfully until you learn to empower yourself.

Everyone in life has to deal with different personalities and difficult situations. Life is a school of lessons constantly forcing people to pursue growth, inwardly as well as outwardly. Every challenge you experience is another grade of learning and the challenges are the teachers of each phase of evolutionary progress. Life is eternal, there is no beginning, there is no end. We have been given life to create, to transcend and to liberate us from the bonds of birth, death and reincarnation.

Example birthdate for the stages of development :

April 18th 1937   Born at: 6:37 pm

(1937 4 18 = $1 + 9 + 3 + 7 + 4 + 1 + 8$ = 33 or $3 + 3$ =6 (Destiny)

STAGES AND CHALLENGES OF DEVELOPMENT

First	9 years of life are ruled by the challenge number	1
Second	9 years of life, 9 thru 18 are ruled by the challenge number	9
Third	9 years of life, 19 thru 27 are ruled by the challenge number	3
Fourth	9 years of life, 28 thru 36 are ruled by the challenge number	7
Fifth	9 years of life 3, thru 45 are ruled by the challenge number	4
Sixth	9 years of life, 46 thru 54 are ruled by the challenge number	1
Seventh	9 years of life, 55 thru 63 are ruled by the challenge number	8
Eighth	9 years of life, 64 thru 72 are ruled by the challenge number	7 (time of birth)
Ninth	9 years of life, 73 thru 81 are ruled by the challenge number	6

(After you have used the full sequence of numbers in your birthdate, use the destiny number, then the directional number. Begin the sequence of numbers all over again after you have used all the numbers.

The stages of development give meaning to all primary numbers and have nothing to do with the challenge or personal year numbers.

CHALLENGE NUMBERS FOR 9-YEAR CYCLES

CHALLENGE NUMBER 1

Entering the number 1 challenge is like coming into spring when everything is beginning to bloom, including you. You feel a force of energy within you greater than you ever felt, almost as if you are being reborn. During this challenge a need to free yourself from any restrictions and forge forward will bring you occasional frustration but definitely success. Any limitations will be resented wanting to be on your own and in charge. During this cycle, your male energy permeates through your veins and entire being feeling the thrust of male assertiveness. You become aggressive, inclined to stand alone--you on one side, the world on the other. The 1 cycle affects females as well as males in an aggressive way because 1 is androgynous energy; it knows no distinction. Associations or contacts in the work force could be mainly with males. During this challenge, if you are a female, you will find yourself thinking and acting in a more assertive and confident manner. No rules, no regulations, just wanting freedom of expression at any cost.

This challenge can be a difficult time for a person who was generally dependent on others. You find that suddenly your lifestyle demands more independence and autonomy, whether by choice or by destiny. Women in a marriage who were taken care of will suddenly decide to get a job wanting financial independence. Either you want to become self-reliant or your lifestyle demands you become self-supporting. You may suddenly feel you want out of the marriage, or your husband abandons you, forcing you to stand on your own. Major changes in life are made, such as moving to another state, quitting a job to go into business for yourself, getting promoted to positions of management, or changing the course of a career.

Regardless of the choices you make, you no longer want to be in a subservient position or take orders from others during this cycle. You want to be in a position of control and independence; if you do not have a spirit of independence the 9 years could be miserable because this challenge exudes a more forceful attitude, demanding you attain expansion through your own efforts. During this 9-year challenge you may feel a lack of support from friends or family. Your new image makes you appear unreasonable even combative, especially if your destiny number is

212

1, 4, 5 or 8. Autonomy takes the place of cooperation, making it difficult to work with others unless you are totally independent or in a managerial role. You will find that it takes extra effort on your behalf to be cooperative, because you will want your own way and will not accept advice easily.

In the 1 cycle you become more erratic and impatient, having little tolerance for outside influences. It is now your time to believe in yourself, to support yourself in your endeavors, to create change in your life and to go for your dream. God knows you certainly will have the inner strength and personal power to handle what you set out to do. Be aware that you will react impulsively with sudden outbursts of tantrums due to your short temper in the 1 cycle. One is not always an easy time because you will feel like a lot of pressure is placed upon your shoulders, regardless of the circumstances. Count to ten before you blow up or just walk away until you cool down.

During a 1 challenge put your ambitions first but do not overlook the feelings of others. This challenge can be a test within itself. While in this cycle learn to control and master your temperament so you can rationally achieve your goals. In asserting your individualism be careful not to react with intolerance, stubbornness or inconsiderateness for others. Enjoy the number 1 cycle in a respectable way, still holding fast to the spirit of compromise without compromising yourself.

This phase will definitely prove to be a challenge requiring maturity and a lot of self-surrender. While it may be a trying and difficult period, it can be a blessing in disguise if you take control of your destiny intelligently. Display your leadership potential in personal aspirations of self-expression and project your abilities to capture what you want. Even if you felt in the past that you have never had leadership abilities, or if those abilities were laying dormant you will now have many opportunities to step into your leadership shoes. Sometimes the shoes will feel tight, sometimes they will be uncomfortable, but most of the time they will get you where you want to go.

At times you will experience loneliness as you stand alone, but the conquest of doing it your way is worth the new experiences and the painstaking process, as you become motivated to leave your imprint in the world. Marriage during this cycle can be difficult, unless you are a destiny 1, 5 or 9, as these numbers will have fewer complications because the energies are in agreement.

Divorce is common during a 1 challenge, unless you have a strong and secure relationship. As a single person, especially a female, marriage opportunities are not always favorable or readily available. Although this is not true in all cases, I would say it is for a high percentage of females of whom I have read for while in their 1 cycle. The partner to the individual experiencing a number 1 challenge needs to honor the mate's desire to stand alone. A 1 must be allowed to be in control of their own lives as they respond to the call of the 1 challenge to evolve into their true potential.

When in a 1 cycle do not allow your energy or desires to be suppressed as you enter into this new period. This cycle does not just affect relationships, it will have its effect in the professional realm as well. Partnerships or business relationships can be turbulent as you demand to have things your way. Going into a new partnership or business arrangement is not always healthy or wise unless you have independent roles and can be flexible enough to make compromises. Demonstrate your leadership quality, but not in an overbearing or forceful way. Always express yourself diplomatically in everything you do and this will be a positive challenge for you.

This is a masculine cycle associated with power, control and independence for advancement or ownership. Follow your lead, push towards your goals and be guided by your instincts to let this be the time you take your life into your own hands. Use good judgment in your decisions, especially if you are making investments. Do not get caught up in fantasies or illusions in your haste to succeed. Be thorough and effective in everything you do.

There is a tendency to become easily frustrated, due to the impulsive temperament of the 1 energy. Your reactions will have strong emotions when your plans do not move as expeditiously as planned. Avoid being impulsive or hasty just for the sake of change. Also make sure your 9-

month cycle is favorable to the 9-year challenge; remember, haste makes waste.

This a special time to shape your life to your liking and to carry the responsibility with pursuit and effort. In your boldness and self-confidence live your life fully. You can regain your spirit and your light from within. Every breath you draw can bring inner satisfaction as you achieve self-confidence in each experience to gain your new individuality. Your true desires, your needs, your aspirations will now win respect in the ocean of life, where you can be recognized, honored and appreciated for your talents.

CHALLENGE NUMBER 2

This 9-year challenge symbolizes the feminine energy. It has the flow of the dolphin's gentleness, yet the strength of its body. Two is a passive cycle of harmony and sensitivity, and its wisdom makes it possible for you to benefit in extraordinary ways. Make this period a time to understand others better, with less emphasis on your own personal needs. This challenge is an important period in learning the art of cooperation and working as a team member. The 2 cycle gives a magnetic aura that helps you to achieve through friendly persuasion. Besides having a busy social life, you will attract new friendships into your life who will turn out to be life-long friends. Influential people will give you their support as you slowly and patiently work toward goals with the assistance of others. Thus, through friendships you will be fortunate to attain fulfilling career achievements.

Two is definitely a period of support through relationships, whether it be friends, lovers or a mate. Friends, relatives, loved ones and co-workers can be your greatest asset for opportunities as you become more involved with people. Look for opportunities where you can gain from partnerships, getting the cooperation of others, yet maintaining your individualism. In this cycle cultivate skills of love and understanding in your everyday communications. This is not a period where you can use force or become aggressive with issues; it is a time you must be more persuasive and skillful in getting the support you need. Two is a great cycle to be in, despite its duality. This 9-year challenge affects improvements in all aspects of your life. This period will definitely bring a relationship into your life if you are single or improve the one you have. You can now expect a commitment of a relationship or marriage as you receive more personal and emotional satisfaction in your life.

Your domestic situation should greatly improve. You will either get a new home or benefits from an improved home environment. Relationships with your personal family and extended family becomes stronger as you actively participate in more family functions. You may experience stronger emotional attachments with some of your family members especially if they were strained in the past. Accept this cycle as your chance to heal the past.

During this period, you will be compelled to change the fashion of your wardrobe, your hairstyle or color, or even invest in cosmetic surgery to enhance your personal appearance. Since this is a feminine number, ruled by the moon, your moods will fluctuate as you become extremely sensitive to your surroundings. Females will play an important role in your lifestyle or in your career whether male or female. Your work could involve around the feminine gender, or your working situation will include a lot of interactions with them. Whether you work through women, with women, or for women, you will be greatly influenced by the female gender and your support system will come through them.

Financial income becomes more satisfying as opportunities for monetary gain occurs and business ventures become more productive. Two cycle is definitely a time that you will improve your luck. Regardless of what destiny number you have, your conditions will upgrade, but more so if the numbers are compatible. If your destiny number does conflict with the 2 challenge, you will experience tension and strife with a certain amount of sacrifice; but the rewards are worth it. A lot of patience and understanding is required during this period for it is not a time of fast paced movement. It is a time where you must give through patience, love, understanding, cooperation and not just to receive benefits. Whatever your gender, you will become more sensitive and intuitive in the 2 challenge. Allow these feelings to flow gracefully to achieve the harmony you want in your domain.

Two is not a period of competition, but a time to surrender and compromise. Let the strength of your inner self guide you, not the force of your outward actions. A 2 is like the beauty of the rose, allow yourself to unfold naturally. Your beauty outwardly will be seen by all as you slowly bloom through the gracefulness of your inner beauty. Be willing to set aside your assertive self to a more subtle, loving being remaining steadfast even when life seems to be at a standstill. Let your inner spirit guide you to your feminine self to help you find harmony within this cycle.

Direct and forthright actions will not work to calm troubled waters. Do not avoid confrontations while in the number 2 challenge; just develop new skills of arbitration and diplomacy. Negotiations through peaceful actions and patience will help you achieve what you want while avoiding arguments and contradictions. Two is generally not a number of leadership by action but more of support through interaction. Success will not be achieved through independent action but through a cooperative spirit of approach. There are times you will assert resistance when you feel you are being pushed beyond your limitation, then you will revolt. Avoid using force for it will only backfire and lead to disappointments and emotional encounters.

Allow your feminine energy to open your sensitivity and your instincts of intuition. Strong flashes of perception will be quite helpful in all your decision making. The 2 will open your chakras intensifying your vulnerability, especially in relationships. Keep guarded when going through a 2 to remain sentimental without becoming melancholy. Also, be wary of people who pretend to want to help you, but instead take advantage of you. Misunderstandings with others can be avoided by not allowing your feelings to stand in the way. Do not become so agreeable that you are unable to stand up for what you believe. Always use high standards of behavior to accomplish your worldly dreams.

The most important goal to achieve while you are in this challenge is to nurture your environment by promoting peace, tolerance and understanding. This 2 cycle is meant to enjoy life and to gain from the feminine energy. Public approval and success will be tied to the people you do business with. Groups and associations will help in projecting you forward. The time has arrived to make your mark in the world according to your destiny. Your most important assets during this period are your charm, the love you show to others and patience, all of which will help you flow gracefully in the ocean of life.

CHALLENGE NUMBER 3

Breathe gently in the fresh air as this new vibration invites you to dance to the music of your soul. Wake up your spirit to expand your creativity and to open new doors to brighten up your life. You will feel the Sun warm your heart and bring a smile to your face as you enter the challenge of magic so let your imagination run wild. The individuals who experience a 3 challenge will find this to be an exciting and creative period, regardless of the destiny number. It will be a period of exploration, expansion, successful endeavors and a time to experience a deep appreciation of your talents. You definitely will seek to broaden your horizons and will gain through social encounters.

Feeling more restless than normal, no matter what you accomplish during this cycle you will never be satisfied, especially if your destiny number is in conflict with the challenge number. It certainly will be an adventurous time, when everything seems to move at a fast pace, opening new rivers and channels through which you may flow. Many talents and skills you never thought were inherent in you could now surface.

Your personal expression will become more buoyant as you find greater pleasure from your undertakings. You will gain both professionally and personally as you approach life in an extroverted and enthusiastic way. Become aware of your special talents making every effort during this challenge to develop those skills to perfection. Capitalize from your business and career experiences, as you make quantum leaps to achieve financial prosperity.

Three is a wonderful challenge for expansion in all areas of life especially in promoting yourself. Your magnetism comes alive, opening doors of opportunity for others to view your capabilities. Open yourself to public exposure as a means of drawing attention to your talents.

You may not be able to accomplish all your dreams, so work with the ones that are most important to you as you reinforce your choice of values. Expand your professional skills to public speaking events giving you exposure through groups, television, radio and the public media. This form of recognition will help to promote satisfaction and opportunities for self growth into your adventurous nature and in the fulfillment of your personal development.

A 3 challenge is a cycle of profound creativity and should be taken full advantage of to broaden your uniqueness. Use your imagination and fantasies to explore activities that give you a lot of freedom of expression and enrich your life. You fear being judged critically. Therefore, work on your skills to master your talents.

Travels and social activities play an important role in the 3 challenge. A lot of travel could even be work-related, whether it is at a distant or just short trips. There will definitely be opportunities for travel especially to foreign countries. You will gain a broad outlook as well as expand your sightseeing through your valuable travels.

This is a period when you will enjoy being in the limelight, and it is important to project your talents as a means of getting the attention you desire. Many artists receive their acclaim during this phase. Fields of entertainment or public communications are encouraged as a means to display your talents. This could be through the art of dance, music, services of beauty, pageantry, comedy or acting. A client of mine started a business as a clown when she was going though her 3 challenge. Another client started stand-up comedy as a part-time fling to satisfy his life-long dream and ended up with offers to do it as a full-time professional. This opportunity made him ecstatic. He not only got his public recognition, but he was enjoying his work bringing happiness and laughter into the lives of others.

Financially, this can be a positive period, but it can also be a time of losses because of extravagance. Be cautious in spending too much time enjoying life and not enough time improving your finances or being irresponsible.

Three is definitely a cycle when you must use discipline to properly focus on your potential or you could abuse this period through frivolous adventures. It is important to expand your life--mentally, physically, and socially.

A problem that needs to be watched during this period is your weight. It may become a problem due to your indulgence of the good life, so pay special attention to what you consume to avoid unwanted weight problems. This is a cycle of enjoyment and success, but also of extravagance that could lead to other problems.

A lot of status symbols can be gained in the 3 challenge. It is definitely a time when you can improve the conditions of your life and to indulge yourself in luxuries. You could find yourself earning a lot of money, but gaining little to show for it if you are not careful about how you spend your money. With practical planning and caution in your investments, this can be a time of bounty and blessings The concerns you have in the 3 challenge will be toward attaining personal pleasures such as new cars, furniture, pleasure boats and summer homes with which to impress your many friends. Be careful in this pleasure seeking cycle that you also prepare yourself for future security.

Brighten this phase of your life through creative and positive activities. Approach life in a playful way and shed any negativity that surrounds you to lighten your personality. Hang out with people who lift your spirits rather than burden you with their heavy baggage. See your life with clarity to bring happiness to every day of your life. This is the time to explore and enrich your outer experiences.

In the 3 cycle opportunities will be many, and challenges will be few. Use discipline and order to be committed to whatever course you undertake. Keep free from negative and destructive situations. Let a good sense of humor and a smiling face be the first activity of your day, not allowing serious conditions to pull you down. This cycle is a time to enjoy life's pleasures. Allow the sun to shine on your life. Use your God-given talents to gain public recognition and respect. You can be successful and appreciated for everything you do. Let your soul experience happiness and freedom in the ocean of life. With blessings of success and enjoyment embrace this wonderful period through professing altruism.

CHALLENGE NUMBER 4

Move gracefully through this challenge as you yield to Mother Earth to strengthen your body and mind to a more practical and disciplined way of life. You must now take control of your health and loved ones, learning about the laws and principles that have to govern all of life. In this 9-year challenge put everything in life on a practical basis as you will definitely feel more responsibility having to become more self-reliant and conservative.

During this phase you will become obsessed with material ambitions, pleasures and security. Financial issues and values will need foundation and structure. Struggles with finances will have an affect on your lifestyle and the pressures of daily living could be a major source of concern for you. Security can be obtained through wise investments and a good sense of financial values.

Domestic issues with home and family will have priority in your surroundings. There will be many family issues to deal with in your domestic life both in your personal family and biological family. Their welfare will seem to consume a lot of your time and energy. Issues of responsibility can be time consuming as you try to fulfill your ambitions in the outer world to create the wealth you deserve. Relatives play a major role in your personal life with a lot of family functions and social gatherings being emphasized.

Through discipline and hard work, this challenge will teach you to live within limitations. It can help you to build a secure foundation through patience and time. You will have to overcome occasional negative setbacks to achieve realization of your overall objectives and to balance your personal life with your career. Remember, even though the 4 challenge can be a hard taskmaster, it is also a companion to wisdom and maturity. A dedicated and spiritual attitude will help you overcome many of your problems as you uplift yourself from the material world. Gain realization of greater things than those of material value. You will not be asked to do more than what is in your power to sustain. The divine hand of destiny will work to convert you to spiritual perfection by placing demands upon you to free you from the bondage of materialism.

Overcome your feelings of insecurity as you release yourself from the tears of pain to prayers and affirmations. The 4 challenge is definitely a time of wisdom and understanding. Through faith and acceptance, this 9-year time frame can be rewarding if you accept your limitations gracefully. When you recognize the positive side of the 4 you will thank God as you benefit from each restriction encountered, setting you free from any limitations that may be placed upon you.

During this cycle do not allow your attitude toward life to become so serious that it reflects in your personality, in dress or attitude. This can be a period of great achievement, building inner strength and establishing a financial foundation for yourself. Your attitude reflects your feelings, so try to maintain a youthful spirit to keep from becoming old. Aging is not meant to grow old through spirit, just in years. A 4 challenge is like the aging of wine. After a certain period of process and refinement the wine becomes mellow and develops its wonderful flavor; so it is with the 4 challenge.

Health issues could be a source of concern, whether your own, a family member's or a friend's. Get physical checkups periodically and make sure you are in good health. This can be a period of great achievement and success but you must be healthy in body and mind. Become more productive in your career and learn to depend more on yourself and not others.

Take this 9-year period and put all your personal affairs in order. Prove to the world and to yourself that you are a responsible and wise individual. Happiness is there for you to enjoy but you need to learn to appreciate the simple things of life. Do not become depressed about life or fall into traps of dull, monotonous routines. Be the rainbow of inspiration to others as you reconnect with yourself on the deepest levels for direction in life..

Socially, you may feel hampered, yet you will draw many devoted and lifelong friends into your life as people from your past and present reach out to you. Choose friends wisely; cut off destructive friendships.

Associate only with rewarding friendships that bring out the best in you. Because of your devotion to friends avoid becoming possessive of those with whom you become close with. Do not become a slave to your feelings. Work toward your goals. Be open to other opinions, but do not live your life by their assessment. This is a period when you can achieve stature and financial status but only through hard work, gaining lifetime value.

A client of mine, who is an artist, received many medals and ribbons for her artistic skills, although it was not easy. She had a young family, worked 40-hours a week, plus housekeeping chores that kept her very busy. A lot of labor and discipline went into her accomplishments, leaving little time for her to play. Yet, she was so driven to achieve recognition that she dealt with the responsibilities and obligations surrounding her lifestyle. Success and reward were not denied to this lovely woman. She learned to deal with the pressures of her life and ultimately received her due reward. She assured me that all the demands were worth the effort, especially now as she admires her rewards and achievements with pride.

Perfect your life through steady development to bring you satisfaction and victory. Devote your life to a cause, because victory comes to all who succeed. Learn to enjoy the things for which you work so hard, and remember when life becomes too dull and gruesome; lighten up. Always make a special effort to add enjoyment and laughter to your daily living.

Know that in this period you are establishing security and a foundation of success that will reward you financially and materially in the future. I have a 4 in the numbers in my birthdate and when I went through my 4 challenge for 9 years it was a time of heavy responsibilities, but yet a very fulfilling period. I was raising four sons, had two homes built within the 9-year period and had a husband who worked six days a week, leaving us both little time to enjoy life.

I raised four sons with little help from their father because of his long hours at work. A lot of energy went into my family and home during that period. Although the 4 challenge was a hard cycle, I loved it. In many ways it was a wonderful time even though it was very demanding. There were many wonderful family gatherings and good times with close friendships that I will never forget.

Remember, as you establish meaningful goals in your struggles, you will produce successful results well worth the effort. This is a time you can shape your life to have long-lasting results. It is a cycle of maturity and responsibility, but also a time you may meet with resistance. Meet your basic needs through persistence without having a sobering attitude or becoming self-destructive. Do not lose your passion for life; your passion is the engine to your life force. When you lose your passion you lose your energy, becoming a slave to life while building up resentment.

This challenge is not without its beauty. It extends to the human conduct of a person and their obligations to a truly moral life, to fulfill the requirements of karma both in this life and the next. In a literal sense, it explains the inequality and suffering with a reasonable explanation.

In a 4 challenge, the attention is focused on home, family, health and financial issues and gaining a responsible foundation. It is not easy to swim upstream in the ocean of life through the battering waves, but you have a life preserver called faith, and it's important to use it.

CHALLENGE NUMBER 5

Awaken your experience to your 5 senses and let your fantasies wonder like clouds in the sky to take you through the gateway of new pastures. Open yourself to your higher consciousness to obtain pure knowledge. This is a 9-year changeable cycle when you learn never to take anything for granted. Inflamed with dynamic energy, you will feel like a burning bush out-of-control, actively aware feeling alive, full of ideas, wanting to live life fully.

Expect the unexpected with life situations constantly changing your lifestyle. Learn to flow with events in a nonconventional way never trying to force situations lest they work against you. Definitely, the 5 challenge is a time of flexibility, a time of totality, love, devotion, joy and sorrow. It is time to let go of outdated ideas, eliminate jobs or people who hold you back or undermine your efforts.

Expand your life. Get used to life-changing effects that will uplift your life force. Be open to new adventures, ideas and opportunities. Life will feel like spring all year long with new buds constantly opening new pathways for you. It is definitely a progressive period when you do not want any restraints of any kind as you look at life from every angle with wandering thoughts.

Regardless of age, you will feel more vibrant and younger because of the youthful presence the 5 activates. Even if you are at a retiring age you will discard any idea of retirement involving yourself in more activities than usual, almost as if you were running away from the time clock. Find a niche in life that will satisfy you and then go on to enjoy it.

There is a certain element of luck during a 5 challenge allowing you to profit from your experiences through your personal charisma. No matter what your destiny number, this period will prove to be an interesting time in life. You will be able to mix pleasure with business, using your contacts for business and social enjoyment.

These will be busy years of activity as you will meet many influential friends and have countless opportunities presented to you. Friends will inspire you in your ambitions, and some may even empower you in your ideas. Be sure to maintain some sort of stability through a home situation. Because of an unwillingness to adapt to routine or domestic responsibilities special efforts must be made to have a normal home life. As a result of your restless energy and active social life you will experience a lot of stress. Hire domestic help to eliminate the workload in your active lifestyle, and try to live life in moderation as much as you can.

Remember, change is necessary and important in the 5 challenge, but avoid the temptation to impulsive changes or quick money schemes that appear questionable or unrealistic. In your abundant energy, be more deliberate in your choices not allowing your restless spirit to take charge. Reduce anxiety and tension by involving yourself in a regime of physical exercises to be in good physical shape.

I have seen people in the 5 challenge become depressed and unhappy because they could not adapt to the changes, and planning ahead for them was not easy. Do not get stuck in a rut just for the sake of security. Always keep an open mind to new ideas. Do not miss opportunities to expand life because of your fears. In this cycle you have to let go of fears and not become a creature of habit.

Relationships are really tested in this cycle so be mindful of the temptations. Make sure you always use good judgment or discrimination in all your associations or relationships. Your attention will not always be connected to the one you love, and your overactive glands will have an eagerness to seek new adventures. Your feelings of love may be sincere to one individual; however, your passion to be sexual is not. This is the curiosity cycle, having a yen to experience the five senses on all levels, wanting a little of everything just for the excitement. Live life through spontaneity, seeking variety in your everyday life, but always do the right thing for yourself and for those you love.

If your destiny number is a 4, 6 or 8, you could appear unconventional to others in your behavior and attitude. This could be a time of short-term marriages, broken relationships, quickie romances and many sexual encounters. If you are not in a loving relationship you will overcompensate your sexual appetite in romantic encounters. Try to satisfy your adventurous nature through a profession, a new career or interests that challenge your unpredictable behavior. Conventional attitudes can help to stabilize your vibratory forces through the many changes.

Regardless of the situation you must maintain command when in a 5 challenge or you will lose control. Do not lose sight of your basic responsibilities. There is always an element of risk with unpredictable changes and 5 is a challenge of unforseen changes. Many situations and opportunities could be short-lived without long-term benefits because of the inconsistency and the spontaneity. Happenings in life will be on a day-to-day basis, both through actions and your thoughts. The desire to spread your wings and explore new horizons will be a motivating factor to satisfy your restless and curious nature during this period.

This challenge can be a great time to be single, for there will be plenty of romantic encounters. It is not the best time to establish a permanent relationship unless you are willing to accept the responsibility of a serious commitment. If you are already married and your destiny is an odd number, this could be a rewarding cycle; but, if the destiny number is an even number, it could bring on problems and separations. Regardless of the destiny number, your sensual nature will certainly play an important role in your adventures. You will seek excitement through pleasurable pursuits or romantic encounters, as your engaging spirit draws romance toward you.

There can now be satisfactory gains in all phases of your life so be open to new expansions. Encourage yourself to become centered as you deal with the turbulence in the ocean of life. Seize opportunities for work which will allow you to reshape your life through expansive choices. Gain the power you desire through public events to obtain achievements for worldly recognition. Open your eyes to unknown dimensions while you bask in the enjoyment of all your five senses.

CHALLENGE NUMBER 6

This challenge stimulates you to respond like Mother earth, supplying the nourishment of love to all without distinction. You will react to life like the soul of a flower looking for sunlight to help you soak in the rays for your inner beauty to blossom. The embodiment of the Divine Spirit will move you beyond your thoughts and actions, into the whole of your being as the presiding force of spiritual devotion takes over.

You will experience powers of hidden forces within your personal magnetism, almost as if a door were opened inside of you. This is a period to experience the genuine pleasures of love, or this could be a challenge when you feel you are lacking in love. Love must now become a spiritual treasure, not merely a physical pleasure. Your outer and inner feelings will now experience a transformation that will be powerful in your spiritual revelations. Emotions and feelings may be tied to family, home, loved ones and friends but, spiritually you will have an inner awakening to unfold the extension of your inner self. It can be a paradox of selfless love or selfish love, depending upon the process born from the experience in this time frame.

Extending yourself to help others will be an ongoing affair, but it should not become a burdensome process. Love gives light to the soul, feeding the seeds of the human emotions. If that light is dimmed or turned off the seed goes dormant, losing its life force as it goes from joy to sadness. This is probably the most emotional cycle of all the numbers, except for the 7 challenge. This is a cycle when you have to respond to the expression of love, but not be bound to love. How you express these emotions in friendships and marriage will be very important to your well being.

This cycle is about money, personal possessions, comforts, love, social and spiritual values. You will feel strong obligations to your home and family life with much of your free time revolving around relatives. Loved ones will demand much of you and make you feel a responsibility in helping them. Be careful not to sacrifice your own needs in helping family members or friends in their struggles. Be supportive to them but do not take on their burdens. Do not involve yourself in family situations by taking on issues that are none of your concern. When family members and friends lean on you for emotional support, respond to them through understanding and compassion, but in an impersonal way. Do not become a victim of others' tribulations by taking on their karmic experiences. Inspiration is important in any situation; however, involvement and interference on your behalf could cause reprisals at a later date bringing you blame and heartache.

If single during this challenge, you will yearn to be in a relationship. It is a period when a lot of focus is centered on marriage, children, grandchildren or having a home. Whether you are in a relationship or in a marriage you will experience emotional growth through love. Rejection, loneliness and disappointments in marriage or personal relationships will magnify emotional turmoil that could have far-reaching consequences in your life. Do not stay in an unhappy relationship to avoid being alone or because of maudlin sentimentality. This challenge is a time when your life requires a lot of affection and security because of your extreme sensitivity. Your life is yourself and without self there is no connection to life. This is what keeps you happy.

Your personal appearance will become important as you become more aware of the clothes you wear and how you look. Your attire will display softer colors and more flattering elegance, as if you are being judged by the public or looking for approbation from others. You will definitely be more into your feminine energy in both your attire and your nature. Perfection will be your main goal, but balance will also be necessary to avoid extremism in that need for perfection.

Look to success from a profession working with the public or in service-oriented fields. School also will be emphasized, as you advance yourself to become specialized in fields that will be looked upon as professional or career-oriented. This cycle is about solving problems and a greater understanding of family, finances, career, relationships and love. These challenges will need to be dealt with in a mature and responsible manner.

This challenge can definitely be a time of ups and downs because of its impassioned nature. Your behavior will be influenced by the amount of nurturing and love you receive. Use good judgment in the affairs of your heart, and put energy into your work and hobbies to avoid depression or misdirection. Use caution in your spending habits since you will find it difficult to be economical. In your extravagance to have nice things, your spending sprees could cause undo financial worries. Money carelessly spent on pleasures will eventually have to be accounted for and if you are not sensible in your spending habits, you may have to sacrifice your pleasures for necessities.

Be open to the many opportunities for achievement and, hopefully, you will be able to bring success into your reality. The 6 challenge can be a difficult time if your destiny number is a 5 or 7, especially with relationships and finances. The ups and downs that challenge you will lead you to frustration and depression. The lesson here is not to dwell on your physical and material bliss but to turn inward for your wealth and your spiritual desires and your rewards will be great.

Weakness during this cycle or refusal to develop strength of character and courage to liberate yourself from dependency will affect you mentally and physically. Do not become unhappy through the suffering of a negative relationship or job situation which has become a prison for you; end it. Your willingness to tolerate unhappiness to keep peace will prevent the natural flow of your loving feelings. Free yourself from adverse situations to experience true love and joys of this Venus cycle. Unconditionally, allow the influence of this Venus cycle to develop a sense of true love, not the misconception of it.

Express openly what you feel without feeling guilty or intimidated. Do not agree to fix everyone's problems, give only loving advice. This is a time to be inspirational, to listen to other people's problems but not become provoked into them. Feel free to choose your destiny and you will find a certain amount of luck favored with your choice.

Performing service or bringing beauty to mankind will be very important during this cycle and significant to your spiritual growth. With your soft heart and your wisdom, you will be able to use your seeds of love to help and inspire others. You can now express your feelings in a romantic and creative way as you merge in the ocean of life. Initiate balance and perfection while cleansing your heart through pure love and compassion.

CHALLENGE NUMBER 7

You are about to discover miracles about your self-worth. The spirit and mind are a connecting link in the physical body, making conscious contact with the Higher self. The body is made up of energy and during this cycle your mind and body will identify with spiritual projection and vibrate healing powers. You will have a coming together of your emotional and mental thought waves to direct your perception. This will be a time to heal yourself and others with the vital healing force of your own being and you will find you have value in your regenerating powers.

The 7 challenge promotes spiritual growth within. It is both a spiritual and intellectual challenge designed to evolve you through the higher mind. While the physical body expresses itself through the mind, it nevertheless has centers within it through which the higher principles will manifest in the spirit. You will feel a need to want to change your life dramatically--you will be different tomorrow then you are today. It may always be understood because that is part of the mystery of the number 7.

You will seek contentment through the earthly pleasures of love and divine wisdom of a pure heart, rather than through materialism. You will be challenged to delve into deeper and more specialized fields, academic and philosophical. Try to attend schools of philosophy, research, parapsychology academic institutes or service oriented fields to help you achieve respect in your educational pursuits to take charge of your destiny.

This is an important period in developing skills so you can gain knowledge and establish security in your vocation and your future. You will experience an increase in your intuitive instincts, developing a greater awareness of your own wisdom and of your life's purpose. Seven is ruled by the planet Neptune, which characterizes delusion and confusion. At times you may appear unrealistic in your attitude and undertakings, and prone to self-delusion. Turn inward for answers when you feel uncertain about your decision making ability. There will be a tendency to keep to yourself because of feelings of detachment which could lead you to depression and loneliness.

In this challenge you may not always get the personal rewards that you deserve, but merit can be gained through your education and the skills you acquire. You cannot trust your luck during a 7 challenge because of the Neptunian influence 7 has. Business or financial investments must be thought out carefully or your financial security could be at risk. Any illegal dealings in which you involve yourself will eventually lead to general dissatisfaction and losses.

Because of your extreme vulnerability during this period you will be reluctant to project your true feelings, keeping many aspects of your life a secret. This is a period to develop objectivity and to acquire technical skills necessary to stabilize your reputation for future years. Nothing is beyond your comprehension when you deal with your intellectual powers and integrity.

If you experience this challenge in your retiring years you will find you keep more to yourself, preferring it that way. There will be a strong interest in religion or spiritual values that will pervade your thought priorities because you feel there is nothing more important for you to act on. Become the observer watching and listening to your inner feelings to help you in seeking the true meaning and purpose of your life's journey.

Do not allow the negative thoughts or actions of others to isolate you from social activities. It is important during this period to feel alive and part of a unity. Peace of mind is gained when you go within to find answers, so be sure to take time to meditate every day. Mediation will not solve all your problems; however, it can help to erase some of the illusions and stress that you create for yourself. Meditation with focus can create positive personality reactions bringing balance to both your mind and body. Avoid mental and emotional turmoil that can result in feelings of repression and solitude. Strive to understand the disturbances that offset your personality--then deal with them

Psychological imbalance can become a problem during this cycle and could turn you on to alcoholism, drugs or anti-depressants to cure your states of depression. Seven is a number of dichotomy, representing the spiritual urge and the escapist urge. In its most positive form 7 is inspirational, sensitive, musical and creative.

Many times you will feel like you are always giving or putting out energy, but never seem to benefit from it. You are developing internally, not externally, for your spiritual rewards. Fanaticism with religious pursuits, religious philosophy and spiritual retreats can lead to obsessions and addictions. Allow your religious philosophy to be spiritual enlightenment, not obsessive extremism.

Children, adolescents and adults in this challenge should be encouraged to continue their education to keep from scattering themselves without a realistic direction. Students could experience social or learning problems if they are not given praise or encouraged to do better. Daydreaming, woolgathering or fantasizing about unrealistic desires can interfere with your academic achievements and add to your mental stress.

A family needs to show great understanding and avoid being critical to any member in a 7 challenge. Putting pressure on you will add additional mental stress to your confused state and create disruption in the home environment. This is a cycle when you need to be encouraged and appreciated to find peace of mind and not be led into confusion because of your vulnerability.

Relationships or marriage are definitely difficult and will be trying because of the detached attitude that you present and feel. It is a cycle you feel more aloof with less attachment in your feelings, yet emotionally and financially you can be quite dependent on your loved ones. You feel quite content when alone and in your peaceful silence you are building power within you.

This challenge is usually not a period of material or financial benefit, but it is a period of intellectual rewards. Moods and feelings will be easily affected by those around you, as you seem to absorb much of other people's energies. It is a time of faith and trust, not only in yourself but in destiny's purpose and plan for you. Keep your physical and mental body balanced by taking an interest in personal fitness or yoga. Although this challenge can be oppressive professionally, it can also be significantly productive in your self-improvement.

Use water frequently to help calm and sooth your nerves. Water has a strong affinity to the number 7, because of its rulership with Neptune and is able to dissolve dismal feelings. It can be used as therapy (cleansing negative energy and thought forms) whether it is taking a bath, shower, swimming in a pool, sitting by a brook or just splashing water on yourself. Water will always refresh and rejuvenate your spirit and is a form of purification.

When unselfish love and understanding are expressed, you will find it easier to enjoy friendships. Make it a point to socialize more often and to fully enjoy your associations with others. It is important to have a special person or friend in your life who you respect and love to become your mentor, helping you to stay in a centered and positive spirit.

The best advice that can be bestowed to an individual in a 7 challenge is not to push or force anything beyond a day-to-day situation. This period is for inner growth and engaging in intellectual aspects for peace of mind. It makes no difference what your problem is when you are at the bottom of the ocean, it is dark and unclear. If use your mind and energy to swim upward to the surface you will see the light shining on you and the ocean. No matter how alone you feel in the ocean of life, a higher power will push you to wholeness to achieve your inward growth and rightful place in life.

CHALLENGE NUMBER 8

Enter the challenge that can lead you to your castle and the world of enchantment. This can be a period of heroic adventure and the time to find your sacred place within the world. In this cycle the importance of accepting death and rebirth is imperative, because it can contain all the magic and sorrow found in the duality of the number 8. Opportunities will now lead to changes; all you have to do is recognize them.

Eight is two 0s connected with the spiral motion of circles. It is the inevitable and onward rush to acquire that well-deserved reward or success which was designed in your past lifetime. It is the time to reap what has been sown. You can turn the 8 sideways to become wings as the imperial eagle to carry you forth into a higher realm; or you can be like the hourglass working through the imperfections. It is important for your soul to transform from the lower dimension of the 8 acquiring wisdom through the physical expression on your course of growth evolving to the higher magnitude of the spiritual 8. Transformation into a higher state of life is necessary regardless of how you achieve it.

In the 8 challenge embrace your leadership abilities to make an impact in your destiny. Eight is the number of transformation and regeneration, bridging the material and the spiritual. Be aware that 8 works to improve opportunities that open doors to financial success and personal gratification. This can be a great cycle to achieve success, power and recognition. You will now be able to enjoy the finer things of life and move into influential circles that will benefit you personally. Your talents and abilities should be put to your best advantage not only to better your life, but to better the lives of others. It is important to share your good luck with others, for what goes around comes around.

This is a period of rewards, success and even fame, especially if it is in your destiny. During this 9-year cycle you will be able to accumulate many material and financial benefits. Wealthy, powerful people can now benefit your career and financial status. The 8 challenge is definitely a time to seize your power and use your knowledge to become an authority figure. Advancement, ambition and attainment all go hand-in-hand. Use the dynamic qualities of this period to promote yourself to your desired pinnacle. Your personal magnetism during this challenge will help to draw important contacts to you. Utilize your talents and power to help you achieve public recognition. Positions of leadership and authority will be offered to you in your profession, as well as having a positive affect in your public relations.

Because of the strong self confidence you feel in the 8 challenge you will be able to project yourself in a effectual manner. Watch that ego though, all the power and success you acquire can make you appear pompous and self-righteous. Come from a loving, humble heart so you will not draw criticism to you, but be accepted with praise and respect. Getting caught up in the glamour and excitement can whither away the wisdom of your spirituality. Blend the material with the spiritual to avoid becoming indulgent through flattery, arrogance and power. Do not lose sight of positive opportunities by being arbitrary and be ready to promote your authority on a worldly scale.

In this cycle you will have a lot to offer; however, success can only be attained when you are willing to take action. Work hard, take on extra responsibility and be careful in careless spending to capture the true meaning of your financial growth. Although you will be successful in financial matters, spending money foolishly without sound judgment in your over-zealousness could work against you. Full responsibility of your actions must be accepted through a mature attitude to help you in your progress. During this cycle nothing in life is too big for you to achieve.

The 8 challenge is a karmic cycle. It is the gift giver for all good deeds and can bestow upon you an incredible amount of success and recognition. Observe how life changes in the 8 challenge and how you are able to master the material world quicker than you could in other cycles. Always remember as you begin to ascend to success not to let your ego stand in the way. Success can be like a big wave in the ocean that can flip your boat off balance, losing self-control. What is down can go up, but what is up can also go down. Build your life on a strong structure of significant and lasting values to show the world your achievements.

This challenge can be a time of historical distinction and the changes in life can be regenerative or degenerative. Nine years is spent in this cycle and it can be a golden time, not only affecting your status but the status of your family and loved ones as well. You and your loved ones will get to enjoy your success through the luxuries of many acquired material assets. Remember, in this period the body must serve the mind, the mind must not serve the body.

In your preoccupation with your success, do not ignore the needs and advice of others. Leave your mark on destiny in a way that will be remembered for your resourcefulness and knowledge, not your inflated ego or manipulative behavior. Do not fall into temptations to use others to advance yourself or to gain from other's resources through deception. Be guided by good moral integrity in gaining the respect of others.

All evil actions or thoughts can be overcome by relying on higher spiritual forces and using your knowledge as the sustainer of your success. Your intelligence will be manifested as that of a developed intellectual being, You will be guided by an unconscious telepathic sensitivity, able to be perceptive to the thoughts and motives of others.

This is a favorable challenge for spiritual leadership, politics, executive positions, institutions, business owners and professionals in all fields. You can become a controversial figure through your leadership as you reform and revive new energy through your farsightedness.

Bring success to humanity, not to your ego. Avoid personal ambitions which will lead you to a preoccupation with power and egocentric gratification. Use the power of love with human understanding. Leave behind old thoughts and beliefs and the desires and pleasures of the material and the flesh. Ascend to the upper half of the 0 of the 8 which is the lotus or the golden boon. During this exciting challenge use yourself as an outlet into which others may plug into. Fulfill your personal ambitions in this ocean of life, reshaping your life to evolve into heavenly divineness from your earthly wisdom.

CHALLENGE NUMBER 9

"Fly Me To The Moon And Let Me Stand Among The Stars"--to keep me safe from the initiation of the 9 challenge. During this challenge you will have to stand on your own initiative until you resign your life and fears to a greater power and commend your spirit to fate.

Nine is the challenge of the Omega. It is not the cycle when you will do it your way, but when you do it God's way. Your destiny is challenged from all the numbers, 1 through 9, and will awaken you to your soul's agreement. The 9 challenge is the most auspicious. You are casting off old molds to acquire new ones.

This is definitely a Uranus period; never knowing what to expect or what you get to keep when you receive it. Nine is a humanitarian number by character, so when you go through a 9-year challenge, this number will bring about a philosophical idealism that you must nurture and express. Learn these lessons without bitterness or losing your idealism.

Nine works through the divine or the damnable. It can lead you to great triumphs with tears of joy or down to a grappling tragedy of tears and sadness. It can bring you windfalls or windstorms, but you will never overlook its power. Ask anyone who has been through a 9-year challenge! The planet Uranus, known to be eccentric, has rulership over the number 9. During this cycle you could experience financial losses, legal problems, ill health, recklessness, scattered behavior, insecurity, uniqueness in your expression and spiritual maturity. In this challenge you will be forced to your knees on several occasions through sacrifices and obstacles that must be endured, forcing you to seek solace through spiritual devotion. The positive side of this cycle is that after you have endured your initiation you become the light of the lantern into a new manifestation of spiritual enlightenment.

Your allegiance must be to the spiritual world and not to the material world. It is a period when you can become a social parasite, working fervently toward spiritual pursuits without exercising practical discipline especially in the stability of your finances. You will be rebellious having radical opinions, emerging into a lifestyle of uncontrolled freedom.

Pursue higher studies in the fields of psychology, religion or spiritual education. It is also a time you want to devote your life to a career or work where you can become of service to others in some benevolent way. Whatever your career or profession, you will feel a desire to break away from the monotonous routine of a regular job, seeking a newfound position without the trappings of a confined environment.

This challenge brings divine protection with it. Luck always seems to come at the last hour, as if providence has placed a protective cloak around you. Be careful in your decisions and your objectives. No matter what you attempt to do in this challenge, remember the end result is "God's will be done".

Due to the suffering and pain you experience in this challenge, you will have a greater understanding of mankind in all its suffering and pain. In many situations you will be faced with mental and emotional despair, bringing greater awareness and appreciation to your life, love and spiritual growth. It is easy to get caught in the web of human suffering due to painful challenges, but pain is the catalyst that bonds you to compassion. Tearful moments will be experienced as you learn the art of unconditional love and lose the stability of financial security. Your psychological attitude toward this vibration is very important as you make way for the new.

Many new friends will enter your life during this cycle; many lifelong friendships will be lost. For some people there could be a lot of travel for business and pleasure. Travels on the sea or ocean could take place as you venture out to experience other countries and cultures. This 9-year cycle brings endings through friends, family, jobs and home situations. Stay steadfast as the tidal waves force you to change your course of action unexpectedly. Hold onto faith and you will be able to ease through this period with a stronger spiritual pipeline and a renewed faith in yourself.

Do not become attached or hold too tightly to any given situation and yet do not allow yourself to become a drifter deluded with the fantasies of life. There will be difficulties through relationships, career, family sickness or even your own health problems, so proper attention to all those areas are necessary. Make sure you get enough rest and have a well-balanced diet.

Your body chemistry will go through some changes as you become more intuitive and resilient in your nature. These changes will make your body sensitive to the energy around you. Little things that normally would not affect you will now cause you to feel insecure. Do not dwell on your needs; instead try to focus your attention on being helpful to others to gain the most out of this cycle.

Nine can be a passage of lessons, but it is also a transit to see your own magnitude of divineness. You will not be expected to be a saint or martyr during this cycle, but to turn experiences into knowledge and use what you learn to help others. Another important thing is to put away fears and arouse victory by surrendering to your destiny. For some, this cycle can be your greatest battle--for others, it can be your greatest spiritual triumph.

Be willing to accept change and place your trust in a higher power. Let go and let in God, because the more you trust and place your life in the hands of God, the easier it becomes to overcome the handicaps that will be a part of your spiritual awakening. Whatever life will be during this challenge, you will feel the excitement of the unknown. You will want to venture out into different lifestyles and to appreciate the unique and unusual opportunities open to you. Be the guiding light for many individuals and reach out to the masses through your abilities and knowledge.

Free yourself from responsibilities so you can move independently and flow with the drama that this cycle will offer. This cycle demands that you free yourself from worldly influences and the desires of materialism. Expect nothing from life to gain everything through life. It is not a time to achieve financial prosperity but to be practical with finances--however, it is definitely a time to let go of the past in favor of a new tomorrow.

Choose carefully what you partake of during this period, and use your intuitive powers to help solve your problems. Focus on the positive aspects of life. Accept that when one door closes it is not the end, but a new beginning. A 9-challenge is like a box of chocolates--mixed blessings. It is a period where anxiety and predictability are magnified. Yet, with a new realization it can give a latitude of insight opening new doors for you to enter to success and fulfillment. You can become successful gaining fame, or be recognized for some important work that you do through your gifts and talents but it cannot be your main focus. It is a period when you can meet with masters and teachers who will guide you on your spiritual journey.

Interest in volunteer work, political projects, involvement in the Peace Corps or other humanitarian groups are pursuits that could change your consciousness and the pathway of your life. Your spiritual thirsts will be strong as your journey in the ocean of life becomes more involved in service and compassion to help others in their sorrows. With a twinkle in your eye, and a smile as bright as the sun. ascend to be a guiding light to others in their darkness, as you connect them with the spiritual source of the universe. AMEN.

Success or excess--you want all or nothing at all. Change is indeed the order of the day as the challenge of the 0 brings about profound changes to your life. This is the cycle where the Spirit of the Lord works with you. It is a time to love who you are and what you do in life without compromising your self, your love or your ambitions. This is the cycle where you will be forced to look into the cosmic mirror to see the part of your life that you have not perfected. When your soul recognizes its higher nature and you realize your unlimited knowledge you will gain powerful inner strength. You will become immersed in all levels of life due to the disturbing influences that will surround you.

Zero is the Alpha and the Omega--in some destinies during this cycle all the numbers within a birthdate will be challenged and felt in action. If you internalize your actions you will develop spiritually similar to a solitary monk seeking to attain heightened dimensions of consciousness--or you can externalize your actions through your spiritual deeds to meet challenges in the world of success and materialism.

There will be many periods of sacrifice and readjustments in this challenge until the lesson of the ego comes into harmony with the internal and the external self. Harsh aspects will make life difficult to function in a balanced way until all energies are concentrated into one focus, and the focal point of the 0 becomes the light of illumination, casting out the obstacle of impairment.

There is considerable difference in how each person reacts to the 0. The person who is spiritually inclined with a 0, and the person who is worldly and materialistic with a 0 will seek different paths of self-realization through their philosophy and actions.

When there are one or more 0s in your birthdate, you will find that in this challenge it is necessary to display a greater sense of direction and balance. It will be important to approach life with a positive spiritual application. In many instances, you will be challenged by situations where you feel trapped or unable to find refuge. It is a feeling as if you are on the outside of life looking in, struggling to pull your fragmented life together into some form--and you are!

In this challenge whether you are looking to move into the circle or trying to find a way out because you feel trapped, 0 signifies challenges in many areas of your life. Zero is the divine working through the materialistic, the realistic and the idealistic. Your existence will experience a full circle of ups and downs to bring about total reform in the course of your life.

Zero is without its partner while going through the 9-year challenge cycle of the 0. This lack of direction leads to frustration in this challenge because it represents options without guidelines. You can be misled by delusions and must learn to live in reality. Zero generally depends upon its partner to find direction and yet in this challenge the 0 has to stand on its own. This can confuse and diffuse the expression of the 0 disturbing the natural flow if its manifestation, attaching itself to the energy of the 9-month cycle and the personal year number for direction. Zero cannot accomplish anything without the energy of its associated number. It feels misguided by the energies of the 9-month cycle and personal year numbers bringing on adverse circumstances into the environment. You must be willing to comply with the winds of change that are initiated in the 0 challenge for appreciable growth--even though "you will be damned if you do, and damned if you don't".

The 0 challenge will be a course in humility and humanity. It will provoke obstacles from every direction of your life--family, finances, career, relationships, security and your self-confidence. It is important to seek as much time as you can to find peacefulness or to meditate, and that may even be difficult.

This is a time to furnish the temple of your soul because your soul is the spiritual vessel that will ultimately help you to attain a positive vibration and an indication of which direction you must follow. Remember, you are an old soul, and you already possess the infinite knowledge necessary to meet the challenge, but you are being forced to evolve spiritually to reach the perfection required in this challenge.

Keep an open mind and use patience in your attempts to rectify difficult circumstances and to remind yourself of what you came here to do. At the end of every tunnel is a light, and while walking through the darkness you may be repeatedly tested and defeated in life, only to be able to wholly identify yourself when you finally stand in the presence of your own light.

Always focus on your objective and maintain a positive attitude to bring about a new sense of order into your life's journey. When you learn to understand and respect the dualism of the ocean with its beauty and its vulnerability, you will not be limited in your vision. You will recognize the ideal balance of the beauty and the beast. The 0 challenge can bring an adventure of struggles, but it can also bring victory when it is mastered.

Destiny	6	6	6	6	6	6	6	6	6	6	6	6	6	6	6	6	6	6
9-Yr Challenge	1	1	1	1	1	1	1	1	1	1	1	1	1	1	1	1	1	1
9-Mo Challenge	1	9	3	7	4	1	8	1	9	3	7	4	1	8	1	9	3	7	4
Dates Cycles Are in Effect	4	1	10	7	4	1	10	7	4	1	10	7	4	1	10	7	4	1	10
	37		38	39	40		41	42	43		44	45	46		47	48	49		50

The 9-month challenge is much like the personal year number except the cycle is shorter by 3 months and is not by sequence of the numbers 1 to 9 as in the personal year rhythm. The orbit of the 9-month cycle is similar to the 9-year challenge, using the same numbers in sequence but only in 9-month cycles. The 9-month cycle affects the 9-year challenge because it is a revolution of numbers circling each other. It is like a circle with another circle going around it. The energy is short-term affecting attitudes differently every 9-months, as the numbers change in revolution. It resembles the motions of a clock where the big hands move slowly for the movement of time and the small (second) hand moves swiftly for the seconds.

The 9-month rotation of the numbers is not your motivational reaction to life. It is the force of energy for 9-months that either enhances the 9-year cycle or debilitates it. When the cycle is positive, it represents gain and opportunities. When the 9-month cycle is negative with the 9-year challenge, it will produce opposition and resistance making that 9-month period difficult. If the personal year number is also inharmonious to the 9-year challenge during that same time period, it will even compound the difficulties you are having.

Use the 9-months to focus energy in positive form. Rise above the short-term effects of a crisis and use it as a reminder to awaken your consciousness of what you need to put more effort into. As you learn to understand the short term cycles you will perceive the events that take place in your life with a different awareness. Events do not change, people do when life is perceived in a positive way. Perspective must be used when dealing with the 9-month challenges, because it is just a transit or a temporary stage and the world, or people, may not be what they appear to be at the time.

You may be exhilarated or feel depressed through the events of those 9-months; but if you were never tested, you could never have merit. Your virtues lie in your quests to master the difficulties that are placed in your path. Do not wait for a crisis to move your life forward or allow your fears to hold you back from your dreams.

The true indicator of progress comes from the 9-year challenge. Then, and only then, can you realize the worldly influences which will identify the greater experiences of which you will encounter. Experiences are based not only on the short-term events you encounter, but also on the major power of the 9-nine year challenge which has a long-lasting effect.

Life is similar to the weather patterns. The seasons of the year are the short-term challenges; the year itself is based on how you approach each season and prepare for it. If the year is entering the winter season, you prepare yourself for the cold and snow. If the season is going into the hot summer you prepare yourself for the heat and humidity. You must also take into consideration that just because it is summer it does not mean there will never be cold or rainy days, as in the winter season there could also be unusually warm and sunny days. Within each season there will be many variables of weather conditions, although the juncture of the season never changes. It is that way with the numbers as well. The 9-year challenge never changes its interval, but the 9-month challenge is the varied condition that will take place within the passage of that 9-year period. You must expect nothing from any given situation and yet be ready for whatever occurs.

Accept and partake of daily living with all its variables. Never take for granted any circumstance or outside influences, for life is not set in concrete. Life is a hidden treasure. You owe it to your soul to follow through each day and find out all that awaits you. Life is like an ocean in constant movement and you need to preserve it from becoming stagnant. Abundant life is brought up from the ocean depths. The level of the ocean never changes, it remains permanent from age to age. It is the land within and around the ocean that upheavals and subsides to a higher or lower level. So it is also with our soul--it never changes. it is permanent from age to age. It is the level of growth and development that changes to indicate the depth of our divine consciousness and is a never ending process.

The number of the 9-month challenge will point to the precipitation, but the 9-year challenge will precipitate the events that occur. The 9-year challenge awakens the soul to what will influence our life; the 9-month challenge initiates the effects of that influence. The combination of the numbers will foretell whether it will be a easy period or a difficult one. A house that is messy needs to be cleaned, especially if it has been overlooked for a long period of time. No one really enjoys cleaning a house, yet to be sanitary, it needs to be cleaned. If the numbers are compatible, you can hire help or get assistance in the cleaning of the house. When the numbers are not compatible you may have to do it yourself. Every agitating activity you have during the course of the 9-month challenge prepares you to face the bigger trials in life. The 9-months should be looked upon as a time of duty to a certain project that needs attention in order to move forward to your next cycle.

One weakness is that most people see problems as punishment; however, they are just duties in life, walking you through your journey to a greater spiritual development. People are always concerned with negative cycles. There are no good or bad situations. Adverse periods are periods of growth to help you determine right from wrong. Growth can only come from a certain degree of discomfort and pain. Sometimes it will take physical effort on your part, like having to get down on your knees to scrub a dirty floor, but the end result brings joy and contentment to see it sparkling clean. To become wholly effective, you need to deal with the discomforts of life to enjoy the state of happiness. Remember, as much as you do not want to clean a dirty house, it is a fact of reality which must be accepted to enjoy living in the ideal, clean home. You cannot always control the situation; however, you can control your attitude about the event.

You are a separate individual and yet you are a greater part of a whole, having an inner connection to the nucleus of life. Living in a house requires effort and responsibility in keeping it up; living your life also requires effort and responsibility. You can either choose to live in a house that is messy and dysfunctional, or you can take the time and effort to restore it to orderliness. When you can become master of your own world, your efforts and involvement in the production of life can overcome obstacles-- despite all the resistance--for a happy ending.

Meaning of 9-Month Challenge

1--------- A time for action or to undertake projects. There can be personal encounters to deal with so be prepared. It is easy to lose your patience, temper or become irritated over little things. Use energy wisely to get things done. Start an exercise program, a new business, make a move or examine your life. Avoid being confrontational, quarrelsome and impulsive. Time to get motivated. Abundant enthusiasm and energy to express yourself. You have a lot more courage now and aggressively will move toward your desires.

2--------- Time to be patient and cooperative. Use this 9 months to improve your physical appearance, buy new clothes, get a new hairstyle or start an exercise program. Great time to meet new friends and renew relationships with old friends. It is a time of love and tranquillity, but also of vulnerability. Use indirect methods to gain what you want through understanding and love, never force issues. In this period you could meet someone if you are single and if you are married, the relationship will seem more content and loving.

3--------- Period of luck and extravagance. Expand yourself socially and professionally. Feeling more extroverted than usual, you will suddenly find yourself bored wanting to become more active. You are more concerned about the joys and pleasures of life than about the responsibilities of life. Your charisma is highlighted without effort. Time to network and travel. Expenses could be highlighted because of a new car or luxuries purchased. Unexpected travel or short trips are commonplace.   Acknowledge your uniqueness.   Add pleasure and variety to your life.

4---------   Get down to business. Take care of loose ends or projects that are uncompleted. Concerns develop in domestic situation with family or friends. You seem to feel more tired than usual, requiring more rest. Pressures of home, business, school or work seems to bog you down. Financial issues become a prime concern and home matters seem paramount. You enjoy more family get-togethers or hosting dinner parties at your home. Time to clean out the closets or cupboards or give the home and yard a good cleaning. Reinforce your choice of values. Let go of the old in favor of the new.

5---------   The pace of life seems restless and jumpy. You want and need to make changes. Flexibility is the key to get best results. Not a time to be too serious. Achievements can be made in work and in social life. Enjoy the excitement that seems to be in your life during this time, with many interesting events to keep you busy. Your sexual energy is in high gear, and so is the intensity of life. Not a good time to make long lasting decisions for when the 5 cycle passes, so can the urgency for change. Your reactions will be swift but not always certain. Travel seems to be on your mind.

6---------   Generally a pleasant and happy time. Good times will be shared with family members and friends. There may be concerns regarding family and friends who need your advice or inspiration. Time to pamper yourself or start a new hobby. Great time to purchase a pet. Redecorate your home or relocate to a new home. Passive period. Accomplishments are gained through persistence, formal education and accepting responsibilities. Mate, children or grandchildren are given priority in this cycle. It is also a time when you enjoy cooking or baking. Take this time to pamper yourself and take inventory of your personal needs.

7--------- Suppressed emotions; you become introspective, pulling away from social activities. Depressing situations keep you from feeling outgoing or active. You pull inward, becoming deeply emotional. A period of sensitivity, pessimism, sadness and worries. Nothing seems to come together. Sabbaticals, therapy or counseling is helpful in this period. Any type of schooling or week-end seminars at this time will be most helpful to your state of mind. Stress when understood and dealt with can lead into a deeper understanding of self. Look for strength through your spiritual interests.

8--------- Major events happen. Money situation improves. Time to influence others through your skills and knowledge. Undertake projects you have been putting off. Anchor your life. Time of blessings and gratitude, also time of extravagance. Kind in heart, but cold and ruthless in mind. Seek a better position or ask for that overdue raise. Time to win at life. There could be undue pressure from a job or career at this time putting in extra hours or having more responsibility in your field of work. A productive and empowering 9 months. Definitely a time to assert your capabilities.

9---------- Reversals of actions are the effect of this period. You feel like you have come to the end of your rope because of stressful situations beyond your control. Be careful of endings or misgivings in your personal contact. Put an end to situations that have no solutions or happy endings. Tie up loose ends. Take a journey. Keep only short-term goals, long-range goals are not dependable. Do not mistake illusions for reality. There could be health problems needing a physician's care for you or people close to you. Time to process your physical, mental and spiritual development to retain your balance and to reap your greatest harvest.

0---------- Pressure seems to be the theme, with irrevocable decisions and choices which must be made. Generally, problems are the result of loved ones or work-related. Many unexpected events arise during this period and you will find it difficult to be relaxed or peaceful. A lack of guidance or purpose becomes a struggling issue during this challenge, whether the crisis is for you or for someone close to you. This is a time to go inward to carry you forward. Your emotions impel you to do so for inner spiritual guidance and awareness. Learn to depersonalize your feelings because of the despondency and the insecurity you will experience during this challenge. Zero is the eternal mystery of spiritual self-giving, demanding everything from you without you expecting any thing in return.

PERSONAL YEAR NUMBER

The personal year is not subject to just the passage of time, it evolves from the need to be functional in your self-expression. Most people go through life on automatic pilot, reacting to their environment through emotions and feelings. You have to be willing to grow and develop through continual challenges to find fulfillment and pleasure. Just think of the positive effect your actions will have on your daily life when you accept your challenges with a healthy attitude. It is like bringing your shadow into the light and facing that part of you that needs to be put into balance.

Of course, life can be disparaging if there are a succession of years when you experience catastrophic hardships. You have to be able to adjust to the ever-constant changes. Be willing to put effort into making life more balanced to accomplish a mature outlook in your progress. The positive effect of your actions will create good karma not only in this lifetime but in your next reincarnation. You cannot enter a human body at birth and not expect to have human experiences. You should not put difficult situations on the back burner, waiting for a miracle to happen, or wish your life free from problems. In order to enjoy a delicious seven course dinner you must turn on the heat. A lot of time and effort must go into the enjoyment of the feast--both before and after.

Everyone progresses differently according to what you have to work with from past incarnations. Many souls are more progressed than others, living in a higher harmonic frequency and can handle personal growth more effectively than individuals living in a lower harmonic frequency. For people in the lower frequency it will take extra effort to adjust to the obstacles within the framework of their experience. Are you plugged into a 20 watt bulb or are you plugged into a 150 watt bulb--that is the determinant.

The personal cycle is a yearly cycle within a 9-year epicycle. It is called an epicycle because it is a period of 9 years rotation of the numbers 1 through 9--taking one year for each number to orbit birthday to birthday within a time frame of 9 years. Revolutions of 9-years with an annual 1-year cycle of each number continually repeats itself every 9-years. Do not confuse this cycle with the 9-year challenge. The 9-year challenge is more intense and longer in duration. One number in orbit lasts for 9 years and the challenge numbers are not in sequence of 1 to 9, those numbers are taken from the sequence of numbers in the birthyear--big difference. The personal year affects the 9-year challenge number forcing it to progress through the value system that the personal year signifies.

Unlike your birthpath numbers, which you chose before your birth, the personal year number is a developmental process to which every individual must succumb. In your birthdate you may lack some of the numbers from 1 to 9, but in the epicycle you experience every number and must perfect every number to serve your greater good, adding wisdom to your character. Pay homage to your personal year cycle respecting it as your classroom teacher, taking you to a new grade each year. If you fail, you lose, because the next year becomes even more difficult as you take on your past problems with your present assignment. The spirit of the personal years are the same for everyone except for the response of the actions and lessons--that will vary with each individual situation.

The birthpath numbers will give you an indication on how the personal year cycle will unfold in your life for that year. The number of the 9-year challenge will indicate the issues that will prevail in the upcoming year. The personal year numbers signify your mood and the mental and emotional processes you need to perfect. Learn to live with the everyday changes and situations, just as you have to learn to live with the weather, never knowing what is coming; however, you must always be prepared.

The personal year number reflects changes of work, finances, relationships and emotional equilibrium. The combined numbers will indicate a passive year, aggressive year or neutral year. Each year you are faced with challenges within your challenges. Knowledge of the personal year is helpful and can be important in accelerating evolvement.

The personal year cycles will have an impact on the 9-year challenge because the numbers are compelled to interrelate with each other, affecting all the primary numbers. The 9-year challenge is a long-term experience of your life, and the personal year awakens that challenge to new levels of development each year.

Think of a beautiful fruit tree that you have planted. Every year you watch its physical changes in wonder. The part of the tree that lives below the ground is always protected from external influences and is heartier than the delicate leaves and blossoms above the ground. The roots and the trunk never change except to constantly grow. The part of the tree that lives above the ground lasts only a single year, then withers away to give change to new growth.

The personal year is similar to the activity and growth of the fruit tree as an annual cycle. There are years the fruit tree will be in full bloom, loaded with fruit; other years it will be more barren with a scant amount of fruit. There may be years when there are heavy winds and drought, producing dryness in the leaves and loosening the foundation, possibly needing a stake to support and strengthen it. There may be years when there are heavy rains or early frost damage to the tree. Years of blight on the leaves or insects that ravage the fruit can make the fruit inedible. I think you have the picture--the tree never changed its position, but the external influences affected the activity and the development of the tree because external influences are always changing and affecting stationary patterns.

The numbers are all separate, yet all have unity in everything you do in life. You are like the fruit on the tree. Every fruit on the tree is different in size, shape and texture; yet it is all the same fruit from the same tree. The numbers are a part of a greater whole, all connected in some way through their own interdependence.

The personal year numbers are a fascinating and intriguing wonder of dimensions, pay close attention to them. I would like to add a word of caution in predicting the personal year and the influence it will have in your life. Predictions can never be definite. For example, returning to the analogy of the tree again, if weather conditions were good all year and the tree was loaded with blossoms it would appear to be a promising year for abundance. One might predict that it will be a good year for bearing fruit. But imagine, because of unforeseen forces that a bad wind storm came unexpectedly while the blossoms were still in bloom, damaging the blossoms and leaves, leaving it changed from its fertile condition. The tree will no longer bear the fruit that was anticipated for that year, yet the tree is not lost, just restricted, and the maturation continues.

YOUR PERSONAL YEAR IS
THE YEAR YOU GIVE TO YOURSELF

PERSONAL YEAR	1--------------------	ASSERT YOURSELF
PERSONAL YEAR	2--------------------	NURTURE YOURSELF
PERSONAL YEAR	3--------------------	EXPRESS YOURSELF
PERSONAL YEAR	4--------------------	SECURE YOURSELF
PERSONAL YEAR	5--------------------	CHANGE YOURSELF
PERSONAL YEAR	6--------------------	LOVE YOURSELF
PERSONAL YEAR	7--------------------	INTERNALIZE YOURSELF
PERSONAL YEAR	8--------------------	TRANSFORM YOURSELF
PERSONAL YEAR	9--------------------	FREE YOURSELF

Personal Year 1

You need to assert yourself to achieve your desires by doing what you long to do. Act decisively with direction. One can be a year to create new situations or make new changes. You will feel bolder in standing on your own. The 1 personal year will be fast-paced with a lot of excitement and activity. You will have less patience and could become argumentative with others, so hold your tongue and your temper. You will also react impulsively to many issues that normally would not affect you. Make sure before you leap that you have a safety net below you. Your energy accelerates similar to riding in a race car, and the temptation to speed up overpowers you. Go for that new job you want, go into business for yourself, start a part-time job. Just get moving.

Personal Year 2

You need to nurture yourself and everyone around you. You become moody and sentimental in a 2 year. Life seems more passive and opportunities are not as readily available as they were in the 1 personal year. In fact, in the 2 personal year you will feel more touchy about yourself as your feelings become more sensitive and your actions more passive. You will feel a lot calmer during the 2 compared with the fast-paced personal 1 year. During the 2 year take time for social pleasures, improving your circle of friends and pampering yourself. Get a new hair style, buy a new wardrobe of clothes softer in color, have cosmetic surgery, go for those facials and massages you never had time for last year.

256

Your conscious mind starts to react based on your subconscious desires, more for self-satisfaction than for ambition. This is the year to have peace of mind and to love yourself for who you are. Indulge yourself.

Personal Year 3

You need to express yourself and expand on your abilities. Communicate your plans, talents and ideas in a public way. Become visible through advertising, soliciting or interacting. Attend functions and seminars, or join groups where you can network. Interaction will be very important for your self-expression and self-exposure. During this personal year you will be able to give form to your ideas and talents making the public aware of you. You will feel in a great mood, full of verve and spirit. Responsibilities seem to be put on the back burner because all that matters to you is to make the most of this positive year expanding on your talents and capabilities. Life will feel like springtime. You are full of new life like a bud about to bloom. With a joyful spirit you love life wanting to enjoy it on all levels. Take time to visit distant shores or take that long journey you have been putting off. Three is a year of friendships and upbeat experiences. Flow into life, celebrate life, live life, however, be careful of being too extravagant, especially during this year. Dance and be jolly.

Personal Year 4

You need to secure yourself and get down to business during a personal 4 year. Outline a long-range plan for the whole year, in which to get things done. This is the year to put more emphasis on the domestic aspect of life through your home, family, relatives or health issues. If your home or business needs attention or improvement, this is the year to get it accomplished and to become more organized. Clear the closets of out-dated and worn-out clothing, have a garage sale, repair broken and run-down equipment. Solve any personal problems with family members. Give the elderly the extra attention they require. Emphasis should be on preservation and your domestic environment. This is a great year for real estate transactions; a move to a new dwelling or to remodel your present home. Four will not feel like a fun year, but it is not meant to be. It is the year to get serious and get the job done. Put money away for a rainy day and give attention to health concerns. Strengthen your domain, get life in order and get the job done.

Personal Year 5

Your need to change yourself by taking chances and risks, but with rational thinking. Important events and surprise opportunities will come up, forcing you to make some choices. You will be more effectual as your charisma is heightened and people begin to listen to what you have to say. Change the direction of your focus during the 5 personal year if you are unhappy with your present situation. As you become more restless and dissatisfied with dead-end situations and dull routines, remove the restraints that keep you from feeling satisfaction with your life. Do not create or institute change just for the adventure or excitement; create change to give substance to a new direction. Open yourself to new ideas through new and creative activities which will benefit you in the future. Open doors to the outside world and dance on the earth letting your soul and mind experience the variety of wonders. Do not just admire the bright stars in heaven, become one.

Personal Year 6

You need to love yourself and to be loved.   Bring heart-centered awareness into your life. This is a year of sentimentality and feelings. Open yourself up to loving experiences becoming closer to people, especially with those about whom you really care. Use the 6 personal year to appreciate your own personal desires, while still attending to the needs of family and friends. People close to you will seem to require your loving support and your divine wisdom. Opportunities to spend more quality time with family and friends will be available for you. It could even be a year when you decide to do some volunteer work, to care for a sick relative or just enjoy your home more. Many adjustments will have to be made in your daily schedule in your desire to help others. To keep peace and tranquillity attend social activities such as operas, plays, concerts or musical. Keep fresh flowers in the home to raise your spirit, for both flowers and music are soothing to the soul and have expressions of human love. Uplift yourself through love.

Personal Year   7

You need to internalize yourself and your energy by seeking more solitude to relieve you of the pressures of life. The personal 1 is a year when you stand alone, in the 7 personal year you choose to be alone. A few months into the 7 personal year you will notice you stopped socializing for no apparent reason, spending more time at home or doing projects you enjoy. In fact, your friends even seem to call you less, causing you to feel insecure about yourself especially if you are normally an outgoing individual. You also seem to lack in energy, requiring more rest and sleep than usual because your body is calling for you to slow down and become whole within yourself.   Your mind thinks a lot more during this period as you feel confused about life regarding different circumstances--both good and bad. You reflect a lot about the past, and become more concerned with the future. Decisions are made to expand your educational pursuits. During my 7 personal year I wrote this book.   It was quiet and lonely because I isolated myself from the world, but I chose to do it.   It was an unexciting year, except for the intensity of my writing. Financially, it can be a rough year, so make sure you have a little extra nestegg as you interrupt your active life to achieve tremendous growth. Go inward.

Personal Year   8

You need to transform yourself.   The serenity of the personal 7 year is over and now in the 8 personal year you make strides to move into the material realm. Eight is a money year, and a period to advance yourself to achieve financial prosperity. Your values are now demonstrated toward mastership and promoting your talents for status and financial gains. Go after your dream and rebuild the foundation which seemed to fall apart in the 7 year.   Life will improve professionally in various ways through people, advancements, pay raises or greater commissions giving you more economic freedom. If careless in the 8 year you could also lose a lot financially, so check your priorities to see where the advantages or disadvantages lie.   This is a year of harvesting and enhancing your power while satisfying your goals. You appear more insensitive and detached from your personal environment. Your presence becomes visible as you exert more wisdom, so go after your dream, and the rainbow will bring you personal satisfaction. It is definitely a year to improve your finances. Go for the dough.

Personal Year 9

You need to free yourself from any kind of bondage by which you feel burdened. Be willing to let go, or you will be forced to do so by forces beyond your control.   A year of struggles and disappointments. The 9 year can make you feel as if doors are closed to you, and in many ways they may be if they are no longer suited for your growth. Plans never seem to go as you expect them to, or you seem to lack personal power. There will be a lot of restlessness in your nature as you become more mentally frustrated due to your fears and the depression that surrounds you. Nine is a year of spiritual awakening. You must learn to let go. Changes may not always come easy and this is a personal year that will have an undeniable effect. It is the end of the nine year epicycle and in this year you must prepare for a whole new personal 9 years. This can be a year when you can be globally social in your travels, meet with a spiritual teacher or expand yourself spiritually and philosophically. Remember, when an old door closes, a new one opens. There can never be a new beginning without an ending. Let go and let God.

The Magic of Candle Burning

CANDLE BURNING

I was asked why I had included a chapter in this book on candle burning since it had nothing to do with numbers. I believe candle burning can assist an individual during a difficult period to help fill conscious thoughts with spiritual support and love. If you believe in miracles (which I do) candle burning can be the divine intervention to shape the purpose of your everyday experiences, similar to medication that is helpful to an illness.

Candle burning assists you in opening your awareness and beliefs to the presence of spirit guides and angels. It is my belief that candle burning is one form of magical healing. The flame of the candle glowing upward is to inspire you to look up and to "lighten up" helping get you through your experiences.

Remember, a flame is a state of illumination imparting mental and spiritual enlightenment, having the power to throw light into your sensory system. Candle burning can be an enlightening and meaningful ritual when you feel spiritless in your well-being. It is like calling on a miracle to help you illuminate your path at a time when you feel your world has turned dark. Every belief, every religion, every faith believes in the power of candle burning. It is considered to be the eternal flame symbolic of the energy of the soul.

Candles are among the earliest symbols to be used as a source for ceremonial practices. As early as 3000 BC candles were in wide use. A composite of vegetable oil, beeswax, carnauba wax, candelilla wax and ozocenite are used as the basic materials to make candles. The wick is made from good quality cotton or braided line which is soaked in solutions of ammonia, chloride, sulfate or phosphorus. The liquid wax from the candle flows upward and is vaporized by the heat as a result of capillary action. The flame is the heat that comes from the burning substances and results in a union with oxygen. As the substance and oxygen burn, the action of the two takes place instantly and heat is given off with light from the flame. Different substances have different effects on the activity of the flame. Some flames will have a faint glow, while others can have a bright glow, depending on the different waxes used.

There are candles which you can buy that are already anointed or dressed. These candles have certain holistic oils or powders, that are diluted or rubbed into the wax which is used to heal different conditions. When a candle is lit with anointed homeopathic oils or powders, the flame burns the oils and powders into the burning wax substance, releasing energy outward through the activity of the flame and smoke. This smoke goes out into the etheric field, creating positive energy. It is similar to someone smoking in a room. You cannot pick up the smoke, you cannot hold it in your hand and you cannot store it in a box, yet the smoke gets into your clothes, hair and furniture, leaving a stagnant telltale sign. There is a similar effect with candle burning, but in a more positive respect. Cigarette smoke works instantly and vanishes hours later. Candle smoke does not work instantly but has a more lasting effect, continuing for an indefinite time.

To understand the process of candle burning keep in mind that your mental attitude plays an important role in the outcome. If you have the right attitude, candle burning can be a positive therapy for healing and mobilizing your will. Candles are produced in a wide variety of colors, shapes and sizes and have become popular decorations for the home, religious ceremonies and spiritual practices. The point of the candlepower produces a source of light and illumination; the intensity of the flame depends on the composites used to make the candle.

The blessing of candles became a popular festivity for the home and for special occasions after the feast of the "Purification of the Virgin Mary". This feast took place forty days after the birth of Jesus, and it was the presentation of Jesus into the temple as the Virgin Mary's firstborn for both to be purified. This feast, Hypapant Kyriou, is celebrated on February 2nd. The feast represents Jesus as the Light of the World and his entry into the world. The feast can be traced in the New Testament (Luke 2:22-39) and marks the end of the Christmas Season. The "Purification of the Virgin Mary" was renamed the "Presentation of the Lord" in 1969. Candlemas and Palm Sunday are holy days when candles are blessed in the Jewish and Catholic services and distributed to worshipers. After the feast of this presentation, in the 12th century the Catholic Church placed candles on the altars and used them as regular observance for all masses and ceremonial functions.

In the 16th century, the use of candles in the home was common among the rich. In the 17th century, they became a classical decoration, not only to wealthy households but also to families of modest budgets. Candles were used frequently for funerals and religious services in absolving sins for the dying and the dead in the Jewish faith. They are now used as rituals of blessings for the sick and the dying by many churches of all faiths. The use of candle burning has become popular today and is used at most ceremonial functions; i.e, initiations, magic spells, witchcraft, exorcizing demons, home decorations, birthdays, and holidays, such as Christmas, Thanksgiving and Easter. Candles provide an outlet of expression to the universe through the flame of the light. They come in many shapes, sizes and colors having their own vibration and symbolism, varying in the purpose and procedure of each custom.

The burning of candles is a sacred form of reverence to be used with devotion to achieve one's wishes and should be respected by the participants and the observers. Candle burning can be used to enhance a difficult situation and requires blessings from a higher power. Wishes should be simple when opening up to candle burning, and there is no guarantee that one's wish will be granted. When burning a candle for a specific wish, do not hope for something that is impossible, so that you do not become discouraged or disappointed. It is blind faith and trust of the individual who lights the candle that will determine the quality of the outcome, and that trust comes from the grace of God. As with any wish, one must be within the bounds of reason. When you ask for a specific wish, make sure it is for your highest good; because if it is not in your destiny, there will be difficulty in the attainment of your wish.

The power of candles can be used to remove worries, pain, grief or anger in one's life. They are used for financial gain, success in finding a job, to attract a loved one or to become more attractive to a loved one. There are a multitude of purposes for candle burning; however this chapter will be on the basic concerns. You must be willing to surrender yourself through your prayers and trust that candle burning will bring blessings and power to your wishes.

Burn candles to help improve a difficult period. Ask for blessings to be granted to give you strength and courage to accept situations beyond your control. Candle burning does not promise to give you what you desire, but it can help you find a place of untroubled rest.

Candles should also be used as a joyous influence for protection and blessings. They should be used to attract positive situations and remove adverse circumstances. They are not meant to perform miracles yet, that is not impossible. The basic function of candle burning is to remove sorrow and unhappiness and bring light into darkness.

The area where you light your candles should be in a secure place, away from children and animals. Any room in your home or office is desirable and should be kept sacred. I prefer to use candles in a glass jar for safety reasons, but any kind of candle can and should be used. It is best to place candles on a cookie sheet or pizza pan for protection from wax drippings or the possibility that the glass jar might accidentally crack. In all the years I have burned candles, I have not had a glass jar break, but it can happen. The candle must stay lit till it burns out, so all safety precautions should be used. When you put the candle out you interrupt the flow of energy terminating a speedier outcome.

Always do your candle lighting when the environment is peaceful, and when you are free from interruptions. The best time is when the sun rises in the morning and the beams are full of radiance. The rising of the sun enhances the power of the flame and the light increases the flow of the wish, just as the rays of the rising sun increase the warmth of the air.

It is best to bathe yourself before you begin candle burning. If that is not possible, wash your hands properly before you prepare your candle. In preparing your candle, you must cleanse it from all impurities previous to others handling it. With a damp, clean, white cloth or white paper towel, gently wipe the candle or glass container. If you wish to inscribe a wish on your wax candle, use a needle; or, for a glass jar write on the inside of the waxed area. If you do not want to write on the wax use white parchment paper to inscribe your wish. Fold the paper and tape it to the bottom of the candle or glass container. A picture can be used of a loved one or, if your desire is for a new home or car, place the picture of what you want under the candle or next to it.

Dressing your candle (rubbing oils or putting magic potions into the candle to produce quicker results) is also very effective and is considered sacred. Special oils can be purchased at a metaphysical store or even regular baby oil may be used. Anointing or (dressing) the candles is not necessary, but it does make candle burning more devotional or sacred in the ritual, enhancing the indulgence of the wish. Place some oil on your right index finger (the finger of the planet Jupiter or Guru). Hold the candle in the left hand, placing the oiled finger on the center of the candle. In a clockwise position, rub the oil upward toward the top of the candle until you have completely covered the top half of the candle or jar. You may have to put oil on your finger several times to insure that there is enough oil to cover the complete surface area. Turn the candle upside down, and from the center of the candle to the bottom half anoint in the same motion as you did in the top half. If you have a glass candle be sure you anoint the inside of the glass and top layer of the candle. Repeat your wish openly, as you rub oil over the entire candle.

You are now prepared to light your candle. Visualize your wish as you light the candle and imagine bright light around you. Verbalize your own special invocation. Fill your heart with love and joy with a firm belief your wish will be answered. Commit to the devotion of your wish and surrender yourself to receive your wish when it is so destined.

Acknowledge your candle daily until it burns out, concentrating on your wish each time you declare it during the course of the day.

Once the candle is lit you must never put it out or allow someone else to touch it. If another person handles your candle for any reason, replace the candle and start over. If you have to put the candle out for any reason, smother it with a funnel or an object that will suffocate it, but *never* blow any candle out *once you have anointed it*. If for some reason you have to put the candle out or it goes out before it is completely burned, relight your candle for the same wish. For added strength in re-lighting, light a gold or white votive candle along with the existing candle or candles. The candles will rekindle the wish, and the gold and white candles will help to speed the recovery of the success. You do not have to oil your candle down a second time to re-light it but you should put oil on the votive candle that you use with it. I always like to burn incense and play Eastern Indian chants at the beginning of the anointing to set a spiritual mood.

When the candle burns out, wrap it in newspaper or a paper bag to keep it free from outside energies and contamination. You can either bury it in the ground or dispose of it with your trash as long as it is wrapped properly. Avoid wrapping two candles in the same paper unless they are both for the same wish. Most of the big, thick candles, or the glass containers, take 5 to 7 days to burn out. If your wish is not fulfilled in the first ritual, you may have to repeat it two or more times until you obtain the desired results.

Never burn candles to bring harm to anyone, for it can backfire and you will end up with the misfortune--even worse than you wished on others. Definitely burn candles for positive manifestations, for family members, relatives, friends or loved ones. It is very powerful to light candles for another person's blessings, but keep it a secret, because the secret wish itself becomes the power. Make sure their name is written on the candle and allow their good fortune to come true.

When your wish comes to pass, always show your gratitude by lighting a small, white votive candle to acknowledge your sincerity. Anointing the thank-you candle in oils is not necessary, but wiping it clean is desirable. The practice of cleansing your candles should be a habit, regardless of what kind of candles you burn--even if it is just for decoration or a social atmosphere. Any candle you use should be free of other's energy, especially for ceremonial purposes. When a candle is lit it becomes a form of electricity that is sent out into the atmosphere, even if it is just to have a candlelight dinner or to burn as an ornament of light.

Any day is good for burning candles but my personal preference is Monday, Thursday, Friday, and Sunday. Monday is the day of the planet Moon, the nurturing essence. Thursday is the day of the planet Jupiter, the guru and benevolence. Friday is ruled by the planet Venus, full of love and compassion. Sunday is ruled by the Sun and is the perfect time to ask for favors from the universe. Burn candles under a new moon to speed the results of your wish; this is not required, but it is the preferred time. Full

Moon candle burning has a special significance because maximum energy is activated, especially if it is also done on a Monday.

It is auspicious to have candle ceremonies on your birthday, New Year's Eve and especially on days of eclipses. I usually burn all the colors on a solar eclipse, when circumstances permit. Any prayer done on the day of an eclipse is threefold in power. Having a wish for each colored candle enhances the mystical energy. Set a special table or altar for all the candles. Place flowers or petals of a rose around them. Flowers teach us how to be silent in beauty and they can lift ones spirits because they are open to all the energy around them. Burning candles with fresh flowers have a radiance of joy and beauty.

CANDLE COLORS AND THEIR MEANINGS

WHITE------ Purest of colors. The color of the sun and Moon. Sunlight consists of white rays and contains all the colors of the rainbow, it only appears to be yellow. The moon is also white, because it is the reflection of the sun. White is the color of milk of the human breast. A baby's christening dress or a bride's wedding dress is white, signifying purity. Always use white to cleanse or purify. White is neutral in energy, and it can be used for any desired wish. Also use white in conjunction with the colored candles to intensify the effectiveness. White is basically used to eliminate depression, purify a negative environment, protect one from evil, and to keep mentally and emotionally healthy. Also use for spiritual realization, household purification, breaking of spells or curses, spiritual healing, strength and truth. White candle magic is used to ward off the effects of black magic.

YELLOW--- The color of the guru and of intelligence. Burn for confidence and charm, to increase knowledge, to better yourself mentally, for academic accomplishment, for new friendships or better relationships with old friends. Use also when writing books or novels, studying for an exam, taking a test or for a safe journey when traveling by airplane. Increases mental clarity and retains knowledge.

ORANGE---- Color Sunyassi's wear for strength of body, character and action to move to another world. Color of courage and the warrior. Use to improve the environment and to live a more cheerful life, to increase energy, to strengthen self-confidence, broaden social activities, dispel pessimism and worry, develop athletically, increase safety and happiness while away from home and to solve legal problems or problems with the IRS. To be victorious.

PINK-------- Color used to attract lasting love and happiness. To receive affection from others or to be more loving. To attract a loyal and sincere mate for marriage. To clear misunderstandings with loved ones. Improving your beauty inwardly and outwardly. For success with cosmetic surgery (also use a gold candle with a pink one for a successful outcome). Entertaining at a party or for a romantic dinner. For peaceful relationships. To help overcome unfulfilling relationships. To restore peace and balance with loved ones. For warmer affections between friends.

RED---------- Color of pure blood that permeates the entire body, the heart--the most powerful organ and the menstrual flow to create life. Use for passion and sex, romantic love, to end celibacy, to improve fertility, to feel more alive, for excitement in social life, for more energy and magnetism, to be attractive to the opposite sex or that special someone, for romantic dinners or in intimate surroundings. Use as inspiration for desires or for abundant energy. Use to win or achieve progress, especially in physical sports. Color of protection and willpower and to bring fast luck and to promote enthusiasm.

GREEN------ Color of nature in growth of grass and trees. Use for wisdom, for purposes of meditation and growth of any kind. to end financial problems, to gain prosperity and material comforts, to find employment, to be able to pay bills, financial security, or for that extra bonus, to adequately provide needs for one's self and family, for healing of the mind and the body or fertility of a new business. To find something that is lost. Use to create a constant flow of money.

GOLD-------- Never tarnishes. Use in situations that require permanence. For luck in general, successful outcomes, new undertakings, gain advantages, and for decision making in achieving the best outcome. For a safe and healthy delivery for mother and child. For protection against evil influences and in happy occasions. To heal a friendship or family disturbance.

BLUE--------   Color of the sky and destiny, unlimited and everywhere. For psychic energy, health and body healing, before and after surgery and to speed recovery of illness. To lift fear and depression, for peace and contentment, to calm one's nerves, for people with insomnia, to have faith in life, for psychic abilities, for journeys or voyages on water, to have prophetic dreams, spiritual awareness and meditation. To attract positive spirit guides. For astral travel or a peaceful and happy death.

VIOLET-----   To uplift one's consciousness, for religious purposes, psychic and spiritual healing, inspiration, clarity of purpose compassion and wisdom. Use during a sabbatical, tranquillity, personal transformation, to attract a spiritual teacher, successful pilgrimage, to become celibate. It is also the Guru of demons to overcome greed and lust. To reverse a curse, or bad omen. For enlightenment. Burn in your bedroom to remember your prophetic dreams.

BROWN----   Color of earth, an important resource to support life on land to grow vegetation. It is for strength and growth in industrial resources, business ventures, and to become ambitious. Focused for practicality and stability. Helpful with household or domestic problems. To overcome addictions, for perfection, determination, to be less critical and fault finding. Use for buying or selling land and real estate or looking for an apartment, planting a garden, protecting pets, taking a trip by car, train or bus, or securing a firm domestic foundation.

BLACK-----   The color of darkness and the night. Used for black magic, rituals and spells because of its supernatural powers. Significant for funerals or associated with death. Color of power or authority. Not a negative energy, but can be used for negative purposes. One should be skilled in the art of candle burning before one engages in the rituals of black candle burning. A black candle is used to reverse a bad spell or overcome evil, for power over a situation or protection in the night. I do not encourage or recommend black candle burning for the novice or the average individual, for its reversals can be dangerous for the individual who lights it. Can be used for transformation along with a white candle.

**SILVER
OR GOLD--** To be used in special ceremonies or rituals of advanced candle burning. Also used for special occasions such as weddings, anniversaries, births, retirement, funerals, etc. Use for intuition, protection, to cancel negativity, to gain lasting and permanent results, for achievements, for winning titles, ribbons or recognition.

*Use sound when lighting candles, especially the "om".
Sound never dies, it is immortal.
Sound brings in protection and destroys negative influences.*

WORD DEFINITIONS

ALPHA-----------------The beginning, the first.

ALCHEMY----------- Combination of chemistry and magic, mysticism.

ANGULAR HOUSES-- Houses in horoscope most important as a source of energy.

ASCENDANT---------Physical manifestation of personality.

ASPECT----------------Relationship of two planets.

APPARITION-------- Something strange comes into view, remarkable vision, or illusion.

AUSPICIOUS--------- Favorable for success, promise of hope.

BEING----------------- Existing form, living creature.

BHAKTI-------------- Love, reverence and devotion.

BLISS------------------ Perfect joy, great happiness, blessedness

BOON------------------Blessing, A favor or good a thing.

CENTURY------------ A period of 100 years.

CHAKRA-------------- Seven points of spiritual power located along the body.

CHALLENGE
NUMBER------------- Cycles that create positive and negative energies of orbit.

CHANNELS---------- To convey through one person to another person or spirit.

CONJUNCTION----- Concentrated mass of planets.

CONSCIOUSNESS-- Power of the mind, cognition, awareness, perception of thoughts.

COSMIC-------------- Having to do with the whole universe and world.

CRYSTAL BALL-----Round glass or crystal to predict the future.

CYCLE----------------Period of time, process of growth or action.

DESTINY------------ Power that determines the course of events in one's lot or future.

DEVI--------------------Female goddess.

DHARMA------------- The eternal law of conduct, righteous way of living, right conduct, duty.

DIRECTIONAL
NUMBER------------- Time of birth, indicating direction of focus for destiny number.

ENLIGHTENMENT   Illumination of the mind, freedom from the material world.

ESOTERIC---------- Highly specialized knowledge intended for the initiated and the enlightened.

EXTERNAL--------- Existence outside one's mind, outward appearance.

FATE---------------- One's destiny, what becomes of a person or thing.

GALAXY------------ Faintly luminous band of countless stars that stretch across sky.

GLOBAL------------- Worldwide, the earth as a whole.

GURU---------------- Religious teacher, revered leader, mentor.

HERMAPHRODITE--- Having the character of both sexes.

HYPNOTIST-------- To dominate or control the will by suggestion.

INCARNATE-------- Embodied in human form, personified.

INTERNAL---------- Subjective inner mind, taken inside, from within.

INTERCESSION--- Act of interceding, prayer or petition on another's behalf.

KABBALAH------- System of esoteric theosophy developed by Rabbis.

KALIYUGA-------- Age of darkness, ignorance, conflict and ego.

KARMA------------- Effect that takes place as the result of prior activity in previous life.

LIBERATED-------- Being set free from political and material oppression.

MAJOR CYCLE---- Nine year challenge of numbers for prediction.

MASTER------------ Someone who serves as an inspiration to others, wise mentor.

MAYA--------------- Illusive power, illusion.

METAPHYSICAL-- Branch of philosophy dealing with the principle of things.

MINOR CYCLE----- Nine day challenge of numbers for prediction

MILLENNIUM------ Period of 1000 years.

MINOR CYCLE----- Nine-week or nine-day challenge of numbers for prediction.

MIRAGE----------- Optical Illusion

MORTAL---------- Inevitably subject to death, living person is mortal.

MYSTIC----------- Esoteric teacher of spiritual truth and doctrine.

MUDA------------- Pride.

NUCLEUS-------- Center of activity, central part of a whole, galaxy, celestial body.

ONENESS-------- Wholeness, singleness, unity.

OMEGA----------- The ending, the last, final.

ORBITAL--------- Range of influence or action to move within an orbit or a wheel.

PALMISTS-------- Foretelling a person's future by reading the lines in their hands.

PARADIGM------ A class of words, a pattern or an example.

PERSONAL YEAR A nine year cycle of numbers of 1 to 9 that change every year on your birthday through a mathematical formula.

PINNACLE---------- Highest point of achievement, a period of time.

PRANA-------------- Life-force.

PRINCIPLE--------- An essential truth.

PRODIGY----------- Person with extraordinary talents

PROPHET----------- Person who foretells the future of events by divine inspiration.

PROPITIOUS------- Omen, promise of success.

PSEUDO-SCIENCE A superficial resemblance, being in abnormal form.

PSYCHIC------------ Able to respond to nonphysical influences, mind or spirit.

PSYCHIC NUMBER Just the day of birth, not month or year.

PURIFICATION-- Cleansing, to remove guilt or sin.

QUIESCENT-------- At rest, dormant, inactive

REINCARNATION- To be reborn into a new body or new form.

REVELATION----- Something which brings a shock or surprise. God's manifestation of Himself to man.

SIGNATURE------- A name or astrological sign used to signify a person's nature.

SHAKTI---------------Female power, energy.

SHIVA LINGAM--- Balance of creation in male and female energies.

SOLAR SYSTEM-- Sun and its nine planets, celestial bodies.

SOUL----------------- Personification or embodiment, immortal divine energy of man.

SPIRIT--------------- Mortal nature of man, supernatural being, regarded as invisible but having power to become visible.

SPIRITUAL------ -- Concerned with soul or spirit, related to religious or sacred matters, having a relationship based on sympathy or sacred thought or feeling.

SUB-CONSCIOUS- Memories or emotions not normally remembered or admitted to the conscious, a dream state.

SUB-MAJOR CYCLE- Nine month challenge.

SUB-MINOR CYCLE-- Nine hour challenge.

SUNYASSI--------- An enlightened being which exists absolutely and without predication.

TAROT-------------- Deck of 52 cards used to predict or foretell the future.

TRANSFIGURATION- To change the shape or appearance.

TRANSFORMATION- Change in composition or structure to change the nature or character radically

TWO-NESS---------- Two or more united in wholeness.

NOTES:

Joice Ashly
P.O. Box 44126
Phoenix, AZ 85064
602/996-9887

Sunset

Picture taken by Richard Dennis of California.